ERNESTO CARDENAL

The Doubtful Strait

El estrecho dudoso

ERNESTO CARDENAL

The Doubtful Strait

El estrecho dudoso

TRANSLATED BY

John Lyons

INTRODUCTION AND GLOSSARY BY

Tamara R. Williams
Project Coordinator

INDIANA UNIVERSITY PRESS
Bloomington & Indianapolis

The paper used in this publication meets the minimum requirements of American National Standard for Information Sciences—Permanence of Paper for Printed Library Materials, ANSI Z39.48-1984.

Manufactured in the United States of America

Library of Congress Cataloging–in–Publication Data

Cardenal, Ernesto.
  [Estrecho dudoso. English & Spanish]
  The doubtful strait = El estrecho dudoso / translated by John
Lyons; introduction and glossary by Tamara R. Williams.
    p. cm.

  Includes bibliographical references.
  ISBN 0-253-31318-X (alk. paper). —ISBN 0-253-20903-X (pbk.: alk. paper)
  1. Latin America—History—To 1600—Poetry. I. Williams, Tamara R., date.
II. Title.
PQ7519.C34E813 1995
861–dc20   94-633

1 2 3 4 5 00 99 98 97 96 95

Contents

Introduction
by Tamara R. Williams

Ernesto Cardenal's prominence as one of Latin America's most important living poets, his reputation as a leading proponent of Liberation Theology, his notoriety as Minister of Culture for the Sandinista government, and his consistent and vocal opposition to U.S. intervention in Latin America represent, in an exemplary way, the fusion of public life and literature that has become characteristic of writers in Latin America.

Born in Granada, Nicaragua, on January 20, 1925, Cardenal was educated at the National Autonomous University of Mexico (1943–1947) and at Columbia University (1947–1949). In Mexico, he was surrounded by a supportive community of poets and writers, including his compatriots Ernesto Mejía Sánchez and Carlos Martínez Rivas, and Mexico's future Nobel laureate, Octavio Paz. The years in Mexico were productive ones. Cardenal completed a master's thesis on contemporary Nicaraguan poetry, later revised to become the introduction to an anthology of works by then-recent poets from Nicaragua, *Nueva poesía nicaragüense* (1949). He published three long poems ("La ciudad deshabitada," "Proclama del conquistador," and "Este poema lleva su nombre"), which were widely acclaimed and established his reputation as a promising young poet. Cardenal's involvement with the intellectual community in Mexico also heightened his consciousness of the political situation in Nicaragua: he began participating in protests against the brutal regime of Anastasio Somoza (dictator of Nicaragua from 1937 to 1947 and from 1951 to 1956). Cardenal's opposition peaked in 1954, when, back in Nicaragua, he participated in the "April Conspiracy," an attempt to overthrow Somoza. The insurrection failed miserably, and the leaders— Adolfo Baez Bone and Pablo Leal—were arrested, tortured, and killed. Cardenal went into hiding. His two major early works, "La hora O" (1956)[1] and *Epigramas* (1961), were composed during this period (1952–1957) and reflect his opposition to the Somoza regime and the United States' intervention in Central America. Mostly autobiographical, his epigrams cover a range of themes. Some attack the hypocrisy and cruelty of absolute tyranny, others equate the love for a woman with a fervor for revolution. "La Hora O" is a three-part poem that begins with an exploration of the United States' political and economic intervention in Nicaragua, and documents in its second part the struggle of Sandino's guerrilla against American marines. The third section deals extensively with the April 1954 insurrection.

At Columbia University, Cardenal focused his attention on learning English and reading the works of North American poets, including Marianne Moore, Charles Olson, Walt Whitman, William Carlos Williams, and Ezra Pound. Among these, Pound emerged the most important poetic influence on Cardenal. The young poet was attracted to Pound's canto as a new poetic form that allowed an unprecedented degree of flexibility and inclusiveness (the inclusion of history, the direct use of sources, the juxtaposition of these sources to produce meaning, and new and often unclassifiable rhythmical patterns).[2] More significant, however, was Cardenal's commitment to Pound's idea of the canto as the manifestation of a larger literary project, one seeking the radical renewal of poetry through a redefinition of its conventional thematic, discursive, and generic boundaries: "[Pound's ambition was] to create a work more inclusive than anything since Homer. He wanted a poetry of the agora, a poetry that could include the genres ordinarily associated with the transactions of economic and political power."[3] Through this project of expansion, Pound believed he could move poetry beyond its enervated state and make it a locus of action and change. Cardenal embraced this project and assumed its implications like no other poet.[4] In New York, he wrote three poems—"Raleigh," "Omagua," and "Las mujeres nos quedaban mirando"—all of which reflect Pound's influence, particularly in their length, their historical focus, and their use of documentary sources.

In 1956 Cardenal experienced a profound crisis and a religious conversion, leading him to enter the novitiate at the Trappist monastery at Gethsemane, Kentucky. At Gethsemane, Cardenal (under the name M. Laurence) received spiritual direction from the famous religious poet and thinker Thomas Merton, who was Master of Novices and whose views on love, non-violence, and Christian communal living would deeply affect the young Nicaraguan's future spiritual development. Due to ill health, Cardenal left the Trappists in 1958 and moved to the Benedictine monastery of Santa María de la Resurrección in Cuernavaca, Morelos, Mexico, where Merton had arranged for Cardenal to pursue his plan to become a monk. Several months into his stay in Cuernavaca, however, Cardenal felt called to abandon his monastic vocation and instead decided to become a priest. He lived and studied with the Benedictines until 1961, when he entered the seminary of Cristo Sacerdote in La Ceja, Antioquía, Colombia. Upon his return to Nicaragua in 1965, he was ordained in Managua on August 15 at the age of forty. Several months later, Cardenal carried out a plan he had conceived with Merton during his years at Gethsemane. He founded an independent Christian community—Our Lady of Solentiname—on the island of Mancarrón (part of the archipelago of Solentiname) in Lake Nicaragua.

Two works underscore Cardenal's Trappist experience. One is *Gethsemaní, Ky.* (1960), a collection of thirty-one brief poems, which Thomas Merton has described as "sketches in the style of the T'ang dynasty."[5] Reflecting the asceticism of monastic living, these poems outline seemingly insignificant details of daily life at Gethsemane simply and objectively, and in their simplicity reveal the poet's mystical experience. *Vida en el amor* (1970)[6] is a series of spiritual reflections in prose on the need for love in everyday living.

The poetry written after leaving Gethsemane displays a greater thematic range. Published in 1965, his *Oración por Marilyn Monroe y otros poemas*[7] contains stunning and formally elaborate critiques of "Americanized" societies, which promote excessive consumerism and materialism and spread a distorted value system that exploits and degrades the human spirit. Implicit in these poems is a fear of, and resistance to, the spread of American cultural values in Latin America. Conversely, in *Homenaje a los indios americanos* (1969)—one of the most comprehensive poetic treatments of Native American cultures in this century—the poet was drawn to anthropological and historical research in pursuit of knowledge about societies whose collective and spiritually oriented existence he perceived as representing the most positive of human values. Cardenal continued to work on both old and new poems about Native Americans well into the 1980s and published some of these in *Los ovnis de oro* (1988). In 1992, *Homenaje* and *Ovnis* were consolidated and published in a bilingual collection, *Los ovnis de oro / Golden UFOs.*

One also finds in Cardenal's post-Gethsemane work an increasing convergence of the political and the religious, a trend crystallized in his brilliant rewriting of the biblical Psalms (*Salmos,* 1967)[8] and reflected later in *Evangelio en Solentiname* (1975),[9] a multi-volume collection of Gospel reflections by the members of the community at Our Lady of Solentiname.

A significant turning-point in Cardenal's spiritual and political development came in 1970, when he was invited to Cuba by the prestigious publishing house Casa de las Américas to serve on the jury for an annual literary prize. The three-month visit inspired what Cardenal has called "almost a second conversion"—to Marxism—giving rise to another book, *En Cuba* (1970).[10] Robert Pring-Mill summarizes Cardenal's reactions to Cuba as follows:

He was far from blind to many shortcomings of the new system, and yet he was persuaded that many things which he had previously considered unattainable this century could indeed be put into practice, given such radical changes in the social order. All the Cuban system seemed to lack to become a viable replacement for the western society whose values and abuses he had so long deplored was a Christian dimension. Cuba simply lacked the firm grounding of that which was done here-and-now in principles which looked beyond this time-bound world towards a timeless reality, from which they might take their being and in which would lie their strength.[11]

Following Cardenal's trip to Cuba, Christianity and Marxism would be inextricably linked in his worldview, laying the foundation for his future commitment to Liberation Theology.

Ten years after its foundation in 1977, the community of Solentiname was bombed and destroyed by Somoza's National Guard. Labeled a subversive, Cardenal was forced into exile. During the next two years he traveled extensively on behalf of the Sandinista National Liberation Front, denouncing the Somoza government and U.S. intervention in Central America. Cardenal quickly emerged as a powerful voice against violations of human rights and national sovereignty in Latin America. Throughout the 1970s, his poetry maintained a characteristic documentary quality, but his focus shifted from the historical past toward current events, particularly those having to do with the dramatic struggle between the Sandinista National Liberation Front and the U.S.-backed Somoza regime. To this period belong his poems "Canto Nacional" (1972) and "Oráculo sobre Managua" (1973), and the collection *Vuelos de victoria* (1978).

When Somoza fell in 1979, Cardenal returned to Nicaragua to become the country's Minister of Culture. In this post, he directed a national campaign for the "democratization of culture," which involved a twofold policy. In an effort to promote popular arts, the ministry encouraged the production of local folk arts and marketed these on a national and international level. Concurrently, the policy sought to familiarize a broad sector of the Nicaraguan population with "art" in the narrow sense, that is, with poetry, painting, dance, and sculpture. It is in this context that Cardenal, inspired by the Costa Rican poet Mayra Jiménez, initiated nationwide poetry workshops which any person, regardless of education and background, could attend. These poetry workshops yielded an enduring body of texts, collected and edited by Mayra Jiménez in her *Talleres de poesía*,[12] which have drawn considerable critical attention. Through the workshops, poetry was produced by those who might otherwise never have had the opportunity to write and express themselves. More important, the workshops granted a broad sector of the Nicaraguan population integration into, and power over, a discourse from which they had been systematically excluded—another mark of the radical cultural change that came with Sandinista rule.

Cardenal retired from his political office and returned to writing full-time in 1988, when the Sandinista government downgraded the Ministry of Culture to an institute as a cost-saving measure. He remains, however, an active supporter and member of the artistic community, primarily as vice-president of The House of Three Worlds, a Managua-based artists' foundation which provides space and funding to artists, musicians, and writers from Central America.

Most recently, Cardenal has completed *Cántico cósmico* (1989).[13] Written over a period of thirty years, the poem is quickly gaining recognition as his greatest poetic achievement and the masterpiece of his literary production to date. Moving beyond an understanding of revolution as a spiritual and political phenomenon, *Cosmic Canticle* embraces the impact of scientific revolutions—relativity, quantum theory, and entropy—and "explores Latin American history by relating the evolution of the Universe to the development of human understanding."[14]

El estrecho dudoso / The Doubtful Strait had its origins in the period following Cardenal's departure from the Trappist monastery Our Lady of Gethsemane. After a year and a half at the Benedictine monastery in Cuernavaca, Cardenal went to Nicaragua for a vacation and stayed at José Coronel Urtecho's farm on the San Juan River. Coronel Urtecho, a distinguished member of the Nicaraguan *Vanguardia* movement, was also a distant cousin and mentor of Cardenal's. It is he who recommended that Cardenal submit a poem to a regional literary competition in El Salvador, advising him to attempt a historical poem about Nicaragua because, he said, Nicaragua's history provided so much rich material for a poem.[15]

Cardenal took his mentor's advice and began collecting material for the project. While still on holiday, he gleaned the multiple volumes of the *Documentos para la historia de Nicaragua* (also known as the Colección Somoza), a rich source of documentation on the conquest and colonization of Nicaragua. Upon his return to Mexico, he continued his historical research at the library of the Museo Nacional de Mexico. A draft of *The Doubtful Strait* was completed six months later and submitted for the Salvadorean competition late in 1961. The poem did not fare well. One of the judges (a Mexican author, Carlos Pellicer) told Cardenal that he had never even seen the poem. Another judge (the Costa Rican poet Alfredo Cardona Peña) reported that he had read the poem but did not recommend it for the award because it was not "lyrical." Others who read *The Doubtful Strait* were impressed, although the poem's length and historical focus apparently conflicted with the competition's established categories and conventional criteria. Cardenal continued to work on the poem in Mexico and again, between 1963 and 1965, in Colombia. The poem was not published in its current form until 1966 (with subsequent reprintings in 1971, 1972, 1982, and 1985). The present edition is the poem's first appearance in English and in a bilingual edition. Moreover, for the first time in its publishing history, the Spanish text of *El estrecho dudoso*—edited by translator John Lyons in collaboration with Cardenal—appears entirely in accordance with the poet's wishes.

Coronel Urtecho's recommendation provided Cardenal with the necessary incentive to embark on a literary project that he had been considering for some time. The idea of writing historical poems was not new to him. As early as 1947, Cardenal had written his first long poem, "Raleigh," and during the 1950s he wrote "Con Walker en Nicaragua," "Drake en la Mar del Sur," "John Roach marinero," "Mr. Squire in Nicaragua," and "Los filibusteros," among others. Yet *The Doubtful Strait* was distinctive, for it emphasized the Spanish discovery, conquest, and early colonization of Central America and focused therefore on Spain rather than Britain or the United States as the imperial power. Moreover, unlike the others, this poem—conceived and produced following Cardenal's religious conversion—would reflect a providential vision of history as a medium of God's work and revelation.

Cardenal dates the beginning of his interest in colonial Central American history to 1959, his last year at Gethsemane, when Merton encouraged him to research the early history of Latin America and of Native Americans in order to gain a more profound understanding of the continent's complex and painful socio-historical reality. As for Cardenal's providential reading of history, it is likely that the election of Pope John XXIII the previous year was of particular significance. Pope John's appeal to Catholics to recognize the value and insights of non-Christian faiths, his summons to Christians to recognize their social and political responsibilities, and his call for reconciliation among those whom history had divided challenged all religious communities at the time to renew their commitment to action and to reconciliation with the poor and the oppressed.[16] Responding to the new pope's priorities, and heeding Merton's advice, Cardenal researched what would become one of the most complete poetic documentations of non-Christian Native American history, ethics, and spirituality, his *Golden UFOs*. He also began to examine the actions and motivations of the "western predators"[17] who initiated one of the most destructive enterprises in history. This story— the story of the Conquest—would eventually be chronicled in *The Doubtful Strait*.

Although one of Cardenal's least-known and least-studied works,[18] *The*

Doubtful Strait is one of his most significant poetic achievements and merits comparison with Pablo Neruda's *Canto general* or Archibald MacLeish's *Conquistador*. Like Neruda's *Canto general*, *The Doubtful Strait* is a book-length narrative poem tracing a history of the American continent from the arrival of European explorers to recent historical events. Divided into twenty-five cantos, the text opens with Columbus's fourth voyage and his discovery in 1502 of Terra Firma near the present Cape of Honduras and reaches an apocalyptic finale with the destruction of León, Nicaragua, by the volcano Momotombo in 1609. Beginning with several accounts of explorations of the Central American region, the text progresses through key events in the conquests of Guatemala, Honduras, El Salvador, Nicaragua, and Mexico, and then elaborates on the colonizing process: the founding of towns, the naming of governors, and the imposition of Spanish rule.

Complementing the interest of the work is its interpolation of a parallel plot that tells the story of the political and economic conditions of more recent Nicaraguan history, mainly of life under the rule of Anastasio Somoza and then under Luis Somoza Debayle, who held power from 1956 to 1963. Specifically, through the use of typology and prefiguration,[19] the tyrannical regime of the Somoza family and its abusive practices are brought into alignment with the notorious colonial governors of Nicaragua: Pedrarias Dávila and Rodrigo de Contreras.

The Doubtful Strait's most remarkable feature is that it is constructed almost entirely from unaltered fragments of documents and histories dating from the colonial era. These include canonical works such as Columbus's "Diario de navegación," Bartolomé de las Casas's *Historia de las Indias*, Bernal Díaz del Castillo's *Historia de la conquista de la Nueva España*, Francisco Antonio de Fuentes y Guzmán's *Recordación Florida*, Francisco López de Gómara's *Historia general de las Indias*, Pedro Mártir de Anglería's *Décadas del Orbe Novo*, Gonzalo Fernández de Oviedo's *Historia general y natural de las Indias*, and Antonio de Remesal's *Historia General de las Indias y particular de la gobernación de Chiapas y Guatemala*. Cardenal also draws extensively from lesser known works such as Fernando de Ixtlilxoxitl's "Relación Décimotercera" and from letters, royal decrees, and legal proceedings in the *Colección de documentos inéditos de Indias* and in *Documentos para la historia de Nicaragua* (Colección Somoza). The only technically non-historical text he uses is in Canto XVII: the Mayan book of prophecies of Chilam Balam. Its inclusion is significant because it marks the presence of an oracular or prophetic discourse and reveals the poem's mythic and Providential dimension.

The intensive use of sources in *The Doubtful Strait* has a dramatic impact on the poem's style, most strikingly in its intertextuality, that is, the concentration and visibility of external discursive structures within the poem. Frequent use of quotation marks to indicate the presence of a source, faithful transcriptions of the sources' stylistic idiosyncrasies and archaisms, and typographical highlighting of segments of pre-text are Cardenal's most immediate means of rendering his borrowing explicit. Cardenal thus exposes the poem's identity as, in the words of Julia Kristeva, "a text constructed as a mosaic of quotations; as an absorption and transformation of other texts."[20]

The consequences of Cardenal's borrowing techniques are best illustrated by some contrasts to Neruda's *Canto general*. Neruda works up his sources into a poetic account that "protagonizes" the poet/narrator of the story. His account, moreover, draws attention to itself as poetry by sustaining a uniformity of tone and style throughout. Cardenal does not rework his sources. He borrows "whole slabs"[21] of the historical records and transcribes them as would an archivist or compiler. What results is the absence of *an* authorial point of view, with the text replaced instead by diverse perspectives, each registered in a distinct voice and style. These perspectives converge, intersect, and oppose one another, producing a text with a distinctive polyphonic quality that is less pronounced in Neruda.

The practice of incorporating other texts into his own is a defining feature of Cardenal's poetic concept of *exteriorismo* and is responsible for the multi-discursive style that has become his trademark. Cardenal attributes this borrowing to the influence of Ezra Pound. From Pound Cardenal learned discursive inclusiveness: the taking of fragments from a broad assortment of pre-existing texts and transposing them into a new poetic context. More significant is Cardenal's profound appreciation of the conceptual motivation behind Pound's practice: to challenge seemingly immutable literary conventions, especially those dealing with the appropriateness of certain themes and types of language for pre-established literary forms.

At the core of Pound's radical innovations was a challenge to the rising popularity of the novel. To "beat the novelists at their own game,"[22] Pound set out to expand the boundaries of poetic content and language by reviving a purportedly exhausted genre—the epic. His models included the Homeric tale and the Renaissance epic, which shared an emphasis on generic heterogeneity and comprehensiveness, what Michael Coyle calls "the ability of one form to include elements and features from others."[23] Both epic forms provided a framework in which poetry, like novelistic prose, could incorporate a broad range of subjects, literary and nonliterary genres, languages, and styles.

In an interview with Mario Benedetti, Cardenal reveals the extent to which he sees his poetic practice linked to Pound's larger effort to destabilize the boundaries between poetry and prose:

> [Pound's influence] consists primarily in making us see that everything fits in poetry; that there are not themes or elements that are appropriate to prose, and others that are appropriate to poetry. All that can be said in a story, or in an essay, or in a novel, can also be said in a poem. In a poem fit statistical facts, fragments of letters, newspaper editorials, news articles, historical chronicles, documents, jokes, anecdotes, things that before were considered elements of prose and not of poetry. Pound, therefore, opened up the limits of poetry so that in it can go everything that can be expressed in language: he has even made us see that neither the novel, nor the story, nor the essay, are necessary, because all can be said with poetry.[24]

To achieve discursive inclusiveness in poetry, Cardenal, like Pound, turned to the epic form. The Nicaraguan poet's relatively few comments regarding the epic genre are significant ones. For example, about *exteriorista* poetry Cardenal states:

> [*Exteriorista* poetry is] "impure" poetry, poetry that is, for some, closer to prose than to poetry, and they have mistakenly called it "prosaic," due to the fact that its subject matter is as ample as that of prose (and due also to the fact that, because of the decadence of poetry in the last centuries, the epic has been written in prose and not in verse).[25]

The parenthetical and nostalgic mention of the epic genre reveals that Cardenal was aware of the epic's decline in importance in the last century. The stated reasons for this decline can be traced to Pound, who saw the epic imperiled by the proliferation of prose paraphrases of the classic epics, which rose in competition with the increasing popularity of the novel. More specifically, Pound was concerned that these prose paraphrases had de-emphasized the Homeric epic's inclusivity to focus on the Homeric tale as *story*, thereby requiring more attention to narrative order.[26] Pound's interest lay in revitalizing the epic's tradition of inclusivity, a position he made known by "programmatically attacking narrative order in his poetic and creative work."[27] Cardenal shared Pound's interest in the epic's generic inclusivity but departed from his mentor by maintaining a solid commitment to the epic as story.

For Cardenal the epic genre was also the most suitable genre for an explicit poetic and political objective: to tell the tale of the Nicaraguan people. In an interview with Margaret Randall in 1984, Cardenal discusses his poem "La Hora 0," and tells how it was originally designed as part of a longer project—a *grande oeuvre*—in which he intended to write about "all the struggles of Nicaraguan history, about the struggle against yanqui imperialism, against the succession of Somozas. It was endless what I had in mind."[28]

With each of Cardenal's publications, the story of Nicaragua (and of Latin America by extension) becomes more inclusive and complex. The factors that influence his country's struggle for survival—politics, economics, cultural imperialism, ethnic conflict, religious persecution, and survival itself—become increasingly intertwined, rendering a multidimensional thematics supported by an equally heterogeneous stylistic configuration.

The Doubtful Strait constitutes a significant part of Cardenal's project "to tell of the struggles of Nicaraguan history." In general, the poem deals with the intricacies of the discovery, conquest, and colonization of this Central American nation. More specifically, it focuses on a sixteenth-century confrontation between what James Brown Scott has referred to as "two antagonistic classes in irreconcilable opposition."[29] The first class, relentlessly depicted in *The Doubtful Strait* as a greedy, ambitious, and deeply divided crew, is represented by the discoverers, conquerors, and governors. It consists of people who seek to gain wealth and defend their interests. The second class comprises people of good will, loyal to the Church, whose aim is to spread faith and civilization in the New World.[30] To this class also belong the resistant Amerindian communities. Ultimately, the central struggle in the text is between those seeking justice and those circumventing it.

Suitable to the nature of his story, Cardenal emplots his account to a structure reminiscent of a Christian contrast epic. History, both past and present, is reworked to reveal a cycle closely identified with an apocalyptic structure, where the movement is from a situation of apparent exile from God toward the arrival of messengers of faith, and finally to a sign of God's redemption and revelation. In Cardenal's story, one series of actions involves characters in ironic human situations, and another outlines the origin or continuation of a divine society.

In the ironic pole of *The Doubtful Strait*, Cardenal reads and writes colonial history counter-hegemonically. He destabilizes the view of the Conquest as a historical event of a complete and coherent significance by undermining and ultimately replacing it with a vision of the event as ambiguous, chaotic, and of uncertain meaning. Cardenal's articulation of this vision results primarily from an elaborate and innovative development of the quest theme. As the title suggests, *The Doubtful Strait* devotes particular attention to the sixteenth-century Spanish obsession with locating an interoceanic waterway—a strait that would enable them to navigate west directly to Calicutt and the Molucas, avoiding the hostility of the Portuguese (who had virtual control over the African route to the spice trade). "The Doubtful Strait" is in fact "the desired strait," a pivotal object of desire, the object of repeated quests, the motivation for complicated action, and the cause of war. Ultimately, however, it is the unattainable, a phantom objective, revealed as a misguided quest that invariably leads to catastrophe.

The pursuit of the strait typically involves a materialistically inclined explorer on a perilous journey that promotes a temporary *agon* and a subsequent death struggle, which he rarely survives. The struggle pits these individuals' preconceptions and illusions regarding the unexplored territory of the "New World" against the overwhelming, diverse, and often threatening realities of the American continent. In an ironic reversal, the explorers' greedy expectations for a wealthy and paradisiacal world are met instead by a hellish world of chaos marked by labyrinthine marshes, impenetrable tropical forests, catastrophic earthquakes, volcanic eruptions, and fierce storms at sea. Where they hope to find gold and emeralds in infinite abundance, they are driven to places of extreme cold where they die in the most grotesque manner or they retreat to a lonely, pathetic insanity. Thirst and hunger lead some survivors to drink sea water and eat poisonous plants and raw shellfish. Some resort to cannibalism.

The opening canto establishes the pattern of ironic reversal. It begins with an account of Columbus's fourth voyage of exploration in 1502 and uses fragments from letters written by Christopher Columbus and by his son Diego Colón, and from those supposedly written to Columbus by Paolo de Pozzo Toscanelli, which appear in Bartolomé de las Casas's *Historia de las Indias*. The collected fragments give a sense of Columbus's fascination with Marco Polo's epic tales of Japan, the East Indies, and India. Marco Polo's descriptions of the castles of the Khans in Cathay, the silk costumes and decorations, golden saddles, precious stones and pearls, spices, and other goods from the orient filter through Columbus's narrative revealing the cupidity that fueled his westward journey:

> "The country is beautiful . . .
> They choose the wisest as rulers.
> Taking the path straight for the West
> you will find the famous city of *Quisay*,
> which means *City of Heaven*,
> in the province of *Mango*, near Cathay.
> From the island of Antilla to the island of Cipango
> the intervals number twenty-six.
> The temples and palaces are faced with gold.
>   Rest assured of seeing mighty Kingdoms.
> Many crowded cities and rich Provinces
> which abound in all manner of precious stones.
> And your arrival will bring great joy to the king
> and to the Princes who rule in these lands."

The reader also learns of Columbus's obsession with locating the inter-oceanic strait and his belief that the strait lay between Cuba and South America, both of which he thought to be part of a single mainland or continent. On previous voyages, Indians had confirmed this notion by telling him that a channel through a narrow neck of land led to a great ocean.

The second half of the first canto concentrates on Columbus's unsuccessful attempt to locate the "uncertain strait." Near the end, we read:

> He found the Strait in Veragua:
> Veragua, in the province of Mango,
> which borders on Cathay . . .
> But it was a Strait of land
> it was not of water.

In his "Carta a propósito de *El estrecho dudoso*," José Coronel Urtecho remarks that these five lines constitute a kind of equation or poetic formula that opens and closes the poem and which in some ways summarizes the entire history of Central America from the time of Columbus to the present day. It embraces the constant tension between the idea of the Strait (and by extension, the idea of Latin America)—a possibility, a dream, a figment of the Spanish geographical and literary imagination—and the reality that the Spaniards never found what they were looking for.[31] This pattern of reversal is exemplified by the experiences of Alonso de Hojeda and Diego de Nicuesa (Canto III), Gil González de Avila (Canto VI), Alonso Calero and Diego Machuca de Suazo (Canto XII), Hernán Cortés (Cantos VIII and XXI), and Pedro de Alvarado (Cantos XV and XVI). The irony produced by these reversals is ultimately reinforced by the overall structure of *The Doubtful Strait*. It opens with a segment from Bartolomé de las Casas's *Historia de las Indias*, expressing the Admiral's greedy expectations of the world he was about to discover. In a marked reversal, however, the poem closes with a detailed description of a world that human desire can only reject. One hundred years later, León—the "excommunicated city," besieged by earthquakes, plagues, and infertility—is destroyed in a volcanic eruption.

A related theme, that of war, also receives ironic treatment in the contrast epic. Here again the action entails a quest, but the parameters of the quest broaden to include the con-quest, that is, the control and subjection of conquered peoples.

To develop this quest series, Cardenal draws from segments of Bernal Díaz's *Verdadera historia* and from Franciso Fuentes y Guzmán's *Recordación Florida*. Hernán Cortés, the conqueror of Mexico, and Pedro de Alvarado, the conqueror of Guatemala, are the central figures in these episodes. Displaying great strength, character, and daring, they are portrayed as individuals of heroic dimensions, and generally appear flanked by a loyal entourage waving colorful flags, pennants, and banners (Canto VIII):

> Cortés had had no further news of las Casas
> and made up his mind to go himself to las Hibueras.
> He went with his captains and with Franciscan friars
> and three thousand Tlascaltec Indians, and with majordomo,
> headwaiter, pastry cook, maker of refreshments
> with the gold and silver dinner service,
> chamberlain, valet, footmen and falconers
> puppeteers, flageolets, sackbutts, flutes,
> and with prince Cuauhtémoc and Coanococh lord of Texcoco

The success of the conqueror, however, turns against itself when the Amerindian communities become permanent underdogs and victims. Unable to measure their power, the conquerors indulge in prolonged brutality, exemplified by the unwarranted execution of Cuauhtémoc in Aclan ordered by an over-suspicious Cortés (Canto VIII), or Alvarado's ruthless burning of villages in the conquest of Guatemala (Canto XIII). The moral significance of these violent actions is explored in a series of episodes incorporating speeches and letters from figures such as Bartolomé de las Casas and Antonio de Valdivieso, texts that denounce the injustices being committed and point up their moral consequences. The shortcomings of these "heroic" conquerors, finally, are reinforced by the introduction of omens or portents such as the strange quetzal which haunts Alvarado (Canto XIII), or Cortés's fall and insomnia after he orders the execution of Cuauhtémoc (Canto VIII):

> And afterwards Cortés could not sleep at night.
> He got up and walked around alone in the darkness
> among the huge idols,
>   and in the dark he fell
> stumbling among the idols, and he cut open his head.
> But said nothing. He merely asked for it to be dressed.

The irony in *The Doubtful Strait* reaches its highest level in the foundation and governance of cities by the Spanish colonizers. To this series belong the cruel provincial governors—Pedrarias Dávila, Rodrigo de Contreras, and his two sons, Pedro and Hernando de Contreras.

The governors, officially appointed to exercise authority on behalf of the king, use their power to oppress: they are thieves and exalt the wicked, they praise perjurers and punish those who are innocent and good, they attack and violate church law and exploit the poor, the weak, and the helpless. In *The*

Doubtful Strait, the satanic governor, a seemingly insuperable enemy of goodness, brings his people to confusion, sterility, darkness, and death. In a chilling representation of Governor Pedrarias (Canto X), Cardenal combines fragments from the Colección Somoza, from Bartolomé de las Casas's *Historia de las Indias*, and from letters in the multi-volume *Colección de documentos inéditos de Indias* pertaining to the discovery, conquest, and colonization:

> The Most Magnificent Señor Don Pedrarias Dávila!
> The Indians killed their children so they would not become slaves
> or the women aborted so as not to give birth or did not cohabit
> so as not to conceive them. And they went to bed tired, without eating.
> And then that year in which the Indians sowed no crops
> (a General Strike) and the Christians took their maize:
> the Indians clutched crosses begging for corn for God's sake.
>
> And if you did not know the way
>   (from León to the mines)
> you needed no guide nor to ask the way:
> you followed the skeletons of the dead Indians:
>
> They went in chains and looking at the roads
> in tears they sang:
>   "Along those roads
>   we went to serve in León
>   and we returned.
>   Now we go with no hope
>   of returning."

The climax in *El estrecho* comes (in Canto XXIV) when Hernando de Contreras, son of Rodrigo de Contreras and grandson of Pedrarias, seeks revenge against Bishop Antonio de Valdivieso for helping oust Rodrigo de Contreras from the Nicaraguan governorship. Hernando Contreras savagely murders the bishop in León in the wake of an uprising against Spanish authority in 1550. Valdivieso, represented as a messianic figure selflessly devoted to delivering his community from evil, emerges as a hero.

His triumph is dramatically supported by the closing canto. Here an episode derived from a segment of Fray Antonio de Remesal's *Historia de las Indias Occidentales* narrates the "excommunication" of the accursed city of León (site of the Bishop's murder) in language reminiscent of catastrophe narratives in the Book of Revelations. As if God were handing down his wrathful judgment, darkness, storms, plagues, infertility, violent earthquakes, and consequent torrential landslides virtually submerge the city in a murky sea of sulphurous-smelling mud. Yet in the sinking city there appears a sign of redemption: a wall bearing the bloody handprint of the murdered

Antonio de Valdivieso:

> The water continued to rise
> 　　　　　　and the *accursed* city
> with the bloodied hand still painted on the wall
> was sinking slowly
> 　　　　　down down
> 　　　　　　　into the water.

The bloody handprint reminds the reader of the violence suffered by Valdivieso, but it also signals vengeance, repossession of the city, its deliverance from evil, and the dawn of a new era. It thus fulfills the prophecy of the Chilam Balam to the afflicted Maya (Canto XVII), announcing the dawning of a new age: "*On the day 13 Ahau I will be established the new age of time.*"

Along with the narration of the ill-founded colonial quest, its progressive corruption, and ultimate self-destruction is the contrasting field of action narrating the origin and continuation of a divine society.

The Doubtful Strait contemplates the Native American community that existed when the Spaniards reached what they believed to be the Indies. The Amerindian communities are virtuous, civilized, and Christian victims of the lawless and godless tyrants. Because they are portrayed as blessed communities struggling against the onslaught of injustice, oppression, and disease that threatens their survival and existence, the poem undermines and ultimately inverts the stereotypical savage/civilized opposition. A selection from Canto XVIII (which draws almost entirely on Bartolomé de las Casas's *Brevísima relación de la destrucción de las Indias*) refers to this inversion directly using animal imagery reminiscent of the biblical parables in which the wolf and the lamb are opposed: "and the Spanish arrived like wolves and tigers, like wolves and tigers to the place of these gentle sheep." Drawing from his own background and experience, las Casas continues his testimony:

> I am of the oldest who went across to the Indies
> and many years have I spent there, during which my eyes have seen,
> not read in histories which could be deceitful, but
> felt, so to speak, with my hands, so many cruelties
> committed upon those meek and peace-loving lambs;
> and one of those who abetted these tyrannies was my father.
> Slaves they are not, they are free *a natura!*
> They are free, and have their natural kings and lords
> and we found them very peace-loving, with their republics well-ordered,
> . . . .
> They were created simply by God, without wickedness or duplicity
> obedient, humble, patient, peace-loving and tranquil.

Limiting the portrayal of the American Indian to the extreme consequences of this savage/civilized inversion would produce a romanticized or allegorical characterization of narrow complexity. Within the poem's narrow Christian framework, the inversion functions on one level as a reminder of the indigenous people's deserved membership in the community of Christ and humankind. Moreover, once the Amerindians have been inscribed into this community, once their words have been uttered, their voices heard, and their actions heeded, their representation moves beyond an othering-type of discourse to their portrayal as agents of their own destiny.[32] Their speeches range from moral judgments to prophetic messages, the most notable being the speeches of Panquiaco (Canto IV), Nicaragua (Canto VI), Cuauhtémoc (Canto VIII), and Lempira (Canto XVII). Actions such as Lempira's abortive attempts at rebellion (Canto XVII) and the Aztecs' initial defeat of Cortés (Canto XXI) reinforce the content of the speeches and both become a vital element, a resisting force, in the complexity and violence of Cardenal's colonial reality. Panquiaco's speech and actions (Canto IV), reminiscent of Christ overturning the tables of the moneychangers, present a case in point:

> And Panquiaco, the eldest son of cacique Comagre,
> appeared (naked) at the door of the palace
> and with a blow of his fist on the scale, scattering the gold
> said: "If I had known you would squabble over my gold
> I would not have given it to you!
> I am amazed that you break up finely wrought jewels
> to make a few bars. Better you were in your own land
> which is so far from here
> if the people there are as wise and refined as you maintain
> than to come to squabble abroad, where we uncouth, barbaric men
> as you call us, live in contentment.

The Amerindian peoples, finally, are portrayed as a chosen people of God. A fragment selected from the prophecies of the Chilam Balam reveals the poem's commitment to las Casas's view that Native Americans were in fact "the scourged Christs of the Indies." It states that, following a sustained period of discord and anarchy, "the true God" will come to guide and protect the people of Itzá, marking the dawn of light and the age of renewal. The inclusion of this millennial prophecy suggests identification with the Babylonian captivity, in that both involve a community experiencing a seemingly endless period of servitude and exile, infernal darkness, victimization, and destruction, to culminate in the coming of a new heaven and a new earth (Canto XVII):

Let knowledge be given to all peoples
of the insignia of Hunab-ku raised up.
Adore it, O Itzalans. You should adore this insignia held on high
and believe in the word of the true God
who comes from the heavens to speak to us.
Multiply your good will O Itzalans,
now that the new Dawn is about to light up the universe
and life is about to enter a new Age.
Have faith in my message, I am Chilam Balam
and I have interpreted the word of the true God.

"The word of the true God" is brought to Native American society by two exemplary messengers: Antonio de Valdivieso and Bartolomé de las Casas. Both emerge well within the dimensions of the messianic hero, whose words and actions struggle to rescue a beleaguered society from demonic tyranny and to restore peace, order, and fertility in a world of hellish confusion. Valdivieso, as mentioned earlier, is murdered in this struggle, a victim of Rodrigo de Contreras's son, Hernando Contreras. Valdivieso's death, followed by the catastrophic destruction of León, is symbolic of the repossession of life, justice, and peace in the midst of a decaying and violently corrupt society. Las Casas lives on in the struggle, leaving the reader with some degree of confidence and hope in a continued fight for a better world.

The Doubtful Strait displays the characteristic expansiveness of the epic achieved primarily through the theme of the quest. The materialistically motivated discoveries, explorations, and conquests lead the reader through an immense and heterogeneous expanse of coastal areas, jungles, forests, swamplands, and mountains, as well as populated spaces. More significantly, however, the story involves a quest of a moral kind—the quest for the just and the right—which is embodied in the actions of las Casas and Valdivieso. This quest identifies spatially and metaphorically with heaven and hell. Its thematic associations—good/bad, order/disorder, darkness/light, barrenness/fertility—ultimately modify and define the moral implications of the territorial quest, creating a textual space that embraces an eschatological vision, history and myth, the physical and the spiritual, the human and the providential.

The Nicaraguan poet Pablo Antonio Cuadra has said of Cardenal's poetry that it has "a common denominator: the vision of America from a foreign eye."[33] In *The Doubtful Strait*, the foreign perspective—the Spanish gaze—is simultaneously exposed and dismantled. This gaze is exposed through the extensive use of fragments from the conquerors' own texts, which, reworked by the poet, constitute a richly nuanced record of the wide variety of intentions, motivations, and attitudes held by the adventurers, explorers, conquerors, and colonizers directly involved in the Conquest, as well as the notions of its chroniclers and historians. The gaze is dismantled, however, when it is forced to reflect upon itself by what Fernández Retamar has called Cardenal's "acid modernizing viewpoint."[34]

Indeed, in *The Doubtful Strait*, the past is not walled off, sacred, and valorized.[35] Rather, it is rendered familiar, relative, and connected to the present: Cardenal's contemporary viewpoint breaks through the spatio-temporal boundaries, connecting the historical past with contemporary reality. This contemporary viewpoint is revealed most notably in his reading of the Conquest as an ironic event: he debunks the traditional view of the glory and greatness of Spain's past actions by collecting fragments that show how greed informed the premises of the Conquest and the motivations and deeds of its actors.

The consequence of this contemporary viewpoint is that the nature and function of the epic bard in *The Doubtful Strait* is radically transformed. The poet abandons the role of singer of national glories and heroic ideals and instead adopts the role of critical reader, re-visor, and rewriter of canonical historical accounts. This role is made evident in a number of ways. In some cases, in recontextualizing borrowed fragments, the poet subverts their original meaning and intention. A case in point can be found in Canto XV, where the poet draws extensively from Alvarado's letter[36] to the King of Spain describing the disastrous outcome of an expedition to the Western Coast of Tierra Firme. In describing his misfortunes, Alvarado had obviously intended to secure the sympathy and continued support of his vitally important adressee. In their new context, however, Alvarado's words discredit him and serve as a bitter attack on his voracious greed and arrogance:

> Tired they clung to the crags
> and in a moment died frozen.
> Pedro Gómez froze with his horse
> and with all his emeralds.
> Their weapons and clothes lay strewn in the snow.
> There the gold remained cast into the snow.
> There the emeralds were cast.
> When they came out of the snow they moved like dead men.
> The Indians were missing fingers, missing feet, and many blind.
> Until they reached the highway of the Incas
> and saw the trail of the Castilians . . .
> The land was Pizarro's!

The poet also sets terse interjections in the text. These vary in form, tone, degree, and intensity, but overwhelmingly they resist mythologizing Spain's glory and power as a conquering nation. At times he emerges as a disputant, questioning the motivations and actions of the characters who appear in the narration. He frequently speaks as a polemicist, challenging the word of the very texts he appropriates. His remarks also function as reminders that the segments of texts we are summoned to read—mostly seventeenth-century historiographical documentation—prefigure the brutal oppression and economic exploitation which characterized Somoza's rule of Nicaragua for nearly half a century. In Canto X, the speaker draws a comparison between the sequence of events following Pedrarias Dávila's death in 1531 and those following Anastasio Somoza's rise to power in 1937. Striking parallels are drawn between the governorship of Rodrigo de Contreras and his rebel sons (Pedro and Hernando) and that of Anastasio Somoza and his two sons (Luis and Tachito). Cardenal has stated that, when writing the poem, he associated the life and death of Antonio de Valdivieso with Augusto César Sandino, the founder of Nicaragua's revolutionary struggle.[37] A more remarkable and prophetic association, however, can be established with the death in El Salvador of Archbishop Romero (assassinated in 1980, fourteen years after the publication of *The Doubtful Strait*). Like Valdivieso, Romero held an important office in the Catholic hierarchy and was murdered because of his denunciation of injustice and unconstitutional practices. An earthquake is also mentioned, establishing yet another parallel—between the earthquake that destroyed León in 1609 and the one that devastated Managua in 1931.

The poet's remarks ultimately reflect concern for a narrative that accurately represents the events at hand (both past and present), the need for which is stated repeatedly in *The Doubtful Strait*. In Canto X, this concern is expressed through the reconstruction of the celebrated dispute between Antonio de Herrera (royal chronicler and author of *Décadas de Indias*) and Francisco Arias Dávila, a grandson of the tyrannical governor of Nicaragua, Pedrarias Dávila. In the poem, Puñonrostro issues a formal complaint denouncing Herrera for defaming his grandfather in his history. The Royal Chronicler's briefly stated rebuttal appears twice: "THE CHRONICLER MUST NOT FAIL TO DO HIS DUTY." Herrera's defense is surrounded by fragments written by numerous individuals that document the atrocities committed by Pedrarias. His commitment to truth, seen in the context of other accounts that sustain his critical view of Pedrarias, undermines the injured grandson's ludicrous complaints and validates the word of the chronicler, and thereby the word of the poet, who concurs with Herrera's account.

In Canto XXI, the poet's compelling attention to truth is mediated through a series of metahistorical statements made by Bernal Díaz del Castillo. Citing the *Verdadera historia de la conquista de la Nueva España*, *The Doubtful Strait* outlines Bernal Díaz's reasons for writing his "true history": he wishes to tell the story of all those explorers, discoverers, conquerors, and colonizers whose names were ignored and omitted in the chronicles of the period. Berating the inaccuracies of Francisco López de Gómara's *Historia de las Indias y conquista de la Nueva España* and advancing the need for a rewriting of history, Castillo initially expresses doubts about his ability to write, and he actually abandons the project for a time. Finally, motivated by the falsities and omissions of the chronicles and histories that precede his, he returns to the idea of rewriting the "true" history of the Conquest. These metahistorical statements establish "truth" as the basic criterion for the writing of history. They advance the need to rewrite history, if necessary, to attain the most accurate account and explanation of the historical sequence selected for narration:

> The old man has reread those chronicles
> and he sees that they tell nothing of what happened in New Spain.
> They are full of lies. They exalt some captains
> and belittle others. They say some took part in the conquests
> who did not take part in them. Then he picks up the pen
> and starts writing again, without elegance,
> without propriety, without beautified arguments or rhetoric,
> according to the common speech of Castilla la Vieja.
> Because graceful composition is the telling of the truth.
> Though he may be doing nothing more than wasting paper and ink . . .
> For he had never written. He is only a soldier.
> But he writes also for his children and his grandchildren,
> so they might know that he came to conquer these lands.
> His history if it is printed they will see is truthful.
> And now as he writes it he pictures it all
> before his eyes as though it happened yesterday!
> He will go on writing, slowly, slowly,
> correcting his errors with care, like the pilot
> who proceeds mapping the coasts, casting his line . . .

The Doubtful Strait, through a careful rereading, selection, and recombination of accounts in "those chronicles," embodies this same critical, corrective approach to the making of history. Like the old *regidor* from Medina del Campo, the poet in *The Doubtful Strait* scans the "old chronicles" like a pilot readjusting his compass and his direction, mapping out alternative coasts, new horizons, new contours of truth, and, ultimately, new meaning.

In her book *Resistance Literature*, Barbara Harlow points out that historical struggles against colonialism and imperialism are usually waged at the same time as a struggle over the historical and cultural record.[38] *The Doubtful Strait* embraces both of these struggles, but the latter is emphasized in the poem's re-reading and rewriting of the dominant historiographical versions of early colonial occupation of Central America. In re-examining the past, moreover, *The Doubtful Strait* redefines the area's symbolic heritage and national mythology, providing a sense of historical coherence and direction to the revolutionary struggle that coincided with the text's production. *The Doubtful Strait* draws on the content of the collective memory, structures it, and from it develops a story in which a community can recognize its own features and experience, and from which it can draw imperatives for belief and action. The story looks back, but also forward, toward the future and its revolutionary possibilities.[39] Ultimately, the poem is an affirmation of collective belief, faith, and action.

Cardenal thus reclaims the functions of the epic bard, for in *The Doubtful Strait* he is historian and record-keeper, poet and storyteller, moralist, prophet, and seer.

The author gratefully acknowledges

Revista Canadiense de Estudios Hispánicos for permission to reprint material from her "Ernesto Cardenal's *El estrecho dudoso*: Reading/Re-writing History" (15, no. 1 [Fall 1990])

Chasqui: Revista de Literatura Latinoamericana for permission to reprint material from her "Reading Ernesto Cardenal Reading Ezra Pound: Radical Inclusiveness, Epic Reconstitution, and Textual Praxis" (21, no. 2 [November 1992])

Inti: Revista de literatura hispánica for permission to reprint material from her "Narrative Strategies and Counter-History in *El estrecho dudoso*" (39, no. 1 [Spring 1994]).

Robert Pring-Mill for his loan of recorded interviews with Cardenal on the subject of *The Doubtful Strait*

the generous support of Hamilton College, which provided funds for the final stages of preparing the manuscript and, with special thanks, Laura and Erin for their assistance.

NOTES

1. Translated in Ernesto Cardenal, *Zero Hour and Other Documentary Poems*, selected and edited by Donald D. Walsh with an introductory essay by Robert Pring-Mill (New York: New Directions, 1980).

2. See Isabel Fraire, "Pound and Cardenal," *Review* 18 (Fall 1976): 36–42.

3. Michael Coyle, *Ezra Pound, Popular Genres, and the Discourse of Culture* (University Park: The Pennsylvania State University Press, forthcoming): 9.

4. See Tamara Williams, "Reading Ernesto Cardenal Reading Ezra Pound: Radical Inclusiveness, Epic Reconstitution and Textual Praxis," *Chasqui* 21, no. 2 (November 1992): 43–52.

5. Thomas Merton, "Prólogo," *Gethsemaní, Ky.,* by Ernesto Cardenal (Bogota: Ediciones La Tertulia, 1965).

6. Available in English as Ernesto Cardenal, *Love,* trans. D. Livingstone (London: Search Press, 1974).

7. Ernesto Cardenal, *Marilyn Monroe and other poems,* trans. and introduction by Robert Pring-Mill (London: Search Press, 1975).

8. Ernesto Cardenal, *The Psalms of Struggle and Liberation,* trans. Emile G. McAnany (New York: Herder and Herder, 1971).

9. *The Gospel in Solentiname,* 4 vols., trans. Donald D. Walsh (New York: New Directions, 1976).

10. *In Cuba,* trans. Donald D. Walsh (New York: New Directions, 1974).

11. See Robert Pring-Mill, "Introduction," *Marilyn Monroe and other poems* by Ernesto Cardenal, trans. Robert Pring-Mill (London: Search Press, 1975).

12. Mayra Jiménez, *Talleres de poesía* (Managua: Ministerio de Cultura, 1983). Translations of a collection of poems from workshops held at the community in Solentiname and an excellent introduction to their nature and function within the context of revolutionary Nicaragua are contained in *Nicaraguan Peasant Poetry from Solentiname,* ed., trans., and introduction by David Gullette (Albuquerque: West End Press, 1988).

13. Ernesto Cardenal, *Cosmic Canticle,* trans. John Lyons (Connecticut: Curbstone Press, 1993).

14. The press release from Curbstone Press, which published *Cosmic Canticle* in 1993, reads: "To try to define *Cosmic Canticle*—narrative poem, mythic song, epic—is to diminish its originality. . . . Throughout, Cardenal blends the visible and invisible, science and poetry, the individual and society, religion and nature, in forty-three autonomous yet integrated cantos."

15. Details about *The Doubtful Strait*'s genesis are from unpublished tape-recordings of an interview with Cardenal by Robert Pring-Mill (August 1972).

16. George Woodcock, *Thomas Merton: Monk and Poet* (New York: Farrar, Straus, Giroux, 1978): 102.

17. See Roberto Fernández Retamar, "Prologue to Ernesto Cardenal," *Caliban and Other Essays* (Minneapolis: University of Minnesota Press, 1989): 104.

18. Only a handful of articles have been devoted to the poem exclusively. These include those by Alstrum, Elías, and Williams (*see bibliography*).

19. See James Alstrum, "Typology and Narrative Techniques in Cardenal's *El estrecho dudoso*," *Journal of Spanish Studies* 8 (1980): 10: ". . . the Nicaraguan poet's abundant use of prefiguration throughout this poem to call the reader's attention to the present situation of his own country and the rest of Central America, represents a clear example of the application of typology—a traditional literary technique first used by the writers of the Bible. Typology

contributes to the development of theme and the arrangement and sequencing of historical events in such a way that they acquire a prophetic significance which transcends history."

20. Julia Kristeva, *Desire in Language: A Semiotic Approach to Literature and Art*, trans. Thomas Gora, Alice Jardine, Leon S. Roudiez (New York: Columbia University Press, 1980): 66–67.

21. Cardenal was influenced the "new historical method" that Pound outlined in *Guide to Kulchur*. In Coyle's description (pp. 6–7), ". . . this 'new historical method' was to be distinguished from more orthodox post-Enlightenment practice because of its inclusion of 'whole slabs of the record.' By 'history' Pound meant actual historical texts—not just academic commentaries upon them, and not just histories but texts of all kinds—the 'concrete evidence of legal codes and poems alike.' By 'including' he meant neither paraphrase or allusion, but the transposition of the language of the sources onto his page."

22. Donald Davie, *Ezra Pound* (Chicago: The University of Chicago Press, 1975): 34.

23. Coyle, 119.

24. A translation by Russell O. Salmon of Mario Benedetti, "Ernesto Cardenal: Evangelio y revolución," *Casa de las Américas* 63 (1970): 175–76.

25. Translation of this fragment of Cardenal's prologue to *Poesía Nicaragüense* is from Russell O. Salmon, "Introduction," *Los ovnis de oro: poemas indios /Golden UFOs: The Indian Poems* by Ernesto Cardenal, trans. Carlos and Monique Altschul (Bloomington: Indiana University Press, 1992): xiii.

26. Coyle, 116–37.

27. Coyle, 135.

28. Margaret Randall, *Risking a Somersault in the Air* (San Francisco: Solidarity Publications, 1984): 99.

29. Citing James Brown Scott, see Venancio Carro, "The Spanish Theological-Juridical Renaissance," *Bartolomé de las Casas: Towards an Understanding of the Man and His Work*, ed. Juan Friede and Benjamin Keen (De Kalb: Northern Illinois University Press, 1971): 246.

30. Carro, 246.

31. José Coronel Urtecho, "Carta a propósito del *Estrecho Dudoso*," *El estrecho dudoso* by Ernesto Cardenal (Managua: Editorial Nueva Nicaragua, 1985): 20–21.

32. For a thorough assessment of the portrait of manners and customs as a limiting and normalizing discourse, see Mary Louise Pratt, "Scratches on the Face of the Country; or, What Mr. Barrow Saw in the Land of the Bushmen," *Race, Writing and Difference*, ed. Henry Louis Gates, Jr. (Chicago: The University of Chicago Press, 1986): 138–62.

33. Jonathan Cohen, "Introduction: To Nicaragua With Love," *With Walker in Nicaragua* by Ernesto Cardenal (Connecticut: Wesleyan University Press, 1979): 7.

34. See Fernández Retamar, 104.

35. See Mikhail Bakhtin, *The Dialogic Imagination*, trans. Caryl Emerson (Minneapolis: University of Minnesota Press, 1984): 14: "The epic past is called the 'absolute past' for good reason; it lacks any relativity, that is, any gradual purely temporal progressions that might connect it with the present. It is walled off absolutely from all subsequent times, and above all from those times in which the singer and listeners are located."

36. Pedro Alvarado, "Carta a S.M. del Adelantado Don Pedro de Alvarado, sobre las contrariedades que el mismo sufría de Pizarro, y estado de los

descubrimientos en Guatemala," *Colección de documentos inéditos de Indias,* vol. 24 (Madrid: Imprenta de Manuel G. Hernández, 1875): 211–35.

37. From unpublished tape-recorded interviews by Robert Pring-Mill with Cardenal (August 1972).

38. Barbara Harlow, *Resistance Literature* (New York: Methuen Press, 1987): 7.

39. Richard Slotkin, *Regeneration through Violence: The Mythology of the American Frontier* (Connecticut: Wesleyan University Press, 1973): 14–16.

WORKS CITED

Alstrum, James. "Typology and Narrative Techniques in Cardenal's *El estrecho dudoso.*" *Journal of Spanish Studies* 8 (1980): 9–27.

Alvarado, Pedro. "Carta a S.M. del Adelantado Don Pedro de Alvarado, sobre las contrariedades que el mismo sufría de Pizarro, y estado de los descubrimientos en Guatemala." *Colección de documentos inéditos de Indias.* Vol. 24. Madrid: Imprenta de Manuel G. Hernández, 1875: 211–35.

Bakhtin, Mikhail. *The Dialogic Imagination.* Trans. Caryl Emerson. Minneapolis: University of Minnesota Press, 1984.

Benedetti, Mario. "Ernesto Cardenal: Evangelio y Revolución." *Casa de las Américas* 63 (1970): 174–83.

Cardenal, Ernesto. *Cosmic Canticle.* Trans. John Lyons. Connecticut: Curbstone Press, 1993.

———. *Los ovnis de oro: poemas indios / Golden UFOs: The Indian Poems.* Ed. Russell O. Salmon. Trans. Carlos and Monique Altschul. Bloomington: Indiana University Press, 1992.

———. *Zero Hour and Other Documentary Poems.* Selected and ed. Donald D. Walsh with an introductory essay by Robert Pring-Mill. New York: New Directions, 1980.

———. *The Gospel in Solentiname.* 4 vols. Trans. Donald D. Walsh. New York: New Directions, 1976.

———. *Marilyn Monroe and other poems.* Trans. and introduction by Robert Pring-Mill. London: Search Press, 1975.

———. *In Cuba.* Trans. Donald D. Walsh. New York: New Directions, 1974.

———. *Love.* Trans. D. Livingstone. London: Search Press, 1974.

———. *The Psalms of Struggle and Liberation.* Trans. Emile G. McAnany. New York: Herder and Herder, 1971.

Carro, Venancio. "The Spanish Theological-Juridical Renaissance." *Bartolomé de las Casas: Towards an Understanding of the Man and His Work.* Ed. Juan Friede and Benjamin Keen. De Kalb: Northern Illinois University Press, 1971.

Cohen, Jonathan. "Introduction: To Nicaragua With Love." *With Walker in Nicaragua* by Ernesto Cardenal. Connecticut: Wesleyan University Press, 1979: 3–17.

Coronel Urtecho, José. "Carta a propósito del *Estrecho Dudoso.*" *El estrecho dudoso* by Ernesto Cardenal. Managua: Editorial Nueva Nicaragua, 1985: 9–38.

Coyle, Michael. *Ezra Pound, Popular Genres, and the Discourse of Culture.* University

Park: The Pennsylvania State University Press, forthcoming.

Davie, Donald. *Ezra Pound.* Chicago: The University of Chicago Press, 1975.

Elías, Eduardo. "*El estrecho dudoso:* del discurso histórico a la épica contemporánea." *Revista iberoamericana* 57, no. 157 (1991): 923–31.

Fernández Retamar, Roberto. "Prologue to Ernesto Cardenal." *Caliban and Other Essays.* Minneapolis: University of Minnesota Press, 1989.

Fraire, Isabel. "Pound and Cardenal" *Review* 18 (Fall 1976): 36–42.

Gullette, David, ed., trans., and introduction. *Nicaraguan Peasant Poetry from Solentiname.* Albuquerque: West End Press, 1988.

Harlow, Barbara. *Resistance Literature.* New York: Methuen Press, 1987.

Jiménez, Mayra. *Talleres de poesía.* Managua: Ministerio de Cultura, 1983.

Kristeva, Julia. *Desire in Language: A Semiotic Approach to Literature and Art.* Trans. Thomas Gora, Alice Jardine, and Leon S. Roudiez. New York: Columbia University Press, 1980.

Merton, Thomas. "Prólogo." *Gethsemaní, Ky.* by Ernesto Cardenal. Colombia: Ediciones La Tertulia, 1965.

Pratt, Mary Louise. "Scratches on the Face of the Country; or, What Mr. Barrow Saw in the Land of the Bushmen." *Race, Writing and Difference.* Ed. Henry Louis Gates, Jr. Chicago: The University of Chicago Press, 1986: 138–62.

Randall, Margaret. *Risking a Somersault in the Air.* San Francisco: Solidarity Publications, 1984.

Salmon, Russell O. "Introduction." *Los ovnis de oro: poemas indios / Golden UFOs: The Indian Poems* by Ernesto Cardenal. Trans. Carlos and Monique Altschul. Bloomington: Indiana University Press, 1992.

Slotkin, Richard. *Regeneration through Violence: The Mythology of the American Frontier.* Connecticut: Wesleyan University Press, 1973.

Williams, Tamara. "Narrative Strategies and Counter-History in *El estrecho dudoso.*" *Inti: Revista de literatura hispánica* 39, no. 1 (Spring 1994): 47–58.

———. "Reading Ernesto Cardenal Reading Ezra Pound: Radical Inclusiveness, Epic Reconstitution, and Textual Praxis." *Chasqui* 21, no. 2 (November 1992): 43–52.

———. "Ernesto Cardenal's *El estrecho dudoso*: Reading/Re-writing History." *Revista canadiense de estudios hispánicos* 15, no. 1 (Fall 1990): 111–21.

Woodcock, George. *Thomas Merton: Monk and Poet.* New York: Farrar, Straus, Giroux, 1978.

Translator's note on punctuation

In general, Cardenal's approach to punctuation is idiosyncratic, which explains why it can appear unmotivated. If there is an underlying motivation, it is the desire not to be bound by convention. More than one publisher has added a lot of commas to Cardenal's poems only to take them out again at Cardenal's insistence.

The Doubtful Strait draws heavily on documents which were themselves totally inconsistent with regard to capitalization, spelling, and punctuation, and it is clear that Cardenal wishes to reflect this in his work. He sometimes switches between archaisms and modern Spanish, also for effect. On occasion, it is clear that he uses (or refuses) commas to adjust the rhythm. Believe me, I have challenged Cardenal on his seemingly arbitrary use of full stops, for example, and he has always stuck to his guns.

ERNESTO CARDENAL

The Doubtful Strait

El estrecho dudoso

"El país es bello"
le había dicho a Colón Toscanelli.

De la isla Ofir, Ophaz o Cipanga
(llamada también la Española) el Almirante
se hizo a la vela a descubrir el estrecho
para pasar a la Tierra firme de las Indias
que estaban hacia el Poniente, decía Toscanelli,
no sólo hacia Levante:

"Los que navegaren hacia el Poniente hallarían las Indias
y los que navegaren hacia Levante las hallarían también."

Hallarían *Zaitón*,
uno de los más hermosos y famosos puertos de Levante,
lleno de barcos cargados de especierías.
Son los reinos del Gran Can
que reside ordinariamente en Catay.
Donde están las doscientas ciudades con puentes de mármol.

"El país es bello . . .
Escogen para gobernadores los más sabios.
Tomando el camino derecho a Poniente
hallaréis la famosa ciudad de *Quisay*,
que quiere decir *Ciudad del Cielo*,
en la provincia de *Mango*, cerca de Catay.
De la isla Antilla hasta la de Cipango
se cuentan veinte y seis espacios.
Los templos y palacios están cubiertos de oro.
     Estad seguro de ver Reinos poderosos.
Cantidad de ciudades poblados y ricas Provincias
que abundan en toda suerte de pedrería.
Y vuestra llegada causaría gran alegría al Rey
y a los Príncipes que reinan en esas tierras."

Después de la Isla Ofir, Ophaz o Cipanga
hubo una tormenta de sesenta días.
Iban con las velas rotas, sin ancla y sin jarcia.
Y después, al doblar un cabo, hubo calma.
Por primera vez vieron el sol y las estrellas.
Tras el cabo la tierra daba vuelta al Mediodía
y los vientos levantes se volvieron favorables.
Y dieron gracias a Dios. Colón le llamó

"The country is beautiful"
        Toscanelli had told Columbus.

From the island of Ofir, Ophaz or Cipanga
(also known as Hispaniola) the Admiral
set sail to discover the strait
to reach the Terra firma of the Indies
which lay to the West, said Toscanelli,
not just to the East:

"Those who sailed to the West would find the Indies
and those who sailed to the East would find them also."

They would find *Zaiton*,
one of the most beautiful and famous ports in the East
full of ships laden with spices.
These are the kingdoms of the Great Khan
who lives mostly in Cathay.
Where one finds the two hundred cities with marble bridges.

"The country is beautiful . . .
They choose the wisest as rulers.
Taking the path straight for the West
you will find the famous city of *Quisay*,
which means *City of Heaven*,
in the province of *Mango*, near Cathay.
From the island of Antilla to the island of Cipango
the intervals number twenty-six.
The temples and palaces are faced with gold.
        Rest assured of seeing mighty Kingdoms.
Many crowded cities and rich Provinces
which abound in all manner of precious stones.
And your arrival will bring great joy to the king
and to the Princes who rule in these lands."

After Ofir, Ophaz or Cipanga Island
a storm blew for sixty days.
With torn sails, without anchor and without rigging they pressed on.
And then, as they rounded the cape, it fell calm.
For the first time they saw the sun and the stars.
Beyond the cape the land turned away to the South
and the easterly winds became favorable.
And they gave thanks to God. Columbus called it

el Cabo de Gracias a Dios.
Unos bancos de arena largos salían al mar.
En *Cariay* andaban desnudos, pintados como berberiscos,
cubiertas sus vergüenzas con corteza de árboles.
Vio animales a los que no puso nombre.
Y en un palacio de madera, cubierto de cañas,
habían sepulturas, y un muerto embalsamado,
adornado con joyas de oro y cuentas.
En *Carambaru* traían un espejo de oro colgado al cuello.
Y dijeron que había mucho oro en *Ciguare*, al Poniente.
Sillas, arcas, mesas de oro. Conocieron la pimienta.
Y hablaron de las grandes ferias que había en Ciguare.
Otrosí que tenían naos con lombardas, arcos, flechas,
espadas, corazas, y que andaban vestidos,
habían caballos y traen ricas vestiduras.
Y a 10 jornadas de Ciguare estaba el río Ganges.
(Como Tortosa con Fuenterrabía o Pisa con Venecia
estas tierras están con Veragua.)
Navegó en 24° al Poniente y hubo eclipse esa noche.
El sol estaba en Libra y la luna en Ariete.
Y en Veragua la mar estaba alta y espumosa y fea,
el agua como hecha sangre, hirviendo como una caldera.
Tronaba, como si en los otros navíos dispararan la artillería.
Después hubo calma, y el mar se llenó de tiburones.

Halló el Estrecho en Veragua:
     Veragua, en la provincia de Mango,
que limita con Catay . . .
     Pero el Estrecho era de tierra,
          no era de agua.

Volvió con los navíos engusanados, comidos de broma,
a la Isla Española o Cipango.
El Almirante desde la popa miró alejarse los palmitos
y mirabolandos de las tierras que describe el Papa Pío,
con gatos monteses y monos colgados de la cola
(aunque no los caballos con frenos de oro del Papa Pío)
y los papagayos que pasaban volando, hacia Catay.

I / 4

Cape Gracias a Dios.
A few long sand banks broke the sea surface.
In *Cariay* they went about naked, painted like Berbers,
their private parts covered with tree bark.
He saw animals to which he gave no name.
In a wooden palace covered in cane
there were tombs and an embalmed body
decorated with golden jewels and beads.
In *Carambaru* they wore a mirror of gold about their necks.
And they said that there was much gold in *Ciguare*, to the West.
Seats, coffers, tables of gold. They knew pepper.
And they spoke of the great bazaars held in Ciguare.
Moreover that they had ships with lombards, bows and arrows,
swords, breastplates, and went about clothed,
they had horses and wore fine garments.
And ten days away from Ciguare was the river Ganges.
(As Tortosa is to Fuenterrabia or Pisa to Venice
these lands are to Veragua.)
He steered along 24° to the West and there was an eclipse that night.
The sun was in Libra and the moon in Aries.
And in Veragua the sea was deep, foaming, and ugly,
the water as though changed to blood, boiling like a cauldron.
There was thunder, as though they were firing guns from the other ships.
Then it fell calm and the sea filled with sharks.

He found the Strait in Veragua:
        Veragua, in the province of Mango,
which borders on Cathay . . .
        But it was a Strait of land
                it was not of water.

With the ships worm-eaten, rotten with teredo,
he returned to the island of Hispaniola or Cipango.
From the stern the Admiral watched the palms recede
and the myrobalans of the lands described by Pope Pius,
with mountain cats and monkeys hanging by their tails
(but not Pope Pius's horses with gold bridles)
and the parrots that flew by, toward Cathay.

Por lo que toca a su vida y sus costumbres,
hombres y mujeres andan completamente desnudos.
Son de mediana estatura y de buenas proporciones.
Su carne tira a roja como el pelo de los leones,
y soy de opinión que si anduvieran vestidos
serían tan blancos como nosotros.
Tienen sus pelos largos y negros,
especialmente las mujeres,
a las que sienta bien la larga y atezada cabellera.
No son muy hermosos sus semblantes
porque tienen las caras chatas o aplastadas
semejantes a las de los tártaros.
Son de extremo ligeros y veloces para correr
tanto los hombres como las mujeres.
Nadan maravillosamente en el agua, como peces,
y las mujeres mejor que los hombres.
Sus armas son arcos y saetas
que fabrican con mucha habilidad.
Carecen enteramente de hierro y otros metales
y arman sus saetas con dientes de bestias y de peces.
No tienen jefes ni capitanes de guerra
sino que andan sin orden, cada uno libremente.
Esta gente vive en libertad, no obedece a nadie
ni tiene ley ni señor. No riñen entre sí.
En el modo de hablar parecen muy sencillos
pero en realidad son muy astutos y sagaces.
Hablan muy rara vez y en tono muy bajo
usando los mismos acentos que nosotros.
Las voces las forman entre los dientes y los labios;
y tienen vocablos distintos de los nuestros.
Su modo de comer es muy bárbaro
y no tienen horas determinadas para ello;
comen cuando tienen hambre, sea de día o de noche.
Para comer se sientan en el suelo;
y no usan manteles ni servilletas,
pues no tienen lienzo ni paño alguno.
Duermen en grandes redes colgadas en el aire.
Son muy aseados y limpios porque se bañan mucho.
Sus casas están construidas a manera de campanas.
Sus riquezas son plumas de aves de varios colores
o cuentas que hacen de los huesos de los peces
o piedrecitas verdes y blancas.
Pero desprecian el oro y las piedras preciosas.

As for their life and customs,
men and women go about completely naked.
They are of medium height and well-proportioned.
Their flesh tends toward red like the fur of lions,
and my opinion is that were they to wear clothes
they would be as white as us.
They have long, black hair,
especially the women,
who are well suited by their long black hair.
They are not very attractive
because they have flattened or pushed-in faces
similar to those of the Tartars.
They are extremely light and swift at running
the men as well as the women.
They are splendid swimmers in the water, like fish,
and the women better than the men.
Their weapons are bow and arrow
which they fashion with great skill.
They are entirely lacking in iron and other metals
and tip their arrows with the teeth of animals and fish.
They have no chiefs or war leaders
moving about uncommanded, each one freely.
These people live in freedom, obey no one
and know neither law nor master. They do not quarrel among themselves.
From their way of speaking they seem very simple
but in reality they are very astute and discerning.
They talk rarely and in a very soft tone
using the same intonations as ourselves.
They form their sounds between their teeth and lips;
and have different words from us.
Their way of eating is very crude
and they have no set hours for this;
they eat when they are hungry, be it night or day.
They sit on the ground to eat;
and use no tablecloth or napkins,
since they have no linen or fabric of any kind.
They sleep in big nets suspended in the air.
They are very clean and fresh because they bathe often.
Their houses are bell-like constructions.
Their riches consist of feathers of many-colored birds
or beads that they make from fishbones
or tiny green and white pebbles.
But they show no interest in gold or precious stones.

. . . allén de estas islas y tierras descubiertas . . .
. . . una grand parte de tierra, que así por su grandeza . . .
. . . como porque han hallado diversos géneros de animales,
que en las otras islas no han hallado animales de 4 pies
se cree que es Tierra-firme . . .

La Tierra Firme fue dividida entre Nicuesa y Hojeda.

Del cabo de la Vela hasta la mitad del golfo de Urabá
para Alonso de Hojeda.
Y de la otra mitad del golfo al cabo de Gracias a Dios
para Diego de Nicuesa.

A vos Diego de Nicuesa . . .
A vos Alonso de Hojeda . . .

. . . que no pertenecen al serenísimo Rey de portugal
Nuestro muy caro y muy amado hijo . . .
Y podían rescatar o haber en otra cualquiera manera
        oro e plata e guanines y otros metales
        e aljófar y piedras preciosas y perlas
        e monstruos e serpientes y animales
        e pescado e aves y especería . . .

                                    (yo El Rey)

Pero allí en Urabá
                Juan de la Cosa quedó hecho como un erizo.
De noche soñaban con él y su fealdad horrible.
Hinchado y deformado por la ponzoña de tantas saetas.
Hojeda fue hallado tiritando en los manglares
de hambre y de frío,
                        herido con ponzoña
y con la señal de trescientas saetas en la rodela.
Y después con el veneno,
                        poco a poco se iba secando.
¡Y la ciénaga! Tenían delante una ciénaga—
Comenzaron a andar la ciénaga, con el lodo a las rodillas,
    pensando que pronto se acabaría, y
andados tres días
                se iba ahondando más y más
y seguían andando
                    esperando que pronto se acabaría
se ahondaba más,

. . . far beyond these discovered lands and islandes . . .
. . . an immense expanse of lande, which by dint of its vastness . . .
. . . so since they have found divers species of animals,
while on the other islandes no four-legged animals have they found
it is thought to be Terra firma . . .

Terra firma was divided between Nicuesa and Hojeda.

From the cape of la Vela to halfway in the gulf of Urabá
for Alonso de Hojeda.
And from the other half of the gulf to Cape Gracias a Dios
for Diego de Nicuesa.

For you Diego de Nicuesa . . .
For you Alonso de Hojeda . . .

. . . provided they do not belong to the most serene King of Portugal
Our very dear and well-loved son . . .
And they could barter or obtain by any other means
     gold & silver and gold ore and other metals
     & seed pearls and precious stones & pearls
     and monsters & serpents & animals
     and fishes & birds & spices . . .
               (I the King)

But there in Urabá
          Juan de la Cosa ended up like a hedgehog.
At night they dreamed of him and his revolting ugliness.
Swollen and deformed by the poison of so many arrows.
Hojeda was found shivering among the mangroves
from hunger and cold,
           a poisoned wound
and with the trace of three-hundred arrows in his shield.
And later from the poison,
             he was gradually wasting away.
And the swamp! A swamp lay ahead of them—
They started into the swamp, with mud up to their knees,
      thinking they would soon be out, and
after three days' walking
           it was getting deeper and deeper
and they kept walking
        hoping that soon it would end
and it got deeper,

         y por no desandar lo andado,
              seguían adelante
y la ciénaga se hacía más honda
(Hojeda iba envenenado)
y anduvieron ocho días, diez días, doce días,
veinte días, con sed, con hambre,
con el lodo a la cintura, noches y días sin dormir,
o durmiendo en las raíces de los manglares
un sueño inquieto, triste y amargo,
                    comiendo las raíces,
bebiendo el agua salobre del pantano.
Anduvieron más
y la ciénaga se hundía más y más.
         El agua hedionda les llegaba a los sobacos,
les llegaba al cuello, a la cabeza, los tapaba,
y se hacía más honda.
         Se iban quedando en el lodo
y ya era muy tarde para volver atrás y desandar lo andado.
Y seguían. Con la esperanza que la ciénaga se acabara.
Anduvieron treinta días en la ciénaga.

         Sólo la mitad salieron.
Y Hojeda salió para morir.
         ¿Fue enterrado de caridad en la Española?
         ¿Se hizo fraile?
Está enterrado en la puerta de San Francisco
donde lo pisan todos los que pasan.

Y los otros que quedaban en Urabá
         (Hojeda no volvía)
eran demasiados para caber en los dos bergantines
y esperaron a que el hambre y las enfermedades y los indios
los diezmaran,
y pudieran caber.
              A los pocos días ya cabían
y sobraba lugar. Se hicieron a la vela,
Pizarro en un navío y Valenzuela en otro.
El de Valenzuela se fue hundiendo en el agua,
con toda su gente
              (unos vieron un pez grande)
y se ahogaron a la vista de Pizarro dando gritos.
Hojeda no volvía;
eligieron por gobernador a Diego de Nicuesa
(y no sabían dónde estaba Nicuesa)
                        y Nicuesa
perdidos los navíos, con sólo un bote pequeño
iba a pie por la costa en busca de Veragua

and rather than retrace their steps
             they pressed on
and the swamp was getting deeper
(Hojeda still poisoned)
and they walked eight days, ten days, twelve days,
twenty days, thirsty and hungry,
mud to their waists, day and night without sleep,
or sleeping among the mangrove roots
a troubled sleep, sad and bitter,
                eating roots,
drinking the brackish marsh water.
They walked on
and the swamp grew deeper and deeper.
      The fetid water came up to their armpits,
to their necks, their faces, covered their mouths,
and still was getting deeper.
      They were caught in the slime
and now it was very late to turn back and retrace their steps.
And they continued. In the hope that the swamp would end.
Thirty days they walked in the swamp.

             Only half came out of it.
And Hojeda came out to die.
        Was he given a pauper's burial in Hispaniola?
        Did he become a friar?
He is buried in the doorway of San Francisco
where he is trodden upon by all who pass by.

And the others who were left in Urabá
        (there was no sign of Hojeda)
were too many to fit in the two brigs
and they waited for hunger and sickness and the Indians
to decimate them,
so they would fit.
             Within a few days they did fit
and with room to spare. They set sail,
Pizarro in one boat and Valenzuela in another.
Valenzuela's slowly sank in the water,
taking all those aboard
              (some saw a big fish)
and before Pizarro's eyes they drowned screaming.
There was no sign of Hojeda;
they chose Diego de Nicuesa as governor
(and they didn't know where Nicuesa was)
                   and Nicuesa
the ships lost, with only a small boat
traveling on foot along the coast in search of Veragua

(y Veragua quedaba atrás).
Su sueño Veragua. La negra Veragua.
Donde un perro sarnoso valía veinte castellanos
y la escudilla de perro a castellano
                2 sapos: 6 ducados.
Vieron una punta tras un gran ancón que hacía el mar
y por ahorrar camino pasaron en bote a la punta
y al llegar encontraron que era una isleta desolada.
Los del bote huyeron cuando vieron esa isla,
                        y que estaban perdidos.
Y cuando Nicuesa y sus hombres se hallaron sin el bote
corrían como locos de un cabo al otro, dando gritos.
Comían las hierbas sin conocerlas, bebían agua salada
y se iban muriendo. Los que quedaban andaban a gatas
paciendo las hierbas, comiendo crudo el marisco.
(Y en la Española le estaban haciendo 1.000 piernas de jamón.)
Eligieron por gobernador a Nicuesa y fueron a buscarlo.
Lo trajeron de Nombre de Dios donde se estaba muriendo.
Y Nicuesa creía que lo recibirían con arcos triunfales.
Ya en la carabela iba dictando decretos contra ellos,
(que les quitaría todo el oro sacado en su jurisdicción).
Cuando llegó Nicuesa salieron armados a recibirlo
gritándole que se volviera a Nombre de Dios.
Nicuesa quedó sin habla. Después habló implorando
y le gritaban que se volviera. (Balboa gritaba en la costa.)
Y él les pedía que si no lo aceptaban por gobernador
que al menos lo aceptaran por compañero.
Y respondían que no querían. Les pidió otra vez
que si no lo querían por compañero que lo aceptaran preso:
prefería estar en cadenas con ellos que en Nombre de Dios!
Y le mandaron que se presentara al rey de España
y no parara hasta llegar a España, so pena de muerte.
Y lo metieron en el bergantín más viejo que tenían
y él protestaba diciendo que ésa era su gobernación
y ellos eran sus súbditos y él era gobernador por el rey
y que se quejaría ante el juicio de Dios por lo que hacían
(ya que no podría quejarse ante el rey)
¡queriéndolo despachar a España en ese navío!
Y lo subieron al navío viejo, sin aparejos,
en el que no sólo no podría llegar a España
pero ni aun a la Española, ni a Nombre de Dios.
El bergantín se hizo a la vela el primero de marzo.
17 hombres iban con él
        (los últimos 17 de una expedición de 800)
y el bergantín se fue alejando en el mar,
y nunca más apareció, ni nadie supo de él
(el cortesano, el alegre tañedor de vihuela

(and Veragua lay to his rear).
Veragua his dream. Black Veragua.
Where one mangy dog went for twenty castellanos
and a bowl of dog meat one castellano
                    2 toads: 6 ducats.
They saw a headland beyond a huge cove in the sea
and to shorten the journey they went by boat to the headland
and when they arrived they discovered that it was a desolate island.
Those in the boat fled when they saw this island
                    and saw that they were lost.
And when Nicuesa and his men found themselves without a boat
they ran from one end to the other like madmen, screaming.
They ate weeds unknown to them, drank salty water
dying one by one. Those who were left walked on all fours
nibbling at the grass, eating raw shellfish.
(And in Hispaniola they were preparing 1000 hams for him.)
They chose Nicuesa as governor and went to find him.
They brought him back from Nombre de Dios where he had been dying.
And Nicuesa thought they would welcome him with triumphal arches.
Already in the caravel he was dictating decrees against them,
(which would take from them all gold produced within his jurisdiction).
When Nicuesa arrived they went out armed to meet him
shouting that he should return to Nombre de Dios.
Nicuesa was speechless. Then he pleaded with them
and they shouted to him to go back. (Balboa on the shore shouting.)
And he begged them that if they wouldn't accept him as governor
that at least they might accept him as comrade.
They said they didn't want to. Again he implored them
that if they wouldn't have him as comrade to accept him as prisoner:
he preferred to be in chains with them than in Nombre de Dios.
And they ordered him to present himself to the King of Spain
and not to stop until he reached Spain, under pain of death.
And they put him in the oldest brig they had
and he protested saying that this was his governorship
and they were his subjects and he was governor by the king
and that he would complain before God's court for what they were doing
(now that he couldn't complain to the king)
wanting to pack him off *to Spain* in that boat!
And they placed him in the old boat, without rigging,
in which not only could he not reach Spain
but hardly even Hispaniola, or Nombre de Dios.
On the first of March the brig set sail.
17 men went with him
        (the last 17 of an expedition of 800)
and the brig drew off into the distance,
and he never appeared again, neither did anyone hear of him
(the courtier, the merry vihuela player

que había sido trinchante de Don Enrique Enríquez)
ni de los que fueron con él, ni dónde ni cómo murió.
Dijeron que hallaron en Cuba unas letras en un árbol:
                AQUÍ PERECIÓ EL DESDICHADO
                DIEGO DE NICUESA

Cuando él había salido de la Española
un fraile había visto un cometa en el cielo
                              como una espada roja.

who had been carver to don Enrique Enríquez)
nor of those who went with him, nor where nor how he died.
On a tree in Cuba they said they found some writing:
                    HERE PERISHED THE WRETCHED
                    DIEGO DE NICUESA

As he left Hispaniola
a friar had seen a comet in the sky
                    like a red sword.

Y Panquiaco, el hijo mayor del cacique Comagre,
salío (desnudo) a la puerta del palacio
y dando un puñetazo en la balanza, desparramando el oro
dijo: "Si hubiera sabido que por mi oro reñiríais
no os lo hubiera dado!
Me maravillo que deshagáis las joyas bien labradas
para hacer unas barras. Más os valiera estar en vuestra tierra
que tan lejos de aquí está
si hay allí tan sabia y pulida gente como afirmáis
que venir a reñir en la ajena, donde vivimos contentos
los groseros y bárbaros hombres que llamáis.
Pero si tanta sed de oro tenéis
que querráis desasosegar y aun matar a los que lo tienen
yo os mostraré una tierra donde saciaréis esa sed.
Pero habréis de pelear con grandes reyes.
Se os opondrá primero el rey Tumanamá,
que tiene más oro que los otros, y está a seis soles.
Además las montañas que hay en medio las ocupan los caribes,
linaje de hombres feroces que comen carne humana,
sin ley, sin imperio y errantes,
pues oprimiendo a los habitantes de las montañas
atraídos por la codicia del oro que abunda en esos montes
ellos dejaron también sus propias moradas como vosotros,
obligando a sacar oro a los pobres montañeses.
Y tienen artífices del oro que hacen joyas,
pues nosotros no estimamos de oro sin labrar
más que si fuera una pelota de barro,
que labrada por mano del artífice
se convierte en una vasija de barro que nos agrade
o sea necesaria. Tendréis que abrir el camino con las armas
cruzando estas montañas (y con el dedo señalaba
los montes del sur). Desde sus cumbres podréis ver
el otro mar, donde hay naves y carabelas como las vuestras
(y señalaba las carabelas) con velas y remos.
Y pasado ese mar hay más oro . . ."
Cuando oyó hablar del otro mar Balboa lo abrazó de alegría.

Un martes a las 10 de la mañana,
      yendo Balboa adelante,
divisó desde un monte,

                                    azul, allá lejos,
bañada de sol,

                                    ¡la mar del Sur!

And Panquiaco, the eldest son of cacique Comagre,
appeared (naked) at the door of the palace
and with a blow of his fist on the scale, scattering the gold
said: "If I had known you would squabble over my gold
I would not have given it to you!
I am amazed that you break up finely wrought jewels
to make a few bars. Better you were in your own land
which is so far from here
if the people there are as wise and refined as you maintain
than to come to squabble abroad, where we uncouth, barbaric men
as you call us, live in contentment.
But if you have such a thirst for gold
that you should want to molest and even kill those who have it
I will show you a land in which to quench this thirst.
But you will have to fight great kings.
First you will be opposed by king Tumanama,
who has more gold than the others and is six suns away.
Furthermore, the mountains that lie in between are held by the Caribs,
a race of ferocious men who eat human flesh,
without law, without empire, wanderers,
thus oppressing the inhabitants of the mountains
drawn by the greed for gold which abounds in these hills
they also left their own homes like you,
compelling the poor mountain people to produce gold.
And they have goldsmiths who make jewels,
since we value unwrought gold
no more than if it were a ball of clay,
which when worked by the craftsman's hand
is transformed into a clay vessel which pleases us
or is useful. You will have to open the path with weapons
crossing these mountains (and he pointed toward
the southern mountains). From their summits you will see
the other sea, where there are ships and brigs like your own
(and he pointed at the brigs) with sails and oars.
And beyond this sea there is more gold . . ."
When Balboa heard him talk of the other sea he embraced him for joy.

One Tuesday at 10 in the morning,
      Balboa going on ahead,
saw from a mountain,
                          blue, away off,
bathed in sun,
                          the South Sea!

Alzó las manos y los ojos al cielo.
Hincó las rodillas en el suelo y todos se arrodillaron.
Cortaron una gran ceiba y con ella hicieron una gran cruz.
Y cantaron el Te Deum:
Te Deum laudamus:
Te Dominum confitemur ...
Y el escribano tomó los nombres de todos los que iban.
Llegaron a la orilla del mar a la hora de vísperas.
El mar estaba menguante, y toda la costa lamosa.
Se sentaron en la arena
a esperar que creciera.
Lo vieron venir creciendo,
y creció mucho y con gran ímpetu hasta donde ellos estaban.
Balboa tomó una bandera y un pendón real
con una imagen de María con el Niño en los brazos
y las armas de Castilla y León pintadas,
y con espada y rodela entró en la mar salada hasta las rodillas
y en nombre de los reyes don Fernando y doña Johana tomó posesión
"de los mares e tierras e costas e puertos e islas australes
con todos sus anexos e reinos e provincias que les pertenecen
o pueden pertenecer por cualquier razón o título que ser pueda
antiguo o moderno o del tiempo pasado o presente o por venir
... en nombre de los Reyes de Castilla presentes o por venir
cuyo es aqueste imperio e señorío de aquestas Indias,
islas e Tierra-Firme septentrional e austral,
con sus mares, así en el polo ártico como en el antártico,
en la una y en la otra parte de la línea equinoxial,
dentro o fuera de los trópicos de Cáncer o Capricornio,
agora e en todo tiempo en tanto que el mundo durare
hasta el universal final juicio de los mortales ..."

Probaron el agua para ver si era salada como la mar del Norte.
El sol se hundió en el mar como un doblón de oro.
Y salió la luna.

He raised his hands and eyes to the heavens.
He dropped to his knees on the ground and all knelt down.
They felled a huge ceiba and with it made a huge cross.
And they sang the Te Deum:

Te Deum laudamus

Te Dominum confitemur . . .

And the notary noted the names of all those present.
They reached the seashore at the hour of vespers.
The tide was going out, and the whole coast slimy.
                    They sat down in the sand
to wait for the water to rise.
                        They watched it gradually rising,
and it rose a great deal in great surges to where they were.
Balboa took a flag and a royal ensign,
with an image of Mary with the Infant in her arms
and emblazoned with the crests of Castille and Leon,
and with sword and shield entered the salt sea to his knees
and in the name of the sovereigns don Fernando and doña Johana took
                                                    possession
"of the seas & landes & coasts & ports & austral yles
with all annexations & kingdoms & provynces which perteyne to them
or may perteyne for whatever reason or deede that might exist
auncient or modern or from tyme past present or to come
. . . in the name of the soveraigns of Castille present or to come
to whome the empire & the dominion of these Indies,
islands & Terra firma north & south belongs,
with theyr seas, in the Arctic pole as in the Antarctic,
on one side & on the other of the equinocctial line,
within or without the tropics of Cancer or Capricorn,
nowe & for all tyme so long as the world should last
till the finall judgment of mortals . . ."

They tasted the water to see if it was briny like the Northern Sea.
Like a gold doubloon the sun sank in the sea.
                        And the moon appeared.

Muchos caballeros e hijosdalgos
vendían en Castilla sus haciendas
o empeñaban sus mayorazgos
        para ir a Italia con el Gran Capitán.
Cuando supieron que Pedrarias iba a Tierra-Firme . . .

Llegaron a Tierra-Firme
a dar un sayón de seda carmesí por una libra de tortillas.
Caballeros con brocados gemían dadme pan, en las calles.
Preguntaban dónde estaba el oro que se pescaba con redes.
Caían muertos de hambre en las calles con vestidos de seda.
Otros salían al campo a pacer las hierbas, como animales,
y las raíces más tiernas. Morían de enfermedad y de modorra,
y morían cada día tantos que en el hoyo para uno
enterraban a muchos juntos, y muchos quedaban sin sepultura
porque los vivos no tenían fuerzas para enterrarlos.
Cuando llegó Pedrarias con su flota al puerto del Darién
envió a uno de sus oficiales a preguntar por Balboa.
"Veislo allí", le dijeron. Creyó que bromeaban.
Balboa estaba en camisa, con camisa de algodón
y alpargatas, ayudando a poner el techo de una casa
y bañado en sudor.

Comenzó la lucha sorda de Pedrarias por eliminar a Balboa.
Llegó el nombramiento de Adelantado de la Mar del Sur.
Pedrarias no quería darle la carta (estuvieron hasta medianoche
reunidos en casa de Pedrarias). Pero tuvo que darla.
Hicieron las paces. Concertó el matrimonio con su hija . . .
Se hicieron los capítulos matrimoniales.
Se desposó con él en nombre de su hija Doña María de Peñalosa
dando la mano por ella (ella estaba en España)
y comenzó a llamar hijo al Adelantado.
Balboa desposado se fue a la mar del Sur
a construir los navíos. Llevaba él mismo
la madera en hombros desde el monte al astillero.
Pero pasó el plazo y no volvía . . .
        Le dijeron a Pedrarias que estaba alzado . . .
Pedrarias lo creyó. O fingió creerlo.
Lo mandó llamar. Balboa llegó donde su suegro.
                        Y Pedrarias lo prendió.
Ordenó al Alcalde que le acumulara todos los cargos
y todos los crímenes que pudiera tener.
        Le acumularon la muerte de Nicuesa.

Many knights and noblemen
were selling their farms in Castille
or mortgaging their estates
        in order to go to Italy with the Great Captain.
When they heard that Pedrarias was going to Terra firma . . .

They came to Terra firma
to swap a crimson silk tunic for a pound of tortillas.
Brocaded knights moaned give me bread, in the streets.
Where, they asked, was the gold that could be fished with nets.
They dropped dead of hunger in the streets clothed in silk.
Others left for the fields to chew grass, like animals,
and the softest roots. They died of disease and exhaustion,
and so many were dying each day that in the grave for one
many were buried together and many went without burial
because the living hadn't the strength to bury them.
When Pedrarias arrived with his fleet at the port of Darien
he sent one of his officials to ask for Balboa.
"There he is," they told him. He thought they were joking.
Balboa was in shirtsleeves, wearing a cotton shirt
and rope sandals, helping to put a roof on a house
and soaked in sweat.

Pedrarias began a secret struggle to eliminate Balboa.
The appointment of Adelantado of the South Sea arrived.
Pedrarias did not want to give him the letter (they were till midnight
assembled in the house of Pedrarias). But he had to hand it over.
They made peace. He arranged the marriage of his daughter . . .
The articles of marriage were drawn up.
He married him in the name of his daughter Doña María de Peñalosa
giving her hand for her (she was in Spain)
and began to call the Adelantado son.
Balboa freshly wed went to the South Sea
to build ships. He himself carried
the timber from the forest to the shipyard.
But the term passed and he had not returned . . .
        They told Pedrarias that he was in rebellion . . .
Pedrarias believed it. Or pretended to believe.
He sent for him. Balboa came to his father-in-law.
                        And Pedrarias arrested him.
He ordered the Mayor to heap upon him all the charges
and all the crimes that he could possibly have.
        They charged him with Nicuesa's death.

Le hicieron una larga acusación.
Vasco Núñez de Balboa apeló al emperador.
Preguntaron a Pedrarias si se le otogaba la apelación
por razón del título de Adelantado.
El gobernador contestó en un papelito: No se le otorgue.
Hágase justicia.
Salió un pregonero gritando por las calles de Acla:
JUSTICIA QUE MANDA HACER EL REY NUESTRO SEÑOR
Y PEDRARIAS SU LUGARTENIENTE, EN SU NOMBRE
A ESTE HOMBRE POR TRAIDOR Y USURPADOR DE LAS TIERRAS
SUJETAS A LA CORONA REAL . . . !
Por la calle vienen los caballos y las yeguas
a pastar en la plaza (porque como pueblo nuevo
estaban llenas de hierba las calles y la plaza)
y entre ellos viene el caballo blanco de Balboa.
Y se ponen a pastar sin oir el pregón.
Balboa oyó el pregón cuando lo sacaban a la plaza.
Alzó los ojos al cielo y dijo:
"Mentira y falsedad que se me levanta.
Nunca en el pensamiento se me pasó tal cosa
ni pensé jamás que de mí tal se imaginara."

Les cortaron la cabeza sobre un repostero.
        Él y los otros 4.
Degollados en fila como carneros en la plaza de Acla.
Desde una casa, cerca de donde los degollaron
Pedrarias estaba mirando, entre las cañas.
Y despúes en un palo en la plaza,
                            la cabeza de Balboa.

Después Pedrarias se hizo recidencia él mismo.
Publicó por pregón que el que tuviera quejas
las fuera a presentar . . . (Ejemplo de democracia.)
Fue fijado en un poste en la plaza de Acla.
Vienen por la calle los caballos y las yeguas
de los conquistadores, a pastar en la plaza,
y viene entre ellos el caballo de Balboa.
Llega con los demás al centro de la plaza verde.
De pronto alza la cabeza, con las crines al viento
corre hacia el poste donde está clavado el pregón
donde estuvo la cabeza,
lo arranca a dentelladas y lo hace pedazos.
Vuelve al trote lento donde están los demás
y comienza a pacer.

Y las noas de Balboa quedaron solas,
                        en la mar del Sur.

They laid lengthy accusations against him.
Vasco Núñez de Balboa appealed to the emperor.
They asked Pedrarias if he should be allowed the appeal
in view of his position as Adelantado.
The governor answered on a slip of paper: It shall not be allowed.
Let justice be done.
A crier went out into the streets of Acla shouting:
EXECUTION BY ORDER OF THE KING OUR LORD
AND PEDRARIAS HIS LIEUTENANT, IN HIS NAME
OF THIS MAN AS A TRAITOR AND USURPER OF THE LANDS
SUBJECT TO THE ROYAL CROWN . . . !
Through the street come horses and mares
to graze in the square (this being a new town
the streets and square were full of grass)
and among them goes Balboa's white horse.
They begin to graze without hearing the crier.
Balboa heard the crier when they brought him to the square.
He raised his eyes to heaven and said:
"Lies and falsehood are being leveled against me.
Never in my mind did I have such an idea
nor ever thought such a thing would be imagined of me."

They beheaded him on an emblazoned drapery.
     Him and the other 4.
Decapitated in a row like sheep in the square of Acla.
From a house close to where they were decapitated
Pedrarias was watching through the bamboo.
And later, on a stake in the square,
                 Balboa's head.

Then Pedrarias instigated his own impeachment.
He broadcast through the crier that whoever had complaints
should go and present them . . . (Model of democracy.)
It was posted in the square of Acla.
Through the street come horses and mares
of the conquistadors, to graze in the square,
and among them comes Balboa's horse.
He arrives with the others in the middle of the green square.
Suddenly he raises his head, and with his mane in the wind
gallops to the post where the proclamation is nailed,
where the head had been,
with his teeth he tears at it until it is in shreds.
He returns at a slow trot to where the others are
and begins to graze.

And Balboa's ships lay abandoned,
                 in the South Sea.

¡La mar del sur! ¡La mar del sur!
Gil González partió de San Lúcar con tres naos
a la mar del sur.
A descubrir el estrecho de la mar del sur.

DC quintales de bizcocho
LIIII fanegas de garbanzos
LII arrobas de alcaparras
L pipas de agua
XXXVIII botas de vino blanco de San Lúcar
pasas almendras sal aceitunas carne salada
chinchorros para pescar brazas de cordeles
anzuelos cadenas hilo para las velas
alquitrán hierro acero madera para hacer navíos
ballestas pólvora arpones barrenas escoplos
hachas para cortar árboles candelas
sillas de montar ornamentos sagrados
3 cartas de marear . . .

A las cinco y media de la mañana partieron las naos.
Gil González presentó a Pedrarias en Panamá la cédula real
para que le entregara las navíos de Balboa
    "todos los nabyos e fustas del dicho Vasco Núñez
    para hazer el dicho descubrimiento"
                    (la Especería).
Y Pedrarias tomó la dicha Çedula en sus manos
y la besó y la puso sobre su cabeza y dijo
que la obedeçia e la obedeçia
con el mayor acatamiento que podía e devya
como Çedula e mandamyento de su Rey e Señor natural
a quien Dios nuestro Señor deje vivir e reinar
por muchos e largos tiempos con acrescentamiento
de muchos Reynos e señoríos
    (pero no la cumplió)
Y Gil González pide y requiere una y dos
y tres veces y más veces cuantas puede y debe de derecho
que torne a ver la dicha cédula de su magestad
y la obedezca y cumpla según y como en ella se contiene.
Y Pedrarias: Que él ya tiene obedecida la dicha Çedula
como a Çedula e mandamiento de su emperador e rey e
señor natural e que a mayor abundancia agora la obedece
con el mayor acatamiento que debe y es obligado
    (y no la cumplió)

The South Sea! The South Sea!
With three ships Gil González set out from San Lúcar
for the South Sea.
To discover the strait in the South Sea.

       DC quintals of biscuit
       LIIII fanegas of chickpeas
       LII arrobas of capers
       L casks of water
       XXXVIII casks of white wine from San Lúcar
       raisins almonds salt olives salt-meat
       dragnets to fish with fathoms of line
       fish hooks chains yarn for the sails
       pitch steel iron wood to make boats
       crossbows gunpowder harpoons augers chisels
       axes to fell trees candles
       saddles sacred ornaments
       3 sea charts . . .

At five-thirty in the morning the ships set sail.
Gil González presented Pedrarias with the royal decree in Panama
so that he would hand over Balboa's ships to him
    "all the shippes and vessels of the aforesaid Vasco Núñez
    in order to make the aforementioned discoverie"
                             (the Spice trade).
And Pedrarias took said Decree in his handes
and kiss'd it and plac'd it on his head and said
that he wolde obey it and obey it
with the greatest respect that he could and should
as Decree and commaund of his King & naturel master
may God our Lord let him live and reign
for many & long yeres with increase
of many Kingdoms & dominions
    (but he did not obey it)
And Gil González asks and insists once and again
and three times and as often as he can and must by law
that he should examine again said decree from His Majesty
and obey and comply accordingly and in the manner prescribed.
And Pedrarias: That he had already obey'd said Decree
beeyng a Decree & commaund from his emperour &
naturel master & that with the utmoste dedication nowe obey'd it
with the greatest respect whych he owes and is oblig'd
    (and he did not obey)

Tuvo que hacer nuevos navíos en la mar del Sur,
pasar la madera a hombros de indios
desde la mar del Norte a la mar del Sur
"donde no avian sino aves y leones y gatos monteses"
y cuando echó al mar los navíos se fueron a pique.
Después ir a Panamá a pedir ayuda a Pedrarias
Pelear con Pedrarias.
                            No se la quiso dar.
Hacer nuevos navíos en la Isla de las Perlas
              —"comiendo paxaros en las islas"
y 100 leguas más allá los navíos se están pudriendo
y el agua de los toneles se derrama
porque no tienen arcos de hierro.
Ir otra vez a Panamá a pedir pez a Pedrarias
y hacer fraguas en la tierra para los arcos de hierro
y Gil González con 100 hombres y 4 caballos
entró en la tierra—

        . . . y caminando yo siempre por la tierra adentro
hacia el poniente
metido algunas veces tan lejos de la costa
que muchas veces me hallé arrepentido
y a causa de pasar los ríos y arroyos a pie y sudando
sobrevínome una enfermedad de tullimiento en una pierna
que no podía dar un paso a pie
ni dormir las noches ni los días de dolor
ni caminar
y me llevaban en una manta atada a un palo
y por las muchas aguas que entonces había pues era invierno
hube de parar en casa de un cacique
en una isla que hacían dos brazos de un río
el más poderoso que yo haya visto en Castilla
y tomé la casa del cacique por posada
y era tan alta como una mediana torre
armada sobre postes y cubierta con paja
y en medio de ella hiciéronme una cámara sobre postes
tan alta como dos estados
y llovió tantos días que crecieron los ríos tanto
que hicieron toda la tierra una mar
y en la casa el agua llegaba a los pechos de los hombres
y la gente de mi compañía se fueron saliendo uno a uno
a subirse a los árboles de alrededor
y yo estaba en esta gran casa oyendo llover a la media noche
y había una imagen de Nuestra Señora
con una lámpara de aceite que la alumbraba
y como la furia del agua creciese mientras más llovía
a la media noche se quebraron todos los postes de la casa

He had to make new ships in the South Sea,
transport the wood on the shoulders of Indians
from the Northern Sea to the South Sea
"where there was naught but birdes and lions & mountain cats"
and when he launched the ships in the sea they foundered.
Then to Panama to ask Pedrarias for help.
To wrangle with Pedrarias.
                                        He didn't want to help him.
Make new ships on the Island of Pearls
        —"eating birdes on the islandes"
and 100 leagues further on the ships are rotting
and the water in the barrels spilling out
because they have no iron hoops.
Once again to Panama to ask Pedrarias for pitch
and make forges in the ground for the iron hoops
and Gil González with 100 men and 4 horses
went inland—

        . . . and still journeying inland
westward
sometimes so far in from the coast
that I often regretted it
and as a result of crossing so many rivers and streams on foot and sweating
I was taken with an infirmity of paralysis in one leg
so that I could not go another step on foot
nor sleep night or day with the pain
nor move along
and they carried me in a blanket attached to a pole
and due to the high waters there were then—it being winter—
I had to stop in the house of a cacique
on an island between two branches of a river
the most powerful I have seen in Castille
and I lodged in the cacique's house
and it was as tall as a medium tower
mounted on posts and covered with straw
and in the middle of it they made me a chamber on legs
as high as two storeys
and it rained so many days and the river swelled so much
that the whole land became a sea
and in the house the water rose to the men's chests
and the people in my company left one by one
to climb into the surrounding trees
and I was in this huge house in the dead of night listening to the rain
and there was an image of Our Lady
with an oil lamp to give it light
and as the fury of the waters grew the more it rained
in the dead of night the posts of the house gave way

y cayó sobre nosotros y derribó la cámara donde yo estaba
y quedé yo con unas muletas el agua a los muslos
y llegaron las varas de la techumbre al suelo
y plugo a Dios que al caer la casa la lámpara no se murió
y como quedamos con lumbre pudimos salir de allí
rompiendo con una hacha la techumbre de la casa
y por allí salieron los compañeros y a mí me sacaron en hombros
y pusiéronme en una manta atada con dos cordeles a dos árboles
y allí estuve hasta la mañana lloviendo todo lo posible
y allí estuvimos dos días hasta que el agua menguó.
Quedó toda la tierra tan enlamada
y lleno de árboles caídos y atravesados
que apenas los compañeros podían andar sobre ella.
Perdimos muchas espadas y ballestas y vestidos y rodelas.
Hicimos balsas de maderos grandes atados unos sobre otros
y fuimos en ellas río abajo hasta llegar a la mar
y como algunos compañeros llegaron de noche
arrebatolos la corriente del río y sacolos a la mar a media noche
metiéndolos la resaca muchas veces debajo del agua
y otro día desde la costa los veíamos dos leguas mar adentro
y como la menguante de la mar los había llevado
la creciente los tornó hacia la tierra
y plugo a Dios que no se perdió ninguno
y caminé por la costa de la mar al poniente.
Prosiguiendo mi descubrimiento por la costa al poniente
llegué a un cacique que se llama Nicoya
el cual me dio de presente XIII.000 castellanos de oro
y se tornaron cristianos VI.000
y tuve nuevas de un cacique que se llama Nicaragua
y muchos indios principales me aconsejaban que no fuese allá
porque era muy poderoso
y aun muchos de mis compañeros me aconsejaban que no fuese
pero yo ya iba determinado de no volver atrás
y cuando llegué a una jornada antes de su pueblo
enviele a decir con las lenguas
que yo era un capitán que el gran rey de los cristianos
enviaba a esas tierras para decir a todos los caciques
que en el cielo más arriba del sol hay un Señor
que hizo todas las cosas y los hombres
y que a todos los caciques de atrás hacia donde el sol nace
lo había dicho y todos lo creen así
y que a todos los caciques de hacia donde el sol se pone
había que decir lo mismo
y que le diré otras cosas muy grandes de este mismo Dios
que habrá placer de saberlas
y él me envió a decir que me esperaba en su pueblo de paz
y llegado me aposentó él mismo en una plaza

and it fell in on us and pulled down the chamber where I lay
and I was left with some crutches water up to my knees
and the beams from the roofing crashed to the floor
and thank God when the house collapsed the lamp did not die
and as we still had light we managed to get out of there
breaking the roofing of the house with an axe
and through there my comrades escaped carrying me out on their shoulders
and placed me on a blanket tied with two ropes to two trees
and there I was till the morning rain coming down as hard as it could
and there we were for two days till the waters went down.
It left the whole land so covered in slime
and full of fallen and twisted trees
that my comrades could scarcely walk on it.
We lost many swords and crossbows and tunics and shields.
We made rafts of huge beams tied one on top of another
and went in them downriver until we reached the sea
and as some comrades arrived in the night
the river current caught them and took them out to sea in the dead of night
the undertow of the sea dragging them many times beneath the water
and the next day from the coast we saw them two leagues out to sea
and as the ebbing tide had carried them off
the floodtide turned them back to the land
and God willed that none be lost
and I traveled along the sea coast to the west.
Continuing my discovery along the coast to the west
I came across a cacique whose name is Nicoya
who presented me with XIII.000 gold castellanos
and VI.000 became Christians
and I had news of a cacique whose name is Nicaragua
and many of the most important Indians advised me not to go there
because he was very powerful
and even my comrades advised me not to go
but by now I was determined not to turn back
and when I came within a day's journey of his village
I sent him word through interpreters
that I was a captain whom the mighty king of the Christians
sent to these lands to tell the caciques
that in the heavens above there is a Lord
who made all things and all men
and that to all the caciques from where the sun rises
I had said the same and all believe it to be so
and that to all the caciques toward where the sun sets
I had to tell the same thing
and that I will tell him other great things about this same God
which he will take pleasure in knowing
and he sent word that he awaited me peacefully in his village
and upon my arrival he himself gave me lodgings in a square

y me presentó quince mil castellanos de oro
y yo le di una ropa de seda y una gorra de grana
y una camisa mía y otras cosas de Castilla
y en dos o tres días que se le habló de las cosas de Dios
vino a querer ser cristiano él y todos sus indios y mujeres
y se bautizaron en un día IX.XVII ánimas chicas y grandes
y vi llorar a algunos compañeros de devoción
y puse una cruz muy grande
en unos montones grandes de grada que hay en la plaza.
Este pueblo del cacique Nicaragua
está a tres leguas de la costa de la mar del sur
y junto a las casas está otra mar dulce y digo mar
porque crece y mengua y yo entré a caballo en ella y la probé
y tomé posesión en nombre de Vuestra Magestad
y preguntando a los indios si se junta con la otra mar salada
dicen que no y cuanto nuestros ojos pudieron ver todo es agua
salvo una isla que está a dos leguas de la costa
y mandé entrar media legua en el agua en una canoa
para ver si el agua corría sospechando que fuese río
y no le hallaron corriente.
Los pilotos que llevaba certifican que sale a la mar del norte
y si es así es muy gran nueva
porque había de una mar a otra
dos o tres leguas de camino muy llano . . .

      ¡El Almirante de la Mar Dulçe!
Gil González pide a su Magestad la merced
      del Almirantazgo de la Mar Dulçe
y de tres islas
            en la dicha Mar Dulce
para él y sus herederos y descendientes
Otro sí: por estas tierras se ha de descubrir la Especería
y la entrada ha de ser por el golfo de las Higüeras
a do él con la ayuda de Nuestro Señor lleva la presente derrota
y piensa hacer navíos para el descubrimiento de la especería
Así mismo le haga merced de la décima de la Especería
      y de todas las cosas que de allá truxeren
pues él ha hallado el pasaje por do se han de traer
a la mar del Norte y para Castilla.
                    firma: gil gs. dávila

Detrás del palacio de Nicaragua
      un lago azul.
Gil González y Nicaragua se sentaron junto al lago.
El conquistador con ropa de hierro,
      el cacique casi desnudo.
Y preguntó Nicaragua:

and presented me with fifteen thousand gold castellanos
and I gave him a silk garment and a scarlet cap
and one of my shirts and other things from Castille
and in two or three days in which he was told about the things of God
he came to desire to be a Christian he and all his Indians and women
and in one day IX.XVII souls young and old were baptized
and I saw a few comrades in tears touched in their faith
and I placed a very tall cross
on some huge stepped mounds that are in the square.
This village of cacique Nicaragua
is three leagues from the coast of the South Sea
and alongside the houses lies another freshwater sea and I say sea
because it has tides and I entered it on horse and tasted it
and took possession of it in the name of Your Majesty
and asking the Indians if it connects with the other salt sea
they say not and as far as our eyes can see all is water
except an island two leagues from the coast
and I ordered a canoe to enter half a league into the water
to see if the water flowed, suspecting it might be a river,
and they found no current in it.
The pilots aboard maintain that it goes out to the Northern Sea
and if true this is a very important discovery
because there was from one sea to the other
two or three leagues of very flat journey . . .

       The Admiral of the Sweet Water Sea!
Gil González requests of His Majesty the title
       of Admiralship of the Sweet Water Sea
and of three islands
              in the said Sweet Water Sea
for himself and his heirs and descendants
Furthermore: through these landes is to be open'd up the Spice trade
and the entry has to be through the gulf of las Higüeras
to which he with the aid of Our Lord is steering the present course
and intends to make shyppes for the discoverie of spice production
In like maner graunt him the faveur of a tythe in the Spice trade
       and of whatsoever might be brought back from there
since he hath discover'd the passage through whych they must be transport'd
to the Northern Sea and on to Castille.
                     signed: gil gs. dávila

Behind the palace of Nicaragua
         a blue lake.
Gil González and Nicaragua sat down beside the lake.
The conquistador in chain mail
         the cacique almost naked.
And Nicaragua asked:

Si los cristianos habían tenido noticias del Diluvio
que anegó la tierra.
¿Y si había de haber otro?
¿Y si la tierra se había de trastornar o caer el cielo?
¿Se voltearía la tierra boca arriba?
¿Cuándo y cómo perderían su claridad y curso el Sol y la Luna?
¿Y las estrellas, qué tan grandes serán?
¿Quién las tenía y movía?
Preguntó del movimiento, cantidad, distancia y efectos de los astros.
Preguntó las causas de la oscuridad de las noches y del frío,
tachando la naturaleza, que no hacía siempre claro y calor,
pues era mejor.
Preguntó sobre el soplar de los vientos
y la variedad de los días y las noches.
Preguntó si se puede sin culpa comer,
beber, engendrar, jugar, cantar, danzar
ejercitarse en las armas.
¿Qué honra se debía al Dios de los cristianos
que hizo los cielos y el Sol a quien adoraban por Dios en aquella tierra,
la mar, la tierra, el hombre que señorea las aves que vuelan
y peces que nadan y todo lo del mundo?
¿Adónde tenían de estar las almas?
¿Y qué habían de hacer salidas de cuerpo,
pues vivían tan poco, siendo inmortales?
Preguntó así mismo si moría el Santo Padre de Roma.
¿Si el Emperador, Rey de Castilla, de quien tanto decían
era mortal?
¿Y para qué tan pocos hombres querían tanto oro?

Had the Christians had news of the Flood
which submerged the world?
And was there to be another?
And would the earth topple backwards or the sky fall?
Would the earth turn upside down?
When and how would the Sun and the Moon lose their brightness and their
                                                         path?

And the stars, how big were they?
Who kept them and moved them?
He asked about the movement, size, distance, and effects of heavenly bodies.
He asked about the causes of darkness at night and of cold,
as these marred nature, which was not always bright and warm,
since it was better.
He asked about the blowing of the winds
and the changeability of days and nights.
Asked if one can eat without guilt,
drink, beget children, play, sing, dance
practice martial arts.
What honor was due to the God of the Christians
who made the heavens and the Sun whom they adored as God in that land,
the sea, the earth, man who rules over the birds that fly
and fish that swim and all that is of the world?
Where were the souls to be found?
And what had they to do once released from the body,
since they lived so little, being immortal?
He asked similarly if the Holy Father in Rome died.
If the Emperor, King of Castille, of whom they so often spoke,
was mortal.
And why did so few men want so much gold?

Gil González fue a las Hibueras a buscar el Estrecho
y Cortés envió a Olid por mar a las Hibueras
y a Alvarado por tierra (a buscar el Estrecho)
y Olid se levantó contra Cortés en las Hibueras
y Cortés envió contra él a Francisco de las Casas
y como no sabía de las Casas fue él mismo a las Hibueras
Y Pedrarias envió a Hernández de Córdoba tras Gil González
y después fue él mismo detrás de Hernández de Córdoba.
Todos los ejércitos convergían en esas "Higüeras"
(Honduras) buscando el estrecho.

Gil González fundó San Gil de Buena Vista
y siguió tierra adentro, hacia la mar del Sur.
Cortes envió a las Casas contra Cristóbal de Olid
con cinco navíos bien artillados, pero en la noche el viento norte
arrojó los navíos a la costa.
40 se ahogaron
              y los demás salieron chorreando agua salada,
desnudos, temblando bajo la lluvia. Olid los apresó,
recibió muy bien a las Casas, lo vistió y lo sentó a su mesa.
(Lo hizo jurar sobre los Evangelios que le obedecería en todo)
y apresó también a Gil González, y lo sentó a su mesa
(y lo hizo también jurar sobre los Evangelios)
muy alegre de tener a dos capitanes presos.
Las Casas le pedía su libertad, y Olid bromeaba,
diciéndole que se holgaba de tenerlo en su compañía.
Y las Casas dijo riendo: "Pues mire bien por su persona
que un día o otro tengo que procurar de le matar."

Estaban en el valle de Naco, cercado de sierras.
Los caminos bordeados de frutales, como Valencia,
y la tierra cruzada de ríos, verde como albahaca,
y después de los llanos verdes, las altas sierras
y más allá más llanos, y más lejos otras sierras.
Y dijeron que estas tierras eran la Tegusgalpa
que quiere decir casa donde se funde el oro,
porque es una casa de fundición donde funden el oro
y hay una calle derecha de muchos oficiales
que hacen cosas de oro . . . Y una princesa dijo
que en esa tierra comían en platos de oro
(señalando un anillo de oro y los platos de peltre).

Gil González went to las Hibueras to find the Strait
and Cortés sent Olid by sea to las Hibueras
and Alvarado by land (to look for the Strait)
and Olid rose up against Cortés in las Hibueras
and Cortés sent Francisco de las Casas against him
and having no news from las Casas went himself to las Hibueras
And Pedrarias sent Hernández de Córdoba after Gil González
and then went himself after Hernández de Córdoba.
All the armies were converging on this "Higüeras"
(Honduras) looking for the Strait.

Gil González founded San Gil de Buena Vista
and continued inland, toward the South Sea.
Cortés sent las Casas against Cristóbal de Olid
with five well-armed ships, but in the night the north wind
dashed the ships on the coast.
40 were drowned
                    and the rest came out dripping salt water,
naked, shivering in the rain. Olid took them prisoner,
he made las Casas very welcome, provided clothes, and seated him at his table.
(He made him swear on the Gospels that he would obey him in everything)
and he seized Gil González too, and seated him at his table
(him too he made swear on the Gospels)
delighted to have two captains prisoner.
Las Casas asked for his freedom, and Olid joked,
telling him that it amused him to have him in his company.
And las Casas said laughing: "Well look carefully to your person
as one day or another I'm bound to try to kill you."

They were in the valley of Naco, surrounded by mountains.
The roads lined with fruit trees, like Valencia,
and the land crossed by rivers, green as sweet basil,
and then the green plains, the high mountains
and more plains beyond and other mountains beyond that.
And they said that these lands were Tegusgalpa
which means the house where gold is smelted,
because it is a smelting house where they smelt gold
and there is a straight street of many skilled craftsmen
who make gold articles . . . And a princess said
that in this land they eat from gold plates
(indicating a gold ring and the pewter plates).

"Que un día o otro le tengo de procurar de le matar"
repetía las Casas riendo. Y un domingo en la noche
(por la tarde habían corrido carreras de caballos)
estaban cenando juntos los tres capitanes
y levantados los manteles bromeaban de sobremesa.
González y las Casas con cuchillos de escribanía
se estaban cortando las uñas.
                              Olid estaba solo.
Sus hombres cenando afuera.
Y habían 30 hombres de Gil González y las Casas,
y otros 50 en la puerta.
                              Olid estaba sin armas.
Levantados los manteles, estaban bromeando y riendo
y las Casas cogió a Olid por las barbas diciéndole
"ea compadre que agora es tiempo",
enterrándole el cuchillo de escribanía en la garganta,
y Gil González le enterró su cuchillo diciendo
"compadre, así se pagan las cosas mal hechas"
y le dieron dieciocho puñaladas.
      Olid gritaba "¡Aquí los míos!"
y los otros gritaban "¡Viva el Rey y Hernando Cortés!"
y Olid salió corriendo y se escondió en la noche.
González y las Casas lo buscaban en la oscuridad.
Estaba metido en un matorral. Uno de sus soldados
también lo andaba buscando. Lo halló en el arbuco.
"¡Ah señor Cristóbal Dolid!"
                              —"¿Es Muñana?"
—"Sí señor. Señor ¿quién os fa muerto?"
Y él le dijo "Gil y las Casas y otros muchos".
Y estaban oyendo el pregón, que quien lo encontrara
lo llegara a decir, so pena de muerte.
Por fin fue hallado, cubierto de heridas y de sangre.
Le curaron las heridas y le pusieron grillos
y un pregón salió por las calles de Naco gritando
"MANDA GIL GONZÁLEZ DÁVILA E FRANCISCO DE LAS CASAS
DEGOLLAR ESTE HOMBRE POR TIRANO"
Al amanecer lo degollaron
y después de muerto le levantaron cabeza de proceso.
Y su cabeza la pusieron en un palo colgada por la boca.

Después Gil González y las Casas se van para México.
Gil González es preso en México. Llevado en un navío a España.
Encerrado en la Tarazana de Sevilla. Murío en Ávila
sin volver a ver la Mar Dulce,
                              su Mar Dulçe.

"And one day or another I'm bound to try to kill you"
repeated las Casas, laughing. And one Sunday night
(that afternoon they'd held horse races)
the three captains were dining together
and after the table had been cleared they remained joking.
González and las Casas with scrivener's knives
were trimming their nails.
                           Olid was alone.
His men were dining outside.
And there were 30 of Gil González's and las Casas's men,
and another 50 at the door.
                           Olid was unarmed.
After the table had been cleared, they were joking and laughing
and las Casas caught Olid by his beard saying to him
"So friend the tyme is nowe come,"
sinking the scrivener's knife into his throat,
and Gil González plunged his knife into him saying
"this is howe one pays for thyngs badly done, friend"
and they stabbed him eighteen times.
        Olid was shouting "In here my men!"
and the others shouted "Long live the King and Hernando Cortés!"
and Olid ran out and hid himself in the night.
González and las Casas searched for him in the darkness.
He was huddled in a thicket. One of his soldiers
was also trying to find him. He discovered him in the undergrowth.
"Ah señor Cristóbal Dolid!"
                           —"Is that Muñana?"
—"Yes señor. Señor, who has killed you?"
And he said "Gil and las Casas and many more."
And they could hear the crier, that whoever found him
should come and report it, under penalty of death.
At last he was found, covered with wounds and blood.
They dressed his wounds and put him in irons
and a crier went out in the streets of Naco shouting
"GIL GONZÁLEZ DÁVILA AND FRANCISCO DE LAS CASAS ORDER
THIS MAN'S DECAPITATION FOR BEING A TYRANT"
At daybreak they beheaded him
and once he was dead raised charges against him.
And they placed his head on a stake hanging by the mouth.

Later Gil González and las Casas leave for Mexico.
Gil González is arrested in Mexico. Brought by ship to Spain.
Locked up in the Tarazana of Seville. He died in Avila
never seeing the Sweet Water Sea again,
                           his Sweet Water Sea.

Cortés no había vuelto a saber de las Casas
y resolvió ir él mismo a las Hibueras.
Fue con sus capitanes y con frailes franciscanos
y tres mil indios tlascaltecas, y con mayordomo,
maestresala, repostero, botiller,
con la vajilla de oro y plata,
camarero, paje, mozos de espuela y halconeros
y titiriteros, chirimías, sacabuches y dulzainas,
y con el príncipe Cuauhtémoc y Coanococh señor de Texcoco
y Tetlepanquetzal de Tlacopan y Oquici de Azcapotzalco
Llevaba en un paño de henequén todo el camino pintado
desde Xicalanco hasta Naco y Nito, y hasta Nicaragua,
con todos los ríos y las sierras que se pasan
y las grandes ciudades y las ventas donde hacen jornadas
cuando van a las ferias.
En todos los pueblos los recibían con fiestas
y con arcos de triunfo.
En los primeros ríos empezaron a perder la plata y la ropa
(los ríos llenos de largatos)
                    pero encontraban siempre arcos de flores.
Grandes ríos pasados en canoas.
Esteros pasados con puentes. Montes,
y después más ríos. Y las ciénagas.
Ríos pasados con balsas, y después más ciénagas.
Los caballos se hundían hasta las cinchas.
En los pantanos habían grandes sapos.
Los bosques cerraban el paso como murallas.
Todo el tiempo llovía. Iban con la aguja de marear
y con pilotos
por las selvas y los montes,
como si fuera el mar —Cortés consultando el paño—
y abriendo los caminos con espadas, hacia el este:
hacia donde estaban los pueblos según el paño.
    Sólo habían bosques.
Y todo el tiempo lloviendo en esos bosques.
No aparecían los pueblos pintados en el paño.
Ríos y más ríos. Esteros cruzados con puentes
y con canoas.
            Ya no tenían qué comer
sino yerbas (quequexques) que abrasaban la boca.
Ya no habían caminos.
                Cortés cogía la brújula:
los abrían con los brazos

Cortés had had no further news of las Casas
and made up his mind to go himself to las Hibueras.
He went with his captains and with Franciscan friars
and three thousand Tlascaltec Indians, and with majordomo,
headwaiter, pastry cook, maker of refreshments
with the gold and silver dinner service,
chamberlain, page, footmen and falconers
puppeteers, flageolets, sackbutts, flutes,
and with prince Cuauhtémoc and Coanococh lord of Texcoco
and Tetlepanquetzal of Tlacopan and Oquici of Azcapotzalco
He carried a henequen cloth depicting the entire journey
from Xicalanco to Naco and Nito, and as far as Nicaragua,
with all the rivers and sierras en route
and the great cities and the inns where they make stops
when they go to the feasts.
In all the towns they were received with festivities
and triumphal arches.
In the first rivers they began to lose the silver and clothes
(rivers full of alligators)
                    but always found floral arches.
Great rivers crossed in canoes.
Inlets spanned with bridges. Mountains,
and then more rivers. And the swamps.
Rivers crossed on rafts, and then more swamps.
The horses were sinking up to their cinches.
In the marshlands there were huge toads.
Forests blocked the way like city walls.
It rained incessantly. They went by the marine compass
and with pilots
through forests and mountains,
as if it were the sea—Cortés consulting the cloth—
and opening paths with swords toward the east:
according to the cloth toward where the towns were.
    There were only forests.
And constant raining in those forests.
The towns painted on the cloth did not appear.
Rivers and more rivers. Marshlands crossed with bridges
and in canoes.
                    By now they had nothing to eat
but grasses *(quequexques)* which burned the mouth.
Now there were no trails.
                    Cortés took the compass:
they opened paths with their arms

y volvían a salir al mismo camino que abrían.
Cortés reventaba de enojo.
                              Querían volverse
pero ya era muy tarde para volver.
Alzaban los ojos y no veían el cielo.
Subían a los árboles para atalayar la tierra
y no veían tierra, sólo árboles y árboles.
Dos guías huyeron de noche. Sólo quedaba un guía
que no sabía el camino. Y el paño de henequén.
En 20 leguas hicieron 50 puentes.
Más ciénagas y ríos que no estaban en el paño.
Ya no habían pueblos. Sólo aldeas abandonadas,
chozas quemadas. Y más ciénagas que pasar.
La lluvia de noche les apagaba el fuego,
y alrededor rugían los animales. A esas horas
algunos desertaban para volver a Tenochtitlán
a donde nunca volvieron.

Los guías decían que estaban perdidos
y que no sabían a dónde iban.
                              Se subían a los árboles
y no veían desde las copas a un tiro de piedra.
Se comían los caballos
                              y los indios ya iban comiendo muertos
. . . y no sólo los indios (un Medrano contó después
que se había comido los sesos de un Montesinos).
No lo cuenta Cortés en las Cartas de Relación.
Nubes de zopilotes seguían al ejército.
Cortés iba a pie, con una pica al hombro,
esforzando a los que quedaban vivos.
A donde llegaban las casas estaban quemadas,
                              y las milpas quemadas.
Hallaron un estero de 500 pasos de ancho.
Hicieron un gran puente de 1.000 vigas.
Cortés decía que tras el estero estaba Acalán,
tierra *abundantísima*, y que allí descansarían,
y cuando cruzaron el puente: ¡una nueva ciénaga!
Los caballos desensillados se iban hasta las orejas
(y hay que ponerles palmas debajo para que no se hundan).
Al fin los caballos pasaron nadando.
Los soldados querían volver a la Nueva España
pero ya era muy tarde para volver. Cortés
no sabía que hacer. Si al otro día
no encontraban poblado,
                              no sabía qué harían.
De pronto árboles cortados y una vereda chica:
                              pero el pueblo despoblado!

and came out again in the same path they had opened.
Cortés was bursting with anger.
                              They wanted to turn back
but now it was very late for turning back.
They raised their eyes and could not see the sky.
They climbed trees to get the lay of the land
and saw no land, only tree after tree.
Two guides fled by night. Only one guide remained
who did not know the way. And the henequen cloth.
In 20 leagues they made 50 bridges.
More swamps and rivers which weren't on the cloth.
Now there were no towns. Only abandoned villages,
burned huts. And more swamps to go through.
The night rain extinguished their fires,
and animals howled all around. At this point
some deserted to return to Tenochtitlán
where they never returned.

The guides said that they were lost
and didn't know where they were going.
                              They climbed trees
and from the treetops could not see a stone's throw.
They were eating the horses
                      and the Indians were now eating the dead
. . . and not only the Indians (one Medrano later disclosed
that he'd eaten the brains of one Montesinos).
Cortés doesn't mention this in the *Cartas de Relación*.
Clouds of buzzards followed the army.
Cortés went on foot, with a pike over his shoulder,
urging on those who remained alive.
Wherever they arrived the houses were burned,
                      and the cornfields burned.
They came to an inlet 500 paces wide.
They built a bridge of 1,000 beams.
Cortés said that beyond the inlet lay Acalán,
a *most bountiful* land, and that there they would rest,
and when they crossed the bridge another swamp!
The unsaddled horses sank up to their ears
(and palm branches have to be placed beneath them so they don't go under).
Finally the horses swam across.
The soldiers wanted to return to New Spain
but by now it was very late to turn back. Cortés
didn't know what to do. If the following day
they didn't find a settlement,
                      he didn't know what they'd do.
Then suddenly trees cut down and a narrow path:
                              but the town was deserted!

Se habían comido a los guías.
Los chirimías y sacabuches y dulzainas
ya no tocaban. Hacía tiempo
que no tocaban. Cuatro chirimías se habían muerto.
Dejaban cruces en las ceibas
con cartas que decían
                POR AQUÍ PASÓ CORTÉS.
                    POR AQUÍ PASÓ CORTÉS.
Y después fue el carnaval aquel, en Acalán.
Cuando en media selva celebraron carnaval.
Habían llegado por fin a Acalán.
Cuauhtémoc iba detrás, despacio,
                            con los pies quemados
                            ("El Águila que Cae")
sin quejarse, sin decir una palabra.
Los indios de Acalán salieron a recibir a Cuauhtémoc.
Dijeron: "Que venga el señor,
nuestro amo y soberano,
que nos trate a sus súbditos sin clemencia."
Y arreglaron los *axóyatl* para los tres Reyes.
Fueron a su encuentro con abanicos de plumas de quetzal,
y le hicieron un dosel de plumas de quetzal y oro
y trajeron mantas reales, y le llevaron sandalias reales
y joyas provistas de pendientes de oro y collares de jade
y brazaletes de jade y la corona real.
Y después les dieron *atole*, y después *pinole*.
Y después comieron y después de la comida
se repartieron los obsequios.
Era el tiempo de carnaval
y los españoles hicieron fiesta durante el día
y durante la noche, andando enmascarados,
celebrando el carnaval.
                    Y los indios también tuvieron fiesta.
Y los Reyes estaban bromeando entre ellos
(mirando desde lejos a los españoles enmascarados)
Cuauhtémoc, y Coanacoch, señor de Texcoco
y Tetlepanquetzal, señor de Tlacopan;
bromeaban como si todavía fueran reyes.
Y dijo bromeando Coanacoch, el chichimeca, a Cuauhtémoc:
"Señor: la provincia que vamos a conquistar
será para mí, pues como sabe V.A.
Texcoco tiene la primacía
según el trato que celebró mi abuelo Nezahualcoyotzin
con su tío Itzcohuatzin, antepasado de V.A."
Y respondió el Rey Cuauhtémoc, también bromeando:
"En esos tiempos, Señor, nuestros ejércitos iban solos,
y entonces esa provincia hubiera sido de V.A.
y estaba bien que así fuese

The guides had been eaten.
The flageolets and sackbutts and flutes
no longer played. Some time now
since they'd played. Four flageolet players had died.
They left crosses on the ceibas
with letters which said
          CORTÉS PASSED THIS WAY
                    CORTÉS PASSED THIS WAY
And later there was that carnival in Acalán.
When in the middle of the forest they celebrated carnival.
They had at last reached Acalán.
Cuauhtémoc went at the rear, slowly,
                              with burnt feet
                              ("The Eagle that Falls")
without complaint, without saying a word.
The Indians of Acalán came out to receive Cuauhtémoc.
They said: "Let the master come,
our ruler and sovereign,
who may treat us as his subjects without mercy."
And they arranged the *axóyatl* for the three kings.
They went to meet him with quetzal-feather fans,
and they made him a canopy of quetzal feathers and gold
and brought him royal shawls and brought him royal sandals
and jewels set in gold earrings and jade necklaces
and jade bracelets and the royal crown.
And then they gave him *atole*, and then *pinole*.
And they ate and after the meal
they distributed the gifts.
It was carnival time
and the Spaniards made merry during the day
and during the night, walking around in masks,
celebrating the carnival.
                    And the Indians also held celebrations.
And the kings were joking amongst themselves
(observing from a distance the masked Spaniards)
Cuauhtémoc and Coanacoch, lord of Texcoco,
and Tetlepanquetzal, lord of Tlacopan;
they joked as if they were still kings.
And Coanacoch, the Chichimec, said in jest to Cuauhtémoc:
"Señor, the province that we are going to conquer
will be mine, since as Your Majesty knows
Texcoco holds the primacy
according to the treaty approved by my grandfather Nezahualcoyotzin
with your uncle Itzcohuatzin, Your Majesty's ancestor."
And King Cuauhtémoc replied, also in jest:
"In those times, Señor, our armies went separately,
and then that province would have been Your Majesty's
and it was right that it should be

porque Texcoco es nuestra antigua patria
de donde procede nuestra estirpe y linaje.
Mas ahora que nos ayudan los hijos del sol,
por lo mucho que a mí me quieren . . . será para mí."
Y habló Tetlepanquetzatzin y dijo:
"No, Señor, será para mí, porque Tlacopan
y el reino de los Tepanecas, que antes era postrero
ahora será el primero." Y habló Temilotizin, el tlaquetactl
poniéndose serio y suspirando: "¡Ah, Señores!
¡Ah, Señores!
¡Cómo se burlan VV. AA.
de la gallina que lleva el codicioso lobo
y que no hay cazador que se la quite!
O del pequeño pollo que se lo arrebata el engañoso halcón
cuando no está allí el pastor,
por más que lo defienda su madre,
como lo ha hecho mi Señor, el Rey Cuauhtémoc . . ."
Y después cantaron romances, tristes romances
que profetizaban todas las cosas que ahora veían,
y padecían, compuestos por los filósofos antiguos.
Y Cortés había visto desde lejos a los señores contentos
y pensó mal. Porque había visto que los reyes se reían.
Y les envió a decir con intérprete que "le parecía mal
que entre nobles y príncipes se burlaran unos con otros".
Y ellos contestaron: "Que no hacían bromas
ni recitaban versos para darle pesadumbre
sino por holgarse y olvidar sus sufrimientos."
Y los señores de Acalán rodeaban al Rey Cuauhtémoc,
en espera de lo que Cuauhtémoc les fuera a decir.
Y les habló el Rey Cuauhtémoc:
"Esforzaos lo más que podáis, con la ayuda de Dios.
Estad contentos.
No vayáis a pueblos extraños.
Sed felices aquí.
Para que no ocasionéis dolor a la gente del pueblo,
a los viejos, a los ancianos, a los niños
que duermen en sus cunas, a los que apenas
empiezan a andar, a los que están jugando . . .
Tened cuidado de ellos y compadeceos de ellos.
Que no se vayan a un pueblo extraño.
Amadlos. No los abandonéis.
Yo os lo recomiendo expresamente, porque nosotros
seremos enviados a Castilla. ¿Qué sé yo
si regresaré algún día, o pereceré allá?
Quizás no vuelva a veros.
Haced todo lo que esté en vuestro poder.
Amad a vuestros hijos tranquilamente y en paz.

because Texcoco is our ancient homeland
whence our race and lineage have their origin.
But now that the sons of the sun help us,
out of their great love for me . . . it will be mine."
And Tetlepanquetzatzin spoke and said:
"No, Señor, it will be mine, because Tlacopan
and the kingdom of Tepanecas, which before us was the last
now will be the first." And Temilotizin, the Tlaquetactl spoke
becoming serious, and sighing: "Ah, Señores!
Ah, Señores!
How Your Majesties make fun
of the hen that the greedy wolf carries off
when there is no hunter who can take it away from him!
Or of the little chicken snatched by the artful falcon
when the shepherd is not there,
no matter how much the mother protects it,
as King Cuauhtémoc, my lord, has so done . . ."
And afterward they sang ballads, sad ballads
which prophesied all the things they were now seeing,
and suffering, composed by the ancient philosophers.
And Cortés had noticed the lords' merriment from a distance
and thought ill of it. Because he'd seen the kings laughing.
And he sent word through the interpreter that "it seemed wrong to him
that among noblemen and princes they should laugh at each other."
And they replied: "that they were not making merry
and reciting poetry to bring him sorrow
but rather to entertain themselves and forget their sufferings."
And the lords of Acalán surrounded King Cuauhtémoc
in expectation of what Cuauhtémoc would say to them.
And King Cuauhtémoc spoke to them:
"Make every effort you can, with God's help.
Be happy.
Do not go to foreign nations.
Be happy here.
Do this to avoid causing pain to the ordinary people,
to the old, the elderly, to the children
who sleep in their cradles, to those who are scarcely
beginning to walk, to those who are playing . . .
Take care of them and have pity on them.
Do not let them go to a foreign nation.
Love them. Do not abandon them.
I give you this advice expressly because we
will be sent to Castille. I don't know
whether someday I shall return or will die there.
Perhaps I may not see you again.
Do all that is in your power.
Love your children calmly and in peace.

No les deis ningún disgusto.
Y yo sólo digo esto:
ayudadme en alguna forma con algo
para que yo pueda dar la bienvenida al gran señor
que es el soberano de Castilla."
Y ellos contestaron:
"Oh señor y amo:
¿Acaso eres tú nuestro súbdito humillándote?
No te intranquilices, porque aquí está tu propiedad.
He aquí tu tributo. Que salgan
ocho tenates de caña con oro amarillo,
con joyas provistas de colgantes
y collares de turquesas. Que salgan
porque es tu propiedad, tu tributo."
Y el soberano contestó:
"Me habéis hecho bien con lo que vuesto corazón me da."
Y después colocaron los teponaxtles
y sacaron las pelotas con plumas de quetzal
y bailaron con los brazos enlazados.
Bailaron Quauhtemoctzin tlácatl
y Counacochtzin de Texcoco
y Tetlepanquetzatzin de Tlacopan.
Pero el enano Mexicatl de los tenochca
estaba solo en su cabaña,
y nadie lo había invitado.
Ve y oye los teponaxtles y el canto y las plumas de quetzal
y se va donde la Malinche y le dice:
"Vente hija mía, Malintzin,
porque veo que Quauhtemoctzin
está completamente encantado con la revista de tropas!
Míralo. Así pereceremos aquí nosotros y él,
el señor Marqués y tú, mi hija Malintzin"
y dijo la Malinche: "¿Es verdad lo que dices?
¿Que Quauhtemoctzin encabeza una conspiración?"
Y él, el enano Mexicatl Cozóololtic, contestó:
"Es absolutamente verdad lo que digo,
porque los hemos oído consultarse en la noche.
Dijeron que iban a quitarnos a los extranjeros,
a los otomí. ¿Cuánto tiempo se necesita
para que los aniquilemos? Que se les asalte.
De este modo los hemos oído consultarse en la noche".
"Está bien Mexicatl lo que manifestaste", dice la Malinche.
Después la Malinche se lo informó a Cortés.

Los tres soberanos se entregaron en manos de los soldados
que se estaban acercando.
Ellos se clavaron a los soberanos

Do not give them any vexation.
And I just say this:
help me in some way with something
so that I might give welcome to the great lord
who is sovereign of Castille."
And they replied:
"O Lord and Master:
Are you our subject to be humbling yourself so?
Do not worry because here is your property.
Here is your tribute. Bring forth
eight cane *tenates* of yellow gold,
with jewels set in earrings
and necklaces of turquoise. Bring them forth,
because this is your property, your tribute."
And the sovereign answered:
"I am much cheered by what your heart gives me."
And then they laid on the *teponaxtles*
and brought out the balls with quetzal feathers
and danced with arms linked.
Quauhtemoctzin Tlácatl and
Counacochtzin of Texcoco and
Tetlepanquetzatzin of Tlacopan danced.
But Mexicatl the Tenochca's dwarf
was alone in his hut,
and nobody had invited him.
He sees and hears the *teponaxtles* and the singing and the quetzal feathers
and goes to find la Malinche and tells her:
"Come my daughter, Malintzin,
because I see that Quauhtemoctzin
is completely enchanted by the inspection of the troops.
Look at him. That's how we and he will perish here,
the lord Marquis and you, my daughter Malintzin"
and la Malinche said: "Is it true what you say?
That Quauhtemoctzin is the head of a conspiracy?"
And he, Mexicatl Cozóololtic the dwarf, answered:
"It is absolutely true what I say,
because we have heard them scheming in the night.
They said they were going to rid us of the foreigners,
of the Otomi. How long will it take us
to annihilate them? Let's take them by surprise.
We have heard them scheming like this in the night."
"You have done well to reveal this," says la Malinche.
La Malinche then informed Cortés.

The three sovereigns surrendered into the hands of the soldiers,
who were closing in.
They latched onto the sovereigns

como perros al cuello de sus víctimas.
Al día siguiente (el martes de carnaval)
fueron ahorcados en el árbol de pochote:
Cuauhtémoc y Cohuanacohtzin de Texcoco
y Tetlepanquetzatzin de Tlacopan.
Los tres fueron ahorcados allá en Ueyemollan
en el árbol de pochote.
Y dijo Cuauhtémoc a Cortés antes de morir
                              ("El Águila que Cae")
"¡Oh Malinche
                —Y Doña Marina era la intérprete—
Oh Malinche: días ha que yo había entendido
que esta muerte me habías de dar
e había conocido tus falsas palabras,
porque me matas sin justicia! Dios te la demande,
pues yo no me la di cuando te me entregué en mi Tenochtitlán"
Y el señor de Tlacopan dijo que moría contento
porque moría junto al Rey Cuauhtémoc, su señor.
Y antes de morir los confesaron los franciscanos
—Y Doña Marina fue la intérprete de la confesión—
Y después Cortés en las noches no podía dormir.
Se levantaba y se paseaba solo en la oscuridad
entre los grandes ídolos,
                          y se cayó en la oscuridad
tropezando entre los ídolos, y se quebró la cabeza.
Pero no dijo nada. Sólo pidió que se la curaran.

Bernal Díaz iba triste, porque era amigo de Cuauhtémoc . . .

Y después las grandes sabanas, verdes y sin árboles
bajo el sol abrasador, llenas de venados mansos
que apenas corrían —adorados como dioses—
Y más allá Tayasal, en mitad del lago, la ciudad de Canek,
con sus casas y sus templos brillantes bajo el sol.
Les dijeron que los hombres con barbas estaban a 10 días.
¡Y el sol! ¡El gran sol! Las corazas calientes los quemaban.
Iban con calenturas sudando bajo el hierro.
¡Y las lluvias! Llovió días y noches sin cesar
y tiritaban dentro de las corazas heladas.
Los pedernales de las sierras cortaban como puñales.
Los caballos se desjarretaban, resbalaban,
caían y se herían. Desde lejos oían rugir los ríos
que venían crecidos y recios.
Pasaron haciendo puentes con vigas y bejucos.
Allí quedaron los grandes troncos cortados:
                              "Los puentes de Cortés".
Y era inútil que Doña Marina preguntara en su lengua

like hounds around the necks of their victims.
The next day (the Tuesday of carnival)
they were hanged on a *pochote* tree:
Cuauhtémoc and Cohuanacohtzin of Texcoco
and Tetlepanquetzatzin of Tlacopan.
The three were hanged there in Ueyemollan
from the *pochote* tree.
And Cuauhtémoc said to Cortés before he died
                                  ("The Eagle that Falls")
"O Malinche!
              —And Doña Marina was the interpreter—
O Malinche, days ago I became aware
that you were to bring me this death
and saw through your false words,
because you kill me unjustly! May God reproach you for it,
since I did not kill myself when I surrendered to you in my Tenochtitlán"
And the lord of Tlacopan said that he died content
because he was dying alongside King Cuauhtémoc, his lord.
And before they died, the Franciscans heard their confessions.
—And Doña Marina was the interpreter for the confessions—
And afterwards Cortés could not sleep at night.
He got up and walked around alone in the darkness
among the huge idols,
                      and in the dark he fell
stumbling among the idols, and he cut open his head.
But he said nothing. He merely asked for it to be dressed.

Bernal Díaz was sad because he was a friend of Cuauhtémoc . . .

And then the great savannahs, green and treeless
under the burning sun, full of tame deer
that hardly ran—adored as gods.
And farther on, Tayasal, in the middle of the lake, the city of Canek,
with its houses and temples gleaming beneath the sun.
They told them that the men with beards were 10 days away.
And the sun! The great sun! The scorching breastplates burned them.
They suffered from fevers, sweating beneath the iron.
And the rains. It rained unceasingly day and night
and they shivered inside their frozen breastplates.
The flints of the sierras cut like daggers.
The horses lost hamstrings, slipped,
fell and were injured. From afar they heard the roar of rivers
which flowed swift and swollen.
They got across, making bridges from beams and rattan.
The huge felled trunks remained behind:
                      "Cortés's Bridges."
And it was pointless for Doña Marina to ask in their language

dónde había caminos. No había caminos.
Cortés estaba furioso. No podía atinar
por más que miraba la aguja . . .
Un día llegaron a un lugar que se llamaba "Tuniha"
(unas chozas de paja) y estaba en el dibujo.
Les dijeron que a dos soles estaban Nito y los españoles.
Y al fin en una huerta junto a un estero:
                    cuatro españoles cortando zapotes.
Al fin Cortés entró a caballo
                            en San Gil de Buena Vista
y salieron a recibirlo y besarle las manos.

where there were paths. There were no paths.
Cortés was furious. He couldn't work it out
no matter how much he studied the compass . . .
One day they reached a place called "Tuniha"
(a few straw huts) and it was on the drawing.
They told them that two suns away were Nito and the Spaniards.
And finally in a vegetable garden near an inlet:
        four Spaniards cutting sapodillas.
Finally Cortés rode on horseback
                          into San Gil de Buena Vista
and they came out to welcome him and kiss his hand.

Pedrarias envió a Francisco Hernández de Córdoba
    al "Estrecho Dudoso"
con caballos y ballesteros, a conquistar y pacificar
las tierras de Nicaragua, y descubrir otras . . .
Luque, Pizarro y Almagro pagaron los barcos.

Fundó las dos ciudades —Granada y León—
junto a los dos lagos:
    el Lago de Granada y el Lago de León.
Y junto a los dos volcanes:
    el Mombacho y el Momotombo.
Trazó con la espada el sitio de la plaza.
El sitio de la iglesia. Y el de la fortaleza.
    Y las fortalezas de las dos ciudades se reflejaban
    en el agua de los dos lagos . . .

Había mucha miel y cera y maizales
y cacao (que usaban como moneda)
y muchos cerdos de montes, venados, conejos,
y mucho algodón, y las indias tejiéndolo.
Tenían libros de pergaminos, de cuero de venado,
con sus tierras pintadas en tinta roja y negra
y los ríos, los caminos y los bosques.
En cada pueblo habían plazas y mercados
y hacían fiestas y arietes y cantares
en los días de la cosecha del maíz.
Hacían mitotes cantando en coro
cuando la recolección del cacao,
con un palo muy alto en mitad de la plaza
y en la punta el dios del cacao
y muchachos atados con cabulla
daban vueltas en el aire alrededor del palo
como si fueran volando,
y abajo danzaban los indios en corro
al son de tambores y atabales
pintados de negro y rojo,
con borlas de algodón y bellos penachos,
y las muchachas daban jícaras de chicha a los príncipes
y ellos encendían un manojo de tabaco
y todos chupaban y echaban el humo por la boca,
y en otras jícaras les llevaban cacao
y pasaban toda la noche tocando los tambores
y tocando los atabales y cantando.

Pedrarias sent Francisco Hernández de Córdoba
    to the "Doubtful Strait"
with horses and crossbowmen, to conquer and pacify
the lands of Nicaragua, and to discover others . . .
Luque, Pizarro and Almagro paid for the ships.

He founded the two cities—Granada and León—
beside the two lakes:
    Lake Granada and Lake León.
And beside the two volcanoes:
    Mombacho and Momotombo.
He traced the site of the square with his sword.
The site of the church. And that of the fortress.
    And the fortresses of the two cities were reflected
    in the waters of the two lakes . . .

There was much honey and wax and corn in the fields
and cocoa (which they used as coins)
and many wild pigs, deer, rabbits,
and much cotton, and the Indian women weaving it.
They had books of parchment, of deerskin,
with their lands painted in red and black ink
and the rivers, the roads and the forests.
In each town there were squares and markets
and they held feasts and battering-ram contests and songs
in the days of the corn harvest.
They held dances singing in chorus
when the cocoa was picked,
with a very tall pole in the center of the square
and on its tip the god of cocoa,
and young men attached with rope
spun around the pole in the air
as though they were flying,
and below the Indians danced in a circle
to the sound of drums and timbrels
painted in red and black,
with cotton tassels and beautiful plumes,
and the girls gave jars of chicha to the princes
and they lit up bundles of tobacco
and they all sucked in and blew out smoke through their mouths,
and in other jars they brought them cocoa
and they spent the whole night pounding the drums
and ringing the timbrels and singing.

Y el fuego del volcán Masaya por las noches
iluminaba todo el cielo como una luna,
y del cráter del volcán salía una vieja
muy vieja y arrugada, con las tetas hasta el ombligo,
a hablar con los indios,
con el pelo parado, los dientes como de perro
y más negra que los indios.
Sacrificaban muchachas a la vieja del volcán.
Y dejó de salir cuando llegaron los cristianos
y dijo que ya no saldría hasta que ellos se fueran
o los echaran de la tierra.

(No se gobernaban por caciques ni por señor ni jefe
sino por un consejo de ancianos elegidos por votos
y éstos elegían un capitán general para la guerra
y cuando moría o lo mataban en la guerra elegían otro
  —y a veces ellos mismos lo mataban
   si era perjudicial para la república—
y se reunían en la plaza a la sombra de una ceiba:
aquel consejo de ancianos elegidos por votos.)

Los hombres de Hernández de Córdoba
  se encontraron con Cortés en Honduras.
Cortés le envió acémilas cargadas de herrajes,
herramientas y ropa y jarrones de plata y joyas de oro
—y unas cartas secretas— ¿Planeó Córdoba sublevarse?
Hernando de Soto y otros nueve fueron a pie a Panamá
a decirlo a Pedrarias. Le hablaron de las cartas.
Pedrarias inmediatamente aderezó los navíos. Le dijeron
a Córdoba que huyera. Que se acordara de Balboa.
Pero él no quiso huir. Dijo soy inocente.
       Espero a Pedrarias.
Pedrarias lo puso preso en su fortaleza de León.
Hernández de Córdoba atravesó tristemente la plaza
que él había trazado; miró por última vez su lago
(el Lago de León) y fue degollado.
Fue enterrado en la iglesia que él levantó,
en la ciudad que él fundó, entre el lago y el Momotombo.

Salía fuego del Momotombo día y noche.

And the fire of the Masaya volcano at night
lit up the whole sky like a moon,
and from the crater an old woman would emerge
very old and wrinkled, with teats down to her navel,
to talk to the Indians,
with her hair standing up, teeth like a dog
and blacker than the Indians.
They sacrificed girls to the old woman of the volcano.
And she ceased to appear when the Christians arrived
and said that she would appear no more until they left
or they were thrown out of the land.

(They were not governed by caciques nor by a lord or chief
rather by a council of elders elected by votes
and these elders chose an overall war captain
and when he died or was killed in battle they chose another
    —and sometimes they killed him themselves
    if he was doing harm to the republic—
and they met in the square under the shade of a ceiba:
that council of elders was elected by votes.)

Hernández de Córdoba's men
    met up with Cortés in Honduras.
Cortés sent him beasts of burden laden with iron-work,
tools and clothes and pots of silver and gold jewels
—and some secret letters— Was Córdoba planning to rebel?
Hernando de Soto and nine others went to Panama on foot
to tell Pedrarias. They spoke to him of the letters.
Pedrarias immediately readied the ships. They told
Córdoba to flee. To remember Balboa's fate.
But he did not wish to flee. He said I am innocent.
                    I'll wait for Pedrarias.
Pedrarias imprisoned him in his fortress in León.
Hernández de Córdoba sadly crossed the square
which he had traced out; he looked for the last time at his lake
(Lake León) and was beheaded.
He was buried in the church he had raised,
in the city he had founded, between the lake and Momotombo.

Fire came out of Momotombo day and night.

El Muy Magnífico Señor Pedrarias Dávila
Furor Domini!!!
fue el primer "promotor del progreso" en Nicaragua
     y el primer Dictador
introdujo los chanchos en Nicaragua, sí es cierto
     "cauallos e yeguas vacas e ovejas
     e puercos e otros ganados . . ."
(pero ganado de él)
y el primer "promotor del comercio" en Nicaragua
(de indios y negros)
                  a Panamá y al Perú
(en los barcos de él)
     "indios y negros y otros ganados"
"para que los pobladores destas partes se rremedien
y la dicha Panamá asimismo"
               dice la propaganda de Pedrarias

     "una yegua rucia vieja————
     "otra yegua rucia de tres años————
     "otra potranca su hija————
     "el negro juan, el negro francisquillo————
     "ysabel la esclava herrada en la cara————
     "perico y su niño que es esclavo y herrado en la cara————
     "marica la esclava————
     "ysabel la de guatemala es esclava y está preñada————
     "martinillo de mateare————
     "catalinilla que está parida————
     "juanillo, juan negro el viejo————
     "los cuales se venden a los precios siguientes————
la potranca rucia trezientos pesos (CCC° p° s)
la potranca su hija dozientos pesos (CC° p° s)
francisquillo quatroçientos e çincuenta pesos (CCCC°L p° s) etc.

     . . . los cuales dichos negros e bestias
     a de vender a los dichos precios . . .

     . . . fiados para el peru por vn año e hipotecados
     los negros e las bestias . . .

. . . los quales a de vender en los preçios siguientes . . .

    ¡ysabel de guatemala, martinillo de mateare, francisquillo,
catalinilla, marica!

The Most Magnificent Pedrarias Dávila
Furor Domini!!!
was the first "promoter of progress" in Nicaragua
        and the first Dictator
he introduced pigs into Nicaragua, yes it's true
        "horses & mares & sheep
        & pigs & other livestock . . ."
(but his own livestock)
and the first "promoter of business" in Nicaragua
(of Indians and negroes)
                        to Panama and to Peru
(in his own ships)
        "indiens & negroes & other livestock"
"so that the settlers of these parts myght prosper
and the sayd Panama likewise"
                        says Pedrarias's propaganda

        "an old silver-grey mare————
        "an other silver-gray mare thre yere olde————
        "an other filly out of her————
        "the negro juan, the negro francisquillo————
        "ysabel the slave branded on her face————
        "perico and his childe who is a slave & branded on his face————
        "marica the slave————
        "ysabel the Guatemalan is a slave & pregnant————
        "martinillo from Mateare————
        "catalinilla who's just given birth————
        "juanillo, old negro juan————
        "whych are for sale at the followyng prices
the silver-gray filly thre hundred pesos (CCC° p° s)
the filly out of her two hundred pesos (CC° p° s)
francisquillo four hundred and fifty pesos (CCCC°L p° s) etc.

        . . . whych sayd negroes & beestes
        are to be solde at sayd prices . . .

        . . . guaranteed for peru for a yeere and mortgaged
        the negroes & the beestes . . .

. . . whych are to be solde at the followyng prices . . .

isabel the guatemalan, martinillo from mateare, francisquillo,
catalinilla, marica!

¡Dulces nombres en los áridos documentos comerciales
de la COLECCIÓN SOMOZA! Dulces nombres
que Pedrarias jugaba al ajedrez.
El conde de Puñonrostro quiso silenciar a Herrera:
don Francisco Arias Dávila é Bobadilla Conde de Puñonrostro
del Consejo de Guerra de Vuestra Magestad, digo:
que habiendo visto las Décadas de la Historia de las Indias
que Antonio de Herrera coronista de Vuestra Magestad
tiene escriptas, en lo que trata de Pedrarias Dávila mi abuelo
. . . se enmienden los pliegos que de esto tratan
antes que la Historia se publique . . .
Contesta Herrera:
NON DEBE EL CORONISTA DEJAR FASCER SU OFICIO

¡Y los ladridos de los perros de Pedrarias!
¡El Muy Magnífico Señor Don Pedrarias Dávila!
Los indios mataban a sus hijos para que no fueran esclavos
o las mujeres malparían para no parirlos o no cohabitaban
para no concebirlos. Y se acostaban cansados, sin cenar.
Y despúes aquel año en que no sembraron los indios
(una Huelga General) y los cristianos les quitaron el maíz:
iban con cruces en las manos los indios pidiendo por Dios maíz.

Y si uno no sabía el camino
                        (de León a las minas)
no necesitaba guía ni preguntar el camino:
seguía los esqueletos de los indios muertos:

Iban encadenados y mirando los caminos
cantaban llorando:
                "Por aquellos caminos
                íbamos a servir a León
                y volvíamos.
                Ahora vamos sin esperanzas
                de volver."

                        (por no abrir la cadena
                                cortarle
                                la cabeça
                        para sacarle la cadena)

Y los perros. Los perros de Pedrarias.
El indio tenía un palo
y le echaban primero los perros cachorros
(para enseñarles montería).
Cuando los tenía vencidos con el palo
soltaban los lebreles y los alanos de Pedrarias.

Sweet names in the arid commercial documents
in the Somoza Collection! Sweet names
with which Pedrarias played chess.
The Count of Puñonrostro tried to silence Herrera:
don Francisco Arias Dávila & Bobadilla Count of Puñonrostro
of Your Majesty's Council of War, I refer to:
who having seen the Decades of the History of the Indies
which Antonio de Herrera chronicler to Your Majestie
has writ, in whych he deals with Pedrarias Dávila my grandfather
. . . should amend the sections which deal with this
before the History is published . . .
Herrera replies:
THE CHRONICLER MUST NOT FAIL TO DO HIS DUTY

And the barking of Pedrarias's dogs!
The Most Magnificent Señor Don Pedrarias Dávila!
The Indians killed their children so they would not become slaves
or the women aborted so as not to give birth or did not cohabit
so as not to conceive them. And they went to bed tired, without eating.
And then that year in which the Indians sowed no crops
(a General Strike) and the Christians took their maize:
the Indians clutched crosses begging for corn for God's sake.

And if you did not know the way
                              (from León to the mines)
you needed no guide nor to ask the way:
you followed the skeletons of the dead Indians:

They went in chains and looking at the roads
in tears they sang:
              "Along those roads
              we went to serve in León
              and we returned.
              Now we go with no hope
              of returning."

                  (to avoid breaking the chain
                        cut off
                        the head
                  to remove the chain)

And the dogs. Pedrarias's dogs.
The Indian had a stick
and first they threw puppies at him
(to teach them hunting).
When he had beaten them back with the stick
they set Pedrarias's greyhounds and wolf hounds loose.

Los indios preguntaron al Demonio
(¿a los brujos? ¿a las brujas? ¿a la Vieja del Volcán?)
cómo se verían libres de los españoles
        y el Demonio les contestó:
Que él podía libertarlos de los españoles
"haciendo que los dos mares se juntaran
        (¿el Canal de Nicaragua?)
pero entonces perecerían los españoles
        (¿el canal Norteamericano en Nicaragua?)
juntamente con los indios"

el pueblo bendice al rey
        por haber mandado que el dicho Pedrarias
vaya a castilla
        y no este mas en estas partes
porque como es hombre de ochenta años e tullido
e muy abarisioso
no piensa sino en acrecentar su hazienda . . .

está muy viejo y tullido casi syempre en la cama
y no puede andar sino es en vna silla sentado
que vuestra magestad le devia dar equivalente provecho
y descanso
                y proveer de rremedio a esta gob ernaçion

Y ya tenía noventa años y no moría nunca
ni iba a Castilla. Estaba tullido y enfermo
y gobernaba con mano de hierro (monopolios
robos sobornos prisiones espionaje elecciones fraudulentas . . .)
y no moría —Se metía en un ataúd todos los años
y hacía que le cantaran el Oficio de Requiem.

Murío de 90 años.
Fue enterrado en La Merced junto a Hernández de Córdoba.
En la Catedral enterrada de un enterrado León
o hundido bajo el agua ¿León Viejo dónde está?
Hay ladrillos, ruinas rojas, en la orilla.
Los pescadores dicen que han visto torres bajo el agua
en las tardes serenas.
                Y han oído campanas.

Campanas tocando solas movidas por las olas

La capital de Nicaragua está allí espectral
bajo el agua. Un borroso sueño . . . Un conquistador degollado
Pedrarias enterrado con todas sus banderas.
Después un Asesinato y un terremoto . . .

The Indians asked the Demon
(male witches? female witches? the Old Woman of the Volcano?)
how they could be rid of the Spaniards
        and the Demon replied:
That he could free them from the Spaniards
"causing the two seas to come together
        (the Nicaraguan Canal?)
but then the Spaniards would perish
        (the North American Canal in Nicaragua?)
along with the Indians"

we the people bless the king
        for having order'd sayd Pedrarias
to go to Castille
        and remayne no more in these partes
because since he is a man of eighty yeres and crippl'd
and verye avaricious
he thinks onely of swelling his fortune . . .

he is very olde and crippl'd allmost alwayes in bed
and he cannot walk but is seat'd in a chair
that your majestie should graunt him well deserv'd reste
and recompens
                and provyde a remedie to this gouvernement.

And by now he was ninety and would not die
nor go to Castille. He was crippled and ill
and governed with an iron fist (monopolies
thefts bribes prisons spying fraudulent elections . . .)
and he would not die—He climbed into his coffin every year
and had them sing the Requiem Service for him.

He died at the age of ninety.
He was buried in La Merced next to Hernández de Córdoba.
In the buried Cathedral of a buried León
or sunk beneath the water. Where is Old León?
There are bricks, red ruins on the shore.
The fishermen say they have seen towers beneath the water
on serene afternoons.
                And have heard bells.

Bells sounding alone moved by the waves.

The capital of Nicaragua lies there, spectre-like
beneath the water. A cloudy dream . . . A beheaded conquistador
Pedrarias buried with all his flags.
Later a Murder and an earthquake . . .

Un gobernador tirano y sus dos hijos
(dos hermanos tiranos).
                         Y salta una mojarra.

El Lago de León Viejo es el Lago de Managua.
¿Hay un nuevo León Viejo?
El mismo Momotombo retumba todavía.
. . . Y los ladridos de los perros de Pedrarias . . .

NON DEBE EL CORONISTA DEJAR FASCER SU OFICIO

A tyrannical governor and his two sons
(two brother tyrants).
                    And a mojarra leaps.

The Lake of Old León is Lake Managua.
Is there a new Old León?
The same Momotombo still rumbles.
. . . And the barking of Pedrarias's dogs . . .

THE CHRONICLER MUST NOT FAIL TO DO HIS DUTY

"En el Estrecho Dudoso
        (escribe Pedrarias a Su Majestad en 1525)
se pobló una villa que se dice Bruselas . . . es
muy buena comarca, tiene buenas aguas y aires
e montería e pesquería en cantidad,
es la tierra fructífera, y de buenas huertas
y a propósito de pan de la tierra que lleva en abundancia . . ."

". . . Y porque soy ynformado que en la costa abaxo de essa tierra
        (escribe Su Majestad a Cortés)
ay un estrecho para passar en la mar del Norte a la mar del Sur,
e porque a nuestro servicio conviene mucho savello,
yo os encargo y mando que luego con mucha diligencia
procureis de saber si ay el dicho estrecho
y envieis personas que lo busquen
e os traigan larga e verdadera relación de lo que en ello allaren
e continuamente me escribireis e enbiareis larga relación
de lo que en ello se hallase, porque como beis
esto es cosa muy ymportante a nuestro servicio . . ."

Y Cortés a Su Majestad:
". . . Así porque tengo mucha información que aquella tierra
es muy rica,
como porque hay opinión de muchos pilotos
que por aquella bahía sale estrecho a la otra mar
que es la cosa en este mundo que más deseo topar,
por el gran servicio que se me representa que dello
Vuestra Cesárea Magestad recibiría . . ."

". . . Así mismo pienso enviar los navíos
        (Cortés a Su Majestad)
que tengo hechos en la mar del Sur,
que, queriendo Nuestro Señor, navegarán en fin del mes de julio
deste año de 524 por la misma costa abajo,
en demanda del dicho estrecho;
porque si le hay,
no se puede esconder a estos por la mar del Sur
y a los otros por la mar del Norte,
porque estos del Sur
llevarán la costa hasta hallar el dicho estrecho
o juntar la tierra con el que descubrió Magallanes
y los otros del Norte, como he dicho

"In the Doubtful Strait
        (writes Pedrarias to His Majesty in 1525)
a small town grew up called Brusselles . . . it is
a very good region, it has good water and air
and hunting and fishing in great supply,
it is fruitful land, and with very good orchards
and well suited to bread of the earth which it has in abundance . . ."

". . . And because I am informed that down coast from that lande
        (writes His Majesty to Cortés)
there is a strayt to go by sea from the North to the South Sea,
and because to our service it is very advantageous to know it,
I charge you and order you that after with much diligence
you seeke to find out if sayd strait exists
and to send people to find it
and for them to bring to you long and trewe account of what they might
                                                                    find therein
and continually that you should write me and send me lengthie accompt
of what you might find in it, for as you see
this is sumthyng verye important to our service . . ."

And Cortés to His Majesty:
". . . Thus because I have much information that that land
is very rich,
as since there is the opinion of many pilots
that around that bay the strait leads into the other sea
which is the thing in this world I most hope to come across,
because of the great service which it appears to me that from it
Your Imperial Majesty would receive . . ."

". . . Thus I intend to send the ships
        (Cortés to His Majesty)
which I have ready in the South Sea,
which, Our Lord willing, will sail at the end of the month of July
of this year of 524 down along that very coast,
in quest of the said strait;
because if it exists,
it cannot be hidden from those by the South Sea
and the others from the North Sea,
because those of the South
will follow the coast until they find said strait
or reach the land discovered by Magellan
and the others of the North, as I have said

hasta juntar con los Bacalaos . . ."

Y Alvarado a Cortés: ". . . También me han dicho
que a cinco jornadas adelante de una ciudad muy grande
que está a veinte jornadas de aquí,
se acaba esta tierra . . . si así es
certísimo tengo que es el estrecho . . ."

/LA REYNA/ Nuestro governador que es o fuere
de la probincia de Nycaragua: yo soy ynformada
que junto a la ciudad de Granada, que es en esa tierra,
ay una laguna de agua dulçe y sale della un Desaguadero
que va a la mar del Norte, que es un río muy grande
como el Guadalquivir que pasa por Sevilla
y que desde allí se llevó el oro que tenia Monteçuma

. . . yo vos mando que luego hagays adereçar los vergantines . . .
/YO LA REYNA/
            (La Reyna era Doña Juana la Loca)

Los navíos podían subir por el río hasta Granada
y de la laguna de Granada sólo hay cuatro leguas
a la mar del Sur, y se podía hacer una carretera
                    —Decía Doña Juana la Loca—

Oh Doña Juana Doña Juana
¡El Canal de Nicaragua!

        ymporta el descubrimiento a nuestro serbycio
        porque por el dicho río arriba
        puede aber nabegación para el Perú
            y para la Espeçeria

Oh Doña Juana Doña Juana
¡El Canal para la Especería!
El Canal de Panamá—
                    ¿En eso acabaron todos los sueños
de la Especería?

until they reach the Bacalaos . . ."

And Alvarado to Cortés: ". . . Also they have told me
that five days' journey beyond a very large city
which is twenty days' from here,
this land comes to an end . . . if it is so
quite certain I am that it is the strait . . ."

/THE QUEEN/ Our governour who is or may be
of the provynce of Nicaraqua: I am informed
that next to the cittie of Granada, whych is in that lande,
lies a lake of sweet water and from it there runs off an Outlet
whych goes to the North Sea, whych is a verie big river
like the Guadalquivir whych runs through Seville
and that from there the gold was brought whych Monteçuma had

. . . I order you forthwith to have the brigantynes made redy . . .
/I THE QUEEN/
            (The Queen was Mad Doña Juana)

Ships could ascend the river as far as Granada
and from the lake of Granada there are only four leagues
to the South Sea, and a road could be made
                            —Said Mad Doña Juana—

O Doña Juana Doña Juana
The *Nicaraguan Canal!*

        the discoverie is ymportant to our service
        because through sayd river upwards
        there may bee navigation to Peru
                and the Spice Trade

O Doña Juana Doña Juana
The Canal for the Spice Trade!
The Panama Canal—
                        Is that where all the dreams of the Spice Trade
came to an end?

Calero llegó a Nombre de Dios con nueve hombres
desnudos, hambrientos y sedientos y descalzos,
para caer en un peligro peor: el doctor Robles.
Tuvo que refugiarse en el monasterio de San Francisco
huyendo del Alguacil y del proceso de oficio del oidor
porque quería el Desaguadero para su yerno
—el dicho señor oidor doctor Robles—
  que presenta el dicho escrito según dicho
  en el dicho año tal y tal, contra el dicho etc. antes dicho
  ante mí el dicho escribano suso dicho . . .
(envolviéndolo en una red de dichos y susodichos).
Y Contreras en Nicaragua lo quería para él.
Pero ellos fueron los descubridores del Desaguadero:
Alonso Calero y Diego Machuca de Suazo.
Podrá decir lo que quiera el dicho doctor Robles.
Podrá decir lo que quiera Rodrigo de Contreras.

Ellos entraron en el río. Asentaron el real en el río,
en el real de los lagartos. Midieron las leguas.
Midieron las brazas. Pasaron los raudales
levantando los bergantines con las manos.
Oyeron los gritos extraños. Oyeron
gritar los congos en la tarde (oían
su ruido ronco sobre los árboles
y no sabían qué era.) Oyeron
en la vuelta del río
     el rumor del raudal
y no sabían qué era.
Vieron aquellos peces pastando como puercos
en las orillas y amamantando a sus crías
      —los manatíes.
No habían casas. Las selvas estaban solas,
y sólo se veían las selvas y el río
reflejando las selvas.

El Capitán Alonso Calero y Diego Machuca de Suazo
partieron de las isletas de Granada
     hacia el Desaguadero.
Navegaron el primer día entre las isletas
y anclaron en la última isla.
     Al otro día
cruzaron el Mar Dulce azul
  y llegaron a la isla de la Ceiba.

Calero reached Nombre de Dios with nine men
naked, hungry and thirsty and barefoot,
to fall into a worse danger: Doctor Robles.
He had to take refuge in the monastery of San Francisco
to escape the Magistrate and the examiner's Crown suit
because he wanted the Desaguadero for his son-in-law
—his honor said examiner Doctor Robles—
      who presents said document according as was said
      in said year so & so, against the said etc. aforementioned
      before me the said notary above-mentioned . . .
(couching it in a web of afore- and above-saids)
And Contreras in Nicaragua wanted it for himself.
But they were the discoverers of the Desaguadero:
Alonso Calero and Diego Machuca de Suazo.
Whatever said Doctor Robles might care to say.
Whatever Rodrigo de Contreras might care to say.

They entered the river. They encamped in the river,
in the alligators' camp. They measured the leagues.
They measured the fathoms. They crossed the rapids
lifting up the brigantines with their hands.
They heard strange cries. They heard
congo monkeys screeching in the evening (they heard
their raucous sound over the trees
and did not know what it was). They heard
in the river bend
               the sound of the rapids
and didn't know what it was.
They saw those fish grazing like pigs
on the shores and giving suck to their babes
                      —manatees.
There were no houses. The forests were deserted,
and all you saw was jungle and the river
reflecting the jungle.

Captain Alonso Calero and Diego Machuca de Suazo
left the isles of Granada
                  heading for the Desaguadero.
The first day they sailed among the isles
and anchored off the last island.
                    The following day
they crossed the blue Sweet Water Sea
     and reached the island of la Ceiba.

Al otro día se hicieron a la vela,
costeando,
        hacia el Desaguadero.
                Hicieron noche
en una punta.
Machuca se fue con los caballos por tierra.
Calero siguió con la armada por el lago.
Tenían buen viento en las mañanas, y paraban
por las tardes
        cuando el viento les daba en las proas.
Llegaron a las islas de Mayali,
                6 ó 7 islas,
y en medio una pequeña con dos buhíos sin gente.
Más adelante otra isla con una mezquita muy ruin
y muchos enterramientos donde se enterraban los indios.
Y llegaron al puerto de Mayali,
                dos buhíos muy ruines.
Más adelante habían otras islas despobladas
        (dos)
        a la izquierda de las islas Solentiname.
En las Solentiname
        tomaron un indio en un bote
para que sirviera de guía,
                y conocía el río
y tres o cuatro lenguas que se hablan en el río.

        El día de San Felipe y Santiago
                'en el nombre de Dios'
entraron en el río
        y comenzaron a navegar río abajo
con las dos fustas, cuatro canoas y una barca
y el Capitán Calero con dos gentiles hombres
iba de pie en una canoa adelante descubriendo.
(Y Machuca por tierra con su gente.)
        Pasaron tres islas grandes, la mayor
tenía un tiro de arcabuz de largo, y unos esteros.
Surgieron al atardecer, y se hizo noche.
Al día siguiente otras dos islas, y un río grande
que venía del mediodía, y esteros pequeños.
El agua corría más recia.
                Calero se adelantó
para ver lo que era.
                Había un raudal
y cuatro indios pescando en medio del raudal.
Cogieron a tres
        (uno se escapó a nado)
y hallaron en las canoas seis pescados

The following day they set sail,
hugging the shore,
                    toward the Desaguadero.
                                        They halted for the night
on a cape.
Machuca took the horses inland.
Calero pressed on with the flotilla along the lake.
They had good winds in the mornings, and halted
in the evenings
            when the wind turned into their bows.
They reached the islands of Mayali,
                        6 or 7 islands,
and in the middle a small one with two empty huts.
Further on another island with a very dilapidated mosque
and many graves where the Indians were buried.
And they reached the port of Mayali,
                        two very dilapidated huts.
Further on there were other uninhabited islands
            (two)
            to the left of the Solentiname islands.
In the Solentiname islands
            they took an Indian from a boat
to serve as guide,
                        and he knew the river
and three or four languages that are spoken on the river.

            On the feast of Saint Philip and Saint James
                        'in the name of God'
they entered the river
            and began to sail downstream
with the two lateen-rigged vessels, four canoes and a ship
and Captain Calero with two gentle men
stood forward on one canoe discovering.
(And Machuca overland with his people.)
            They passed three large islands, the largest
was a crossbow-shot in length, and some inlets.
They anchored at dusk, and night fell.
The next day two other islands, and a great river
which came from the south and small inlets.
The water was running more strongly.
                        Calero went ahead
to see what it was.
                    It was a rapids
and four Indians fishing in the middle of the rapids.
They caught three
                    (one escaped by swimming away)
and in the canoes they found six fish

cada uno con dos arrobas de peso,
                                    y una gran red.
Después Pocosol
                  con un cacique y cuatro viejas
Y les dijo el cacique:
que hacía diez lunas había llegado Boto,
un cacique que estaba río arriba,
y le mató muchos indios
y le llevó muchas indias y muchachos.
Y hacía una luna había llegado Tori,
un cacique que estaba río abajo,
y le mató los demás, y sólo quedaron
él y cuatro viejas.
                        Pasaron el Raudal del Diablo.
Hallaron otro río a mano derecha viniendo de Nicaragua
y un pueblo quemado.
                        Salieron al mar del Norte
creyeron todavía que era una laguna
porque el mar hacía allí un gran ancón.
            Machuca no aparecía.
Fueron hasta el río Yari buscando a Machuca,
subieron tres días por el río,
hallaron su rastro, las huellas de los caballos,
y lo perdieron.
                  Machuca se había ido.
Y Calero volvió al mar en la fragata, con calentura.
Comenzó a arreciar el mar
y se volcó la fragata.
Quedaron montados a horcajadas en la quilla
azotados por el mar.
Fueron nadando a la costa con tablas y remos.
Calero no sabía nadar; los indios lo llevaron en una escotilla.
Salieron desnudos y descalzos,
        y comenzaron a andar por la costa
y vieron la fragata
                        encaramada en dos peñas.
Recogieron los remos en la costa,
y echaron otra vez al mar la fragata.
                                Vieron una vela
y supieron que estaban en la mar del Norte
y no en una laguna.

Y Calero llegó con nueve hombres a Nombre de Dios
comiendo lobos marinos y pájaros en las islas
y bebiendo agua de mar.

Machuca se había vuelto a Nicaragua comiendo los caballos
y no sabía de Calero, y creía que había muerto.

each one weighing two arrobas,
                    and a large net.
Later Pocosol
                with a cacique and four old women.
And the cacique told them:
that ten moons ago Boto had arrived,
a cacique who was upriver,
and he killed many Indians
and took off many Indian women and children.
And one moon ago Tori had arrived,
a cacique who was downriver,
and he killed the rest, and all that were left
were he and the four old women.
                            They passed the Devil's Rapids.
They found another river on the right coming from Nicaragua
and a burned town.
                    They emerged into the North Sea
they still thought it was a lake
because the sea widened into a big cove.
        There was no sign of Machuca.
They went as far as the river Yari searching for Machuca,
three days they traveled upriver,
they found his trail, the tracks of his horses,
and they missed him.
                    Machuca had left.
And Calero returned to the sea in the frigate, with a fever.
The sea began to turn rough
and the frigate capsized.
They were left sitting astride the keel
lashed by the sea.
They swam toward the coast with planks and oars.
Calero could not swim; the Indians bore him along on a hatch-door.
They emerged naked and barefoot,
        and began to walk along the coast
and they saw the frigate
                        perched on two rocks.
They recovered the oars on the shore,
and put the frigate back to sea.
                    They saw a sail
and realized that they were in the North Sea
and not in a lake.

And Calero arrived with nine men in Nombre de Dios
eating sea wolves and birds on the islands
and drinking sea water.

Machuca had returned to Nicaragua eating the horses
and he had no news of Calero, and believed that he was dead.

Corrió Pedro de Alvarado por la tierra como un rayo . . .
En Soconusco se rindieron.
    Pasó a Zapotitlán
y los venció, y le pidieron la paz.
    Marchó hacia Quetzaltenango
y en la cumbre de un puerto halló una hechicera gorda
y un perro sacrificado (que significa guerra).
    Peleó en las barrancas
y los venció. Peleó en un llano
y los venció. Pelearon junto a una fuente
y volvió a vencerlos.
                  Murió el príncipe Ahuzumanche.
La sangre de los indios corrió como un arroyo
por la falda del monte,
    y bajó hasta el río Olintepec
y lo tiñó de rojo
y desde entonces se llamó Xequiquel ("río de sangre").
    Quetzaltenango estaba desierto.
Pero llegó Tecún-Umán, el rey de los quichés,
el gran elegido de Cawek, el del solio de cuatro doseles,
en unas andas adornadas con plumas y pedrerías,
cubierto de joyas y plumas,
con una esmeralda en el pecho que parecía un espejo,
conducido por los nobles del reino,
y Alvarado desplegó el ejército en dos alas
y él se puso en el centro,
y Tecún-Umán desplegó también el suyo en dos alas
y él se puso en el centro,
en el llano enfrente de Quetzaltenango
    (y un quetzal volaba por los aires).
Los indios fueron arrollados por los caballos.
Alvarado en su corcel se encontró con Tecún-Umán
que iba en sus andas,
y Tecún-Umán se bajó de sus andas y se fue contra Alvarado
tratando de derribarlo del caballo
    (mientras el quetzal daba gritos en el aire)
y le mató el caballo, y Alvarado
atravesó el pecho del rey del quiché con su lanza.
Estuvo mirando largo rato su cadáver.
Y el quetzal fue hallado muerto cuando murió el indio
(atravesado por una lanza)
                y lo acometieron perros.
Dijo Alvarado: "Nunca vi en México más extraño *quetzal*."

Pedro de Alvarado tore through the land like a bolt of lightning . . .
In Soconusco they surrendered.
      He went on to Zapotitlán
and conquered them, and they asked for peace.
      He marched toward Quetzaltenango
and at the top of a mountain pass he came across a fat sorceress
and a sacrificed dog (a war sign).
      He fought in the gorges
and conquered them. He fought on a plain
and conquered them. They fought by a spring
and again he conquered them.
                        Prince Ahuzumanche died.
The blood of the Indians flowed like a stream
down the mountainside,
      and descended to the river Olintepec
and dyed it red
and ever since it has been known as Xequiquel ("blood river").
      Quetzaltenango was deserted.
But Tecún-Umán arrived, the king of the Quiché,
the great elected of Cawek, he with the canopied throne with four portières,
in a litter adorned with feathers and precious stones,
covered with jewels and feathers,
and on his chest an emerald that looked like a mirror,
led by noblemen from the kingdom,
and Alvarado deployed his army in two flanks
and positioned himself at the center,
and Tecún-Umán also deployed his army in two flanks
and positioned himself at the center,
on the plain by Quetzaltenango
      (and a quetzal soared overhead).
The horses rode rough-shod over the Indians.
Alvarado on his charger came face to face with Tecún-Umán
who was traveling in his litter,
and Tecún-Umán got down from his litter and set upon Alvarado
trying to unseat him from his horse
      (while in the air the quetzal screeched)
and he killed his horse, and Alvarado
ran the king's chest through with his lance.
For a long time he stared at the dead body.
And the quetzal was found dead when the Indian died
(run through by a lance)
                and the dogs set upon it.
Alvarado said: "Never in Mexico did I see a stranger *quetzal*."

Después pidieron las paces
Llegaron Oxib-Queh el Ahau-Ahpop del reino,
y el príncipe Beleheb-Tzy el Ahpop-Camhá del reino,
con todos los nobles y príncipes de la familia real
a pedir paz.
     Invitaron a Alvarado a la corte de Utlatlán
(pero ellos seguían al acecho en las barrancas de Utlatlán).
Y Alvarado vio que Utlatlán sólo tenía dos puertas,
una con 30 escalones,
y la otra con una calzada destruida,
y las casas muy juntas y las calles angostas,
     ni mujeres ni niños,
y la ciudad rodeada de barrancas,
y los caciques muy demudados en sus parlamentos
(y los de Quetzaltenango dijeron que los querían quemar)
y se salió de Utlatlán antes que fuera de noche
con todo su real al campo
     —y los indios muy tristes cuando los vieron salir.
Oxib-Queh y Beleheb-Tzy llegaron a su real
y los encadenó.
               Y los hizo juzgar por consejo de guerra.
La sentencia del consejo: ser quemados vivos.
Se encendió la hoguera en el campamento
y en presencia de todos los príncipes de la familia real
que lloraban,
          fueron quemados vivos.
     "el día *4 Kat* (Semana Santa de 1524)
     "los príncipes Ahpop y Ahpop Camhá
     "fueron quemados vivos por Tonatiuh
     "oh hijos míos."
Y después quemó la corte de los quichés.
Partió para Iximché (Tecpan-Quauhtemalan)
     la corte de los cakchiqueles.
Fogatas encendidas de volcán en volcán
(Hunhpú, Pacaya, Chingo, Lamatepec, Quetzaltepec, Chicontepec)
anunciaban de noche de volcán en volcán
la llegada de Alvarado (*Avilantaro*)
Lo salieron a recibir los reyes Belehé-Qat y Cahi-Imox
en ricas andas adornadas de joyas y plumas
con todos los señores de la corte y los nobles del reino
y lo alojaron en el palacio real de Tzupam Hay.
Preguntó a los jefes cuáles eran sus enemigos
y los jefes dijeron:
     "mis enemigos son dos:
     Tzutuhil, Panatacat, oh Dios"
     (porque creían que Tonatiuh era dios)
y Alvarado fue contra los tzutuhiles de Atitlán,

Then they sued for peace.
Oxib-Queh the Ahau-Ahpop of the kingdom arrived
and prince Beleheb-Tzy, the Ahpop-Camhá of the kingdom,
with all the noblemen and princes of the royal family
to sue for peace.
They invited Alvarado to the court of Utlatlán
(yet still they lay in ambush in the ravines of Utlatlán).
And Alvarado saw that Utlatlán had only two gates,
one with thirty steps,
and the other with a ruined causeway,
and the houses very close together and the streets narrow,
     no sign of women or children,
and the city surrounded by ravines,
and the caciques very agitated in their parleying
(and those from Quetzaltenango said that they wished to burn them)
and he went out of Utlatlán before night fell
with all his camp into the fields
     —and the Indians very sad when they saw him leave.
Oxib-Queh and Beleheb-Tzy arrived at his camp
and he put them in chains.
                         And he had them tried by court-martial.
The court's sentence: to be burned alive.
The fire was lit in the camp
and in the presence of all the princes of the royal family
who were in tears,
                    they were burned alive.
     "on day *4 Kat* (Holy Week of 1524)
     "the princes Ahpop and Ahpop Camhá
     "were burned alive by Tonatiuh
     "O my children."
And then he burned the Quiché's court.
He departed for Iximché (Tecpan-Quauhtemalan)
     the court of the Cakchiquels.
Bonfires lit from volcano to volcano
(Hunhpú, Pacaya, Chingo, Lamatepec, Quetzaltepec, Chicontepec)
announced by night from volcano to volcano
the arrival of Alvarado (*Avilantaro*)
Kings Belehé-Qat and Cahi-Imox came out to greet him
in rich litters adorned with jewels and feathers
with all the lords of the court and the noblemen of the kingdom
and they gave him lodgings in the royal palace of Tzupam Hay.
He asked the chiefs who their enemies were
and the chiefs said:
     "my enemies are two:
     Tzutuhil, Panatacat, O God"
     (because they believed that Tonatiuh was God)
and Alvarado attacked the Tzutuhils of Atitlán,

la bella corte de Atitlán junto al lago:
>Tzutuhil ("Flor de las naciones").
En un islote del lago tenían su castillo.
Salieron a pelear con atabales, penachos y divisas.
Los venció. Tomó el islote del lago.
Entró en la corte de Atitlán
>(la nación que nunca había sido conquistada)
y la destruyó.
>>"El 7-*Muerte* (20 de abril de 1524)
>>"los Tzutuhil fueron matados por Tonatiuh.
Despúes fue a Panatacatl.
>>>>Los caminos estaban cerrados.
Era una noche oscura de los primeros días de junio.
Llovía mucho y los de Itzcuintlán estaban dormidos.
No distinguieron la arcabucería de los truenos.
Despertaron con los españoles dentro de Itzcuintlán.
Murió el señor del reino esa noche.
>>>>Quemó Itzcuintlán.
Pasó a Nancintlán, y de allí a Paxaco.
Habían estacas puntudas hincadas en el camino
y un perro descuartizado (en señal de guerra).
Los venció y los hizo huir.
>Mojicalco, Acatepec
estaban despoblados.
>>Y llegó a Acajutla
donde bate el mar del Sur.
En la llanura ondeaban los plumeros de los jefes.
Peleaban con sacos de algodón, blancos y de colores,
que les llegaban hasta los pies
>>>>(no podían levantarse)
y tenían grandes flechas y lanzas de treinta palmos
y le arrojaban las flechas diciéndole:
>>>>*toma tu oro Tonatiú*
y una flecha lo atravesó a Alvarado en una pierna
clavándole la pierna en la silla de montar.

Cuzcatlán estaba lleno de huertas de cacao
que producen flor y fruta casi todas las lunas.
Era una tierra fértil y con venados blancos.
Los Itzalcos estaban en las faldas de un volcán
que siempre estaba humeando,
>y alrededor del volcán
estaban las huertas de cacao.
Habían unas fuentes con mucho ruido,
de agua caliente, y en unas el agua era clara
y en otras roja, amarilla y de otros colores.
Y un río corría de tarde y de noche, y desaparecía de día.

the beautiful court of Atitlán beside the lake:
>Tzutuhil ("Flower of the nations").
He had his castle on an islet in the lake.
They came out to fight with tambours, pennants and emblems.
He conquered them. He seized the island in the lake.
He entered the court of Atitlán
>(the nation that had never been conquered)
and he destroyed it.
>"On *7-Death* (20 April of 1524)
>"the Tzutuhil were killed by Tonatiuh.
Then he went on to Panatacatl.
>The roads were closed.
It was a dark night in the first days of June.
It was raining heavily and the people of Itzcuintlán were asleep.
They could not hear the harquebus firing amid the thunder.
They awoke to find the Spaniards inside Itzcuintlán.
The lord of that kingdom died that night.
>He burned Itzcuintlán.
He went on to Nancintlán, and from there to Paxaco.
There were pointed stakes driven into the road
and a quartered dog (as a sign of war).
He conquered them and put them to flight.
>Mojicalco, Acatepec
were deserted.
>And he reached Acajutla
where the South Sea beats.
The chiefs' plumes fluttered on the plains.
They fought in white and colored cotton coats
which reached to their feet
>(they could not get up)
and they had long arrows and lances measuring thirty palms
and they hurled their arrows at him saying:
>*take your gold Tonatiú*
and an arrow pierced Alvarado's leg
pinning the leg to the saddle.

Cuzcatlán was full of cocoa groves
which produce blossom and fruit almost every moon.
It was a fertile land with white deer.
The Itzalcos were on the flanks of a volcano
which was always smoking,
>and around the volcano
were the cocoa groves.
There were some very noisy springs,
of hot water, and in some the water was clear
and in others red, yellow and other colors.
And one river flowed in the afternoon and night, and disappeared by day.

Habían muchos volcanes y lagunas,
y habían grandes árboles de bálsamo
y en la ribera del río Lempa unos árboles pequeños
daban una goma olorosa como el benjuí
y una flor olorosa.
De la laguna salía el río Lempa, muy grande,
y en un peñol en la laguna sacrificaban los indios.
El Gran Sacerdote pipil vestía una ropa larga y azul
con una mitra de muchos colores y un báculo de Obispo.
Tenían dos grandes sacrificios:
        uno al comienzo del invierno,
cuando empezaban las lluvias,
        y otro al comienzo del verano.
Tañían las trompetas y los demás instrumentos
cuando salía en la tarde la estrella Quetzalcoatl.
Al otro día se juntaba todo el pueblo, y venían
los cuatro sacerdotes, con vestiduras de colores
y con sus braseros con olor;
        se volvían al sol naciente
y arrodillados lo incensaban,
        y venía el Gran Sacerdote
con el muchacho que se había de sacrificar;
lo ponían sobre la piedra de sacrificio, le sacaban el corazón
y asperjaban con la sangre los cuatro vientos.

Y volvió a Iximché o Tecpan-Quauhtemalan
y fundó la ciudad de Santiago de Quauhtemalan
        en aquel valle verde y bello,
entre el Volcán de Agua y el Volcán de Fuego.
De un volcán manaban arroyos y fuentes
y del otro salían llamaradas de fuego.

Se comenzaron a hacer las casas.
A traer los horcones para los postes.
Caña y lodo para las paredes,
        y heno para los techos.

There were many volcanoes and lakes,
and there were huge balsam trees
and on the banks of the river Lempa some small trees
which gave a gum which smelled like benjamin
and a strong-scented bloom.
The river Lempa ran off from the lake, very wide,
and on an outcropping in the lake the Indians held sacrifices.
The Pipil High Priest wore a long blue robe
with a many-colored miter and a Bishop's crook.
They had two great sacrifices:
        one at the start of winter,
when the rains began,
        and the other at the start of summer.
They played trumpets and other instruments
when Quetzalcoatl the star appeared in the evening.
The following day the entire people came together, and the four
priests came, with gold vestments
and with their fragrant censers;
        they turned to the rising sun
and kneeling down incensed it
        and the High Priest came
with the boy who was to be sacrificed;
they laid him on the sacrificial stone, they took out his heart
and sprinkled the blood to the four winds.

And he returned to Iximché or Tecpan-Quauhtemalan
and founded the city of Santiago de Quauhtemalan
        in that beautiful and verdant valley,
between Volcán de Agua and Volcán de Fuego.
From one volcano flowed streams and springs
and from the other came tongues of fire.

They began to build houses.
To bring wooden beams for supports.
Mud and cane for the walls
        and straw for the roofs.

El día del apóstol Santiago amaneció sereno y claro
con el campo verde recién llovido, y con tambores y pífanos
y descargas de mosquetes y arcabuces.
Resplandecían los arneses, tremolaban las plumas
en el aire fresco de la mañana, cabriolaban los caballos
enjaezados y cubiertos de jireles de oro y seda.

Se trazó primero el cerco, y después las cuatro calles:
Calle Norte   Calle Sur   Calle Leste   Calle Hueste
y en el cruce de las cuatro
cuatro solares para la plaza
y dos solares junto a la plaza para la Catedral.
        "Otro sí un sitio para el Hospital de la Misericordia
        "Item el adoratorio de Nuestra Señora de los Remedios
        "Otro sí el sitio para la fortaleza. Otro sí el Cabildo.

        "E visto e leído por mí el dicho escribano,
        "el dicho testimonio, el dicho Capitán dijo,
        "e mandó a mi el dicho escribano que asi lo sentase."

Y después fue dado su solar a cada vecino:
González, Rojas, Gutiérrez, López, Juan Pérez.
Y el Cabildo estableció el precio del puerco,
el precio del huevo (a real de oro),
el orden de la procesión del Santísimo Sacramento
el día del Corpus:
        Detrás del Santísimo Sacramento los armeros,
        y luego los plateros,
        los mercaderes,
        los barberos,
        los sastres,
        los carpinteros,
        los herreros,
        los zapateros . . .

En las faldas del Volcán de Agua, y alrededor
de Guatemala,
                se extendían las milpas cuadradas,
    los cuadros de frijoles,
                        los cuadros de potreros,
    cuadros de hortalizas
                    y cuadros de frutales,

The day of James the Apostle the dawn was clear and serene
with green fields fresh with rain, and with fife and drums
and discharges of musket and crossbow.
The harnesses were gleaming, the plumes were fluttering
in the cool morning air, the horses were cavorting
harnessed and decked out in gold and silken caparisons.

The enclosure was traced, and then the four streets:
North Street   South Street   East Street   West Street
and where the four crossed
four plots for the square
and two plots adjoining the square for the Cathedral.
  "In addition a site for the Hospital of Mercie
  "Item the churche of Our Ladie of Succour
  "In addition the site for the fortress. In addition the Council.

  "And seen and read by me the sayd notary
  "the sayd testimony, the sayd Captain sayd,
  "and he commaunded me sayd notarie that I should thus recorde it."

And afterwards each neighbor was given his plot of land:
González, Rojas, Gutiérrez, López, Juan Pérez.
And the Council established the price of pork,
the price of eggs (one golden real),
the order of the procession of the Most Blessed Sacrament
the day of Corpus:
  Behind the Most Blessed Sacrament the armorers,
  and then the silversmiths,
  the merchants,
  the barbers,
  the tailors,
  the carpenters,
  the blacksmiths,
  the shoemakers . . .

On the foothills of Volcán de Agua, and around
Guatemala,
    the square cornfields stretched out,
  the squares of beans,
      the squares of pasture,
  squares of vegetables
     and squares of orchards,

unos cuadros cultivados
　　　　　　　　y otros cubiertos de breña
como un tablero de ajedrez.

Y todas las mañanas las indias bajaban a Guatemala
con pértigas de ramilletes tejidos de flores:
claveles, siemprevivas, mirtos, amapolas,
retamas, tulipanes, romero, adormideras,
varas de San José, narcisos, floripondios,
y las que llaman reinas, que crecen en las quebradas.
Unas flores para las boticas,
　　　　　　　　otras en su cabeza.

Corrían arroyos medicinales en los prados.
Fuentes de claras linfas en las vegas.
En alegres campiñas pastaban las vacadas.
Y pastaban los ciervos entre las breñas
hierbas medicinales, con las que crían
sus piedras bezares. Corrían los conejos,
tepesqüintes, guatuzas y pizotes. Volaban
los sensontes, los cenicientos, los pintados,
los carpinteros, los tordos y las tórtolas,
los cardenales jaulines, los quetzales.
Y los gorriones sutiles y tornasolados
que se vuelven en el vuelo verde, azul, leonado,
oro finísimo, libaban el humor de las flores:
duermen en los bosques umbríos del volcán,
en la estación seca, pegados a los árboles,
y salen de los bosques buscando las flores
al comienzo del invierno, cuando oyen
los primeros truenos . . .

En las Fiestas Reales se celebra *la fiesta del Volcán*.
Acaece esta fiesta ordinariamente
en noches de luna y de verano.
En la plaza mayor ponen un volcán de maderos
y lo visten y adoran como un monte natural,
con muchas yerbas y flores,
y esconden en las ramas muchos monos,
guacamayos, chocoyos, ardillas y otros animalillos,
ciervos, jabalíes, pizotes en sus grutas,
y empiezan a tocar muchos instrumentos:
trompetas, flautas, caracoles, chirimías y atambores,
y concurren muchas carrozas y mucha gente a caballo,
y la plebe a pie.
Todos los balcones y andamios están ocupados.
Está presente la Audiencia Real,

some squares under cultivation
and others covered with brambles
like a chessboard.

And each morning the Indian women came down to Guatemala
with rods of nosegays of braided flowers:
carnations, poppies, myrtle, immortelles,
broom, opium buds, tulips, rosemary,
narcissus, floripondios, sprigs of San José,
and those they call queens, which grow in the ravines.
Some flowers for the pharmacies,
others on their heads.

Medicinal streams flowed in the meadows.
Clear water springs on the lowlands.
In merry fields herds of cattle grazed.
And stags fed among the brambles
on medicinal herbs, from which they extract
their bezoar stones. Rabbits,
pacas, agoutis, and pizotes ran. Zenzontles,
cenicientos, gold finches, woodpeckers,
starlings and turtle doves,
cardinals, quetzals flew.
And subtle and iridescent sparrows
which in flight turn green, blue, tawny,
finest gold, sucked the nectar of the flowers:
they sleep in the shady forests of the volcano,
in the dry seasons, clinging to the trees,
and leave the forests in search of flowers
at the onset of winter, when they hear
the first thunder . . .

In the Royal Feasts the *feast of the Volcano* is celebrated.
This feast usually falls
on moonlit nights and in summer.
In the main square they build a volcano from timbers
and they dress it up and adorn it like a natural hill,
with many grasses and flowers,
and among the branches they hide several monkeys,
macaws, budgerigars, squirrels and other small animals,
deer, wild boar, red cratis in the gaps,
and they begin to play many instruments:
trumpets, flutes, flageolets, conches and tambours,
and many carriages take part and many people on horseback,
and the populace on foot.
All the balconies and walkways are filled with people.
The Royal Audience is present,

y entran a la plaza dos compañías de caballería
y después entran marchando dos de infantería
y se tienden por toda la plaza de armas.
Y después entran los indios desnudos
con sus maztlates y embijados,
con plumas de guacamayos y pericos
y con arcos y flechas,
y después de ellos vienen muchos instrumentos
y trompetas, y tras ellos otros danzando
con danzas bien ordenadas y vistosas:
        Es *la danza del Volcán* . . .

and two companies of knights enter the square
and then two of infantry march in
and cover the entire parade square.
And then naked Indians enter
with their *maztlates* and vermilion paint
with macaw and parakeet feathers
and with bows and arrows,
and after them come many instruments
and trumpets, and behind them others dancing
with very attractive and orderly dances:
This is *the dance of the Volcano* . . .

"Si Vuestra Magestad me imbiase licencia para que yo vaya a esos
Reynos . . ." (Escribe Pedro de Alvarado)
Tal vez, dice, por el Estrecho de Magallanes
podría pasar a alguna Isla, o Tierra firme
de la otra Costa de la Especiería
y desde allí descubrir por diversos rumbos y vientos
las Islas de la Especiería y Maluco.
        "todo lo demás que por este Mar está por descubrir . . ."
¡el Sur¡
las Islas que debía haber en el Mar del Sur
y la costa de Tierra-firme en el Mar del Sur!
        ". . . Cualquier Islas en la mar del Sur . . ."
Su Majestad regalaba a Don Pedro de Alvarado
cualquier islas en el mar del Sur de la Nueva España
"e TODAS las que halláredes hacia el Poniente della"
y Alvarado hizo las naos
        para descubrir las islas y la Especiería
        —"descubrir lo no sabido"—
pagó la flota con su bolsa
se endeudó con $40.000 (pesos oro)
Salió de la Provincia de León
a descubrir por la Mar del Sur
        hacia el Poniente
pero después de 400 leguas de mar
las corrientes y los vientos contrarios (o la codicia)
lo llevaron al Perú.
No halló sino ciénagas
y montañas.
            No habían caminos
de pueblo a pueblo,
y la lengua en cada pueblo
            era diferente.
Abrieron los caminos con las espadas, y con las manos
por espacio de 160 leguas
y algunos se volvían locos.
El volcán de Quito les arrojaba cenizas desde lejos
y sus truenos y relámpagos se veían a 100 leguas.
Tardaron en atravesar las montañas 7 meses.
Y después la tierra era tan alta y sin árboles
y tan fría. Después las grandes Sierras de Nieve
donde soplaba un aire tan frío!
Se metieron por la nieve,
sin saber dónde acababan aquellas Sierras.

"If Your Majestie wolde sende me licence so I might go to those
Kingdoms . . ." (Writes Pedro de Alvarado)
Perhaps, he says, through the Strait of Magellan
I could get through to some Island, or Terra firma
of the other Spice Coast
and from there discover by diverse routes and winds
the Spice Islands and Molucca.
        "anything else that through this Sea remaynes to be discovered . . ."
the South!
the Islands bound to exist in the South Sea
and the coast of Terra firma in the South Sea!
        ". . . Whatever Islands in the South Sea . . ."
His Majesty was giving to Don Pedro de Alvarado
whatever islands in the South Sea of New Spain
"and ALL those you might finde West of there"
and Alvarado built the ships
        to discover the islands and the Spices
        —"to discover the unknown"—
he paid for the fleet from his own wealth
he took on debts of $40,000 (gold pesos)
He set out from the Province of León
to make discoveries in the South Sea
        sailing Westward
but after 400 leagues at sea
the currents and contrary winds (or greed)
brought him to Peru.
There he found only swamps
and mountains.
                There were no roads
from one town to the next,
and the language in each town
                was different.
They opened paths with their swords, and with their hands
over a distance of 160 leagues
and some went mad.
From afar the Quito volcano rained ash on them
and its thunder and lightning could be seen 100 leagues away.
It took them 7 months to cross the mountains.
And later the land was so high and treeless
and so cold. Then the mighty Snow Sierras
where such a cold wind blew!
They went into the snow,
not knowing where those Sierras ended.

Los grandes copos de nieve los cegaban.
Les daba calentura. Y morían. Y se volvían locos.
Los enfermos eran llevados a caballo
amarrados para que no se cayeran,
    o los que se habían vuelto locos.
Se les daba sepultura en la nieve
y se hacía almoneda de sus bienes.
    Los pueblos quemados y despoblados.
Los indios de Guatemala gritaban llamando a sus amos.
La nieve a los indios les quemaba los ojos,
y se les caían los dedos de las manos y los pies,
y se quedaban parados, enteramente helados.
De noche en el campamento no tenían fuego
y sólo se oían quejidos en las tiendas
y suspiros en el viento helado.
El viento era frigidísimo y furioso
y en el camino no tenían abrigo.
Cansados se arrimaban a los peñascos
y al momento morían helados.
Pedro Gómez se heló con su caballo
y con todas sus esmeraldas.
Las armas y la ropa iban quedando en la nieve.
Allí quedó el oro tirado sobre la nieve.
Allí quedaron tiradas las esmeraldas.
Cuando salieron de la nieve iban como difuntos.
Los indios iban sin dedos, sin pies, y muchos ciegos.
Hasta que llegaron al gran camino de los Incas
y vieron el rastro de los castellanos . . .
    La tierra era de Pizarro!

The huge snowflakes blinded them.
They caught fever. And they died. And they went mad.
The sick were carried on horseback
tied down so they would not fall,
      or those who had gone mad.
They were buried in the snow
and their possessions were auctioned.
      The towns burned or deserted.
The Guatemalan Indians cried out, calling their masters.
The snow burned the Indians' eyes
and their fingers and toes fell off,
and they were stopped in their tracks, completely frozen.
At night in the camps they had no fire
and only moans were heard in the tents
and sighs in the icy wind.
The wind was freezing and furious
and as they traveled they had no shelter.
Tired they clung to the crags
and in a moment died frozen.
Pedro Gómez froze with his horse
and with all his emeralds.
Their weapons and clothes lay strewn in the snow.
There the gold remained cast into the snow.
There the emeralds were cast.
When they came out of the snow they moved like dead men.
The Indians were missing fingers, missing feet, and many blind.
Until they reached the great highway of the Incas
and saw the trail of the Castilians . . .
      The land was Pizarro's!

Partió otra vez de Guatemala Pedro de Alvarado
con su flota, a descubrir nuevas tierras,
hacia China
         y California . . .
Con vistosos estandartes, banderas de cuadra,
         flámulas, grímpolas y gallardetes!

Pero al llegar a Jalisco estaban los indios alzados.
Porque Vázquez de Coronado se había ido a la Cibola
y Oñate había quedado con poca gente en Guadalajara.

Los caxcanes y sus valles estaban sublevados,
las sierras de Tepec, el valle de Xuchipila,
el valle de Nochistlán y el valle de Teocaltipiche,
toda la indiada estaba sublevada en las sierras.
Y bajaron, y mataron a los españoles en un eclipse.

Y Alvarado resolvió a socorrer Guadalajara
(pacificar la tierra en 4 días
         y embarcarse otra vez)
Hizo compañía con el Virrey . . . (la Compañía de la Çibola)
Mitad y mitad en lo que se descubriera en la Çibola . . .

Los indios estaban en las sierras, entre rocas.
Rocas cortadas, donde sólo suben los gatos.
         Chichimecas robustos,
             y grandes flecheros.
Arrojaban flechas y varas tostadas.
         Y los comían.

Alvarado tuvo que retirarse (no fue tan fácil como creía)
         por tierra pantanosa
                 llena de cardones y magueyes.
                     Los caballos atascándose.
Los hombres quedando pegados en el lodo.
Él se apeó del caballo,
         peleando a pie
                 con espada y rodela.
Muchos se quedaron pegados en los pantanos
         sin poderse mover.
Y después ya iban subiendo la cuesta, los indios ya no venían,
pero Baltazar Montoya espoleaba el caballo cansado

Pedro de Alvarado set out from Guatemala once again
with his fleet, to discover new lands,
toward China
        and California . . .
With colorful standards, checkered flags,
        pennants, streamers and ensigns!

But when he reached Jalisco the Indians were in revolt.
Because Vásquez de Coronado had gone off to la Cibola
and Oñate had been left with few people in Guadalajara.

The Caxcans and their valleys had risen up,
the sierras of Tepec, the valley of Xuchipila,
the valley of Nochistlán and the valley of Teocaltipiche,
all the Indian populations were in revolt in the sierras.
And they came down, and they killed the Spaniards during an eclipse.

And Alvarado resolved to assist Guadalajara
(to pacify the land in 4 days
        and to set sail again)
He formed a partnership with the Viceroy . . . (The Çibola Company)
Half and half of what would be discovered in la Çibola . . .

The Indians were in the sierras, among the rocks.
Sharp-edged rocks, where only cats can climb.
        Robust Chichimecas,
            and great bowmen.
They hailed down arrows and hardened spears.
        And they ate them.

Alvarado had to withdraw (it was not so easy as he thought)
        because of the swampy ground
                full of thistles and maguey.
                    The horses getting bogged down.
The men getting stuck in the mud.
He dismounted from his horse,
        fighting on foot
            with sword and buckler.
Many were left stuck in the swamps,
        unable to move.
And later they climbed the hillside, the Indians no longer in pursuit,
but Baltazar Montoya spurred his tired horse on

creyendo que todavía venían. El caballo resbalándose
y Alvarado atrás a pie:
       sosegaos Montoya
          SOSEGAOS MONTOYA.
Seguía espoleándolo y el caballo fue rodando
cuesta abajo arrastrando con él al Adelantado.
Crujieron sus armas y su pecho bajo el caballo.
Y fueron rodando Alvarado y caballo hasta el arroyo.
Lo recogieron y tenía las armas y el pecho quebrados.
Le preguntaron qué le dolía y dijo "el alma".
Lo llevaron con cuidado en tapextle hasta Atenguillo.
Quería ir aprisa en tapextle para confesar los pecados.
Se confesó sollozando bajo unos pinos,
y murió abrazando el crucifijo,
y diciendo: "tengo enferma el alma."
     La Armada de la Especiería
la dejó en testamento a Doña Beatriz de la Cueva.
Y a 350 leguas de distancia
exclamó a esas horas Doña Beatriz:
     ¡Haya buen siglo el Adelantado!
Y el día antes llovió sangre en Toluca.

Doña Beatriz mandó pintar todo el palacio de negro
por dentro y por fuera, salones, patios, cocinas,
corredores, caballerizas, ranchos, excusados,
y hasta los tejados,
              todo pintado de negro,
y con cortinas negras,
porque el Adelantado había muerto en Muchitiltic
que quiere decir "Todo Negro"
porque desde Muchitiltic hasta Iztlán
tanto la tierra como las piedras, todo es negro.
Y la Catedral estaba también cubierta de paños negros
y toda la ciudad enlutada
celebrando las honras del Adelantado.
Y Doña Beatriz estaba encerrada en un aposento muy oscuro,
de paredes negras, sin querer ver la luz,
ni la luz de una ventana, ni la luz de una vela,
con una falda negra, y cubierta con una toca negra,
y sólo era llorar y llorar, y gemir, y hablar sola
y dar grandes voces y gritos.
Y no comía ni bebía ni dormía
ni quería que nadie la consolase,
y decía
     que ya Dios no la podía hazer mas mal
       del que la avia hecho.
Decía:

thinking they were still coming. His horse missing its step
and Alvarado was behind on foot:
        easy Montoya
        EASY MONTOYA.
He kept spurring him and the horse went sliding
downhill dragging the Adelantado with him.
His weapons and his chest were crushed beneath the horse.
And Alvarado and horse went careering down toward the stream.
They picked him up, and his weapons and his chest were broken.
They asked him where it hurt and he said "my soul."
Carefully they carried him by *tapextle* to Atenguillo.
He wanted to go quickly on the *tapextle* so as to confess his sins.
He made his confession sobbing beneath the pines,
and died embracing the crucifix,
and saying: "my soul is sicke."
        The Spice Trade Armada
he bequeathed to Doña Beatriz de la Cueva.
And 350 leagues away
at that time Doña Beatriz exclaimed:
        Godde speede the Adelantado!
And the day before it rained blood in Toluca.

Doña Beatriz ordered the whole palace to be painted black
within and without, rooms, patios, kitchens,
corridors, stables, huts, latrines,
and even the roofing,
                        all painted black,
with black curtains,
because the Adelantado had died in Muchitiltic
which means "All Black"
because from Muchitiltic to Iztlán
the earth as much as the stones, all is black.
And the Cathedral was also covered in black draperies
and the whole city in mourning
observing the Adelantado's obsequies.
And Doña Beatriz was shut away in a very dark room
with black walls, not wishing to see the light,
neither the light of a window, nor the light of a candle,
wearing a black dress, and on her head a black wimple,
and she did nothing but weep and weep, and groan, and talk to herself
and utter loud cries and shouts.
And she did not eat or drink or sleep
neither did she want anyone to console her,
and she said
        that now Godde could do her no greater harme
                then he had allready done her.
She said:

¿Por ventura tiene Dios mas mal que hazerme
despues de averme quitado al Adelantado, mi Señor?
Y decía que se llamaba Doña Beatriz la Sin Ventura.
Y se reunió el Cabildo para elegir Gobernador
y eligió a Doña Beatriz de la Cueva, Gobernadora.
Y fueron los Señores Alcaldes y Regidores
a su aposento, donde estaba encerrada,
y le dijeron que la elegían y nombraban
en nombre de Su Majestad, Gobernadora.
Y ella aceptó la Gobernación,
y juró sobre la cruz de la vara de la Gobernación
y firmó en el libro del Cabildo:

La sin ventura

Dª Beatriz

y después tachó su nombre con una raya de tinta,
con una raya gruesa de tinta, más larga que el nombre,
para que sólo se leyera:

La sin ventura
████████████

Y el cielo de Guatemala se nubló
y se fue llenando de nubarrones
    con relámpagos y rayos,
y el jueves 8 de septiembre comenzó a llover,
y llovió ese día,
        y el otro,
            y el otro,
mientras el Volcán de Fuego vomitaba llamas.
Y el domingo, dos horas después de medianoche
hubo una tormenta de rayos en el Volcán de Agua
y después fue el primer temblor, con retumbos
como si muchas carrozas corrieran bajo la tierra,
debajo de Guatemala, y después más temblores
y más retumbos, y el Volcán de Agua saltaba
como si quisiera arrancarse de la tierra, y ya el agua
venía bajando del volcán, despeñándose
y arrastrando árboles y piedras del tamaño de carabelas
y aquel río de tierra y agua y árboles y piedras
fue corriendo hacia la casa del Adelantado Pedro del Alvarado
llevándose las paredes y los tejados de las casas,
saliendo por las ventanas,
y echando de las ventanas a los hombres,
mientras el Volcán de Fuego retumbaba
      y arrojaba ríos de fuego
    Despedía como rayos y cometas ardientes.
Y el agua ya subía a la recámara de Doña Beatriz.
Ella salió de la recámara envuelta en una colcha,
y llamó a sus doncellas, y corrió con ellas al Oratorio.

Could Godde possibly have any greater harme to do me
having bereft me of my Lord, the Adelantado?
And she said her name was Hapless Doña Beatriz.
And the Council met to choose a Governor
and chose Doña Beatriz de la Cueva, as Governess.
And the Lord Mayors and Aldermen went
to her room, where she was shut away,
and they said to her that they were choosing and nominating her
in the name of His Majesty, Governess.
And she accepted the Governorship,
and swore on the cross on the Governor's staff
and placed her signature in the Council's book:

Hapless
Dᵃ Beaţriz

and afterwards she crossed out her name with a line of ink,
with a thick line of ink, longer than the name,
so you could read nothing but:

Hapless
███████████

And above Guatemala the sky clouded over
and began to fill with storm clouds
    with thunder and lightning,
and on Thursday the 8th of September it started to rain,
and it rained that day,
           and the next,
                and the next,
while Volcán de Fuego was spewing flames.
And on Sunday, two hours after midnight
there was a lightning storm on Volcán de Agua
and then came the first tremor, with rumbling
as though many carriages were running under the earth,
under Guatemala, and later more tremors
and more rumblings, and Volcán de Agua was leaping
as though it wished to wrench itself from the earth, and now the water
was coming down the volcano, headlong
and dragging with it trees and rocks the size of caravels
and that river of earth and water and trees and rocks
came rushing toward the house of Adelantado Pedro de Alvarado
sweeping away the walls and roofs of the houses,
coming out through the windows,
and throwing the people from their windows,
while Volcán de Fuego was rumbling
        and hurling out rivers of fire.
    It gave off what looked like bolts of lightning and burning comets.
And the water was now rising to Doña Beatriz's chamber.
She left her chamber wrapped in a bedcover,
and called her maidservants, and hurried with them to the Oratory.

Y el agua iba subiendo la escalera de piedra
          llegaba
al primer descanso,
     seguía subiendo de grada en grada,
llegaba al segundo descanso,
y llegaba al piso del Oratorio.
Doña Beatriz estaba sobre el altar con sus doncellas
abrazada a una imagen de Cristo crucificado
y abrazando a la hijita del Adelantado, y el agua negra
subió la primera grada del altar,
la segunda grada,
          cubrió el altar,
les llegaba a las rodillas,
comenzó a salir por las ventanas,
     tembló otra vez la tierra
y las paredes del Oratorio se desplomaron
sobre Doña Beatriz la Sin Ventura y sus doncellas.

Y el río de piedra y cieno corrió de calle en calle
y de barrio en barrio, derrumbando las casas,
arrastrando las casas con sus gentes,
llevando las casas a otros sitios de la ciudad.
La noche estaba oscurísima, no se veían los rostros,
y seguían los grandes truenos,
     seguían los relámpagos,
y se veían pasar por las calles
     a la luz de los relámpagos,
las piedras enormes flotando en la corriente como corchos
revueltas con muertos, muebles, caballos ahogados y portales.
El viento hacía crujir los árboles
y se oía el rugido de las fieras, el ruido del agua,
el estruendo de las piedras que bajaban rodando,
el mugido de las vacas, los gritos
de las mujeres y los niños, de calle en calle
y de barrio en barrio.
Y algunos vieron como demonios en el aire dando gritos
y una vaca negra con sólo un cuerno
en la puerta del palacio de la Sin Ventura.

Sólo su aposento quedó intacto en el palacio
pero Doña Beatriz había salido de su aposento
y cuando llegaron estaba la cama todavía caliente.

Murieron Alonso Velazco y su mujer y sus hijos
y no se halló nadie en la casa ni muerto ni vivo
y de la casa no quedaron ni los cimientos.
De la casa de Martín Sánchez

And the water was coming up the stone stairs
                    it reached
the first landing,
        it continued to rise step by step,
it reached the second landing,
and it reached the floor of the Oratory.
Doña Beatriz was on the altar with her maids
embracing an image of Christ crucified
and embracing the Adelantado's little daughter, and the black water
rose to the first altar step,
the second step,
                    it covered the altar,
and reached their knees,
it began to pour out the windows,
        the earth trembled again
and the Oratory walls fell in
upon Hapless Doña Beatriz and her maidservants.

And the river of rock and mud ran from street to street
and from district to district, knocking down houses,
sweeping houses away with their inhabitants,
carrying the houses to other parts of the city.
The night was exceedingly dark, you could not see faces,
and the great thunder continued,
        the flashes of lightning continued,
and you could see moving through the streets
        by the light of the lightning
the enormous rocks floating like corks in the current
mixed up with dead bodies, furniture, drowned horses and porticoes.
The wind made the trees creak
and you could hear the roar of wild animals, the rush of the water,
the crash of the rocks that tumbled down,
the lowing of cattle, the cries
of women and children, one street after another
and one district after another.
And some saw what looked like demons in the air screeching
and a black cow with a single horn
at the gates of Hapless's palace.

Only her room remained intact in the palace
but Doña Beatriz had left her room
and when they reached there the bed was still warm.

Alonso Velazco died with his wife and his children
and no one was found in the house neither dead nor alive
and of the house not even the foundations remained.
From Martín Sánchez's household

no se volvió a ver ninguno.
Murió Francisco Flores, el manco.
Murió Blas Fernández, el ciego.
Murió Robles, el sastre, y su mujer.
Murió la mujer de Francisco López,
y la de Alonso Martín y sus nietas,
murieron los hijos de Juan Páez.

Al amanecer el Volcán de Agua estaba descabezado.
La ciudad llena de lodo y piedras y árboles y muertos.
No se distinguían las plazas, las calles, los barrios,
ni los sitios de las casas.
                    Todavía llovía un poco.

Se hizo la procesión de los muertos cantando las letanías
y el obispo ordenó quitar el luto de las iglesias
y que se suspendieran las exequias del Adelantado.

no one was ever seen again.
One-handed Francisco Flores died.
Blas Fernández, the blind man, died.
Robles the tailor and his wife died.
The wife of Francisco López died,
as did Alonso Martín's, and his granddaughters,
the children of Juan Páez died.

When day broke Volcán de Agua was decapitated.
The city full of mud and rocks and trees and dead bodies.
You could not find the squares, the streets, the districts,
or where the houses had stood.
                              It was still raining a little.

The procession for the dead was made singing the litanies
and the bishop ordered the mourning to be removed from the churches
and the funeral rites of the Adelantado to be suspended.

Se levantó en las sierras un indio
        llamado Lempira ("Señor de las Sierras")
y reunió los indios de 200 pueblos,
y más de 2.000 señores y caballeros conocidos
y los juntó en Piraera ("Sierra de las Neblinas").
Les dijo: que era vergonzoso
que tantos hombres estuvieran en servidumbre
de tan pocos extranjeros, en su propia tierra.
Ofreció ser su capitán y ponerse en los mayores peligros.
Y les aseguró que si estaban unidos vencerían.
Y le siguieron. Y empezó la guerra.
Empezaron a pelear entre los precipicios y los cactus.

La palabra de Lempira corrió de peñol en peñol,
de valle en valle,
                y de sierra en sierra.
Se subió al peñol más alto con 30.000 mil hombres.
Un peñol derecho como una lanza,
sin camino ninguno.
                Los españoles lo cercaron
y duró el sitio 6 meses.
Unos le decían que hiciera las paces
porque al fin tendría que perder,
pero él rechazaba las ofertas de paz
y desde su peñol retaba a los españoles.

Los reunió en el año *Ix*. Y el año *Ix*
estaba anunciado de muchas miserias.
Un año "de gran falta de agua y de muchos soles
los cuales habrán de secar los maizales,
y tendrían muchas discordias y guerras entre sí
Y CON OTROS PUEBLOS,
y habrán mudanzas en el mundo de los Señores
y de los sacerdotes,
por razón de esas guerras
Y LOS QUE QUIERAN SER SEÑORES NO PREVALECERÁN".
Ese año *Ix* (1535–36)
¡el de las muchas miserias!
fue el de la llegada de Montejo a Honduras
¡y la llegada de Pedro de Alvarado!
        Y Lempira se levantó en ese año *Ix* . . .

Y se acercaba el final del "Katún 13 Ahau"

In the mountains there rose up an Indian
    called Lempira ("Lord of the Sierras")
and he gathered together the Indians from 200 towns,
and more than 2,000 known lords and knights
and he brought them together in Piraera ("Sierra of Mists").
He told them that it was shameful
that so many men should be in servitude
to so few foreigners, in their own land.
He offered to be their captain and to expose himself to the greatest of dangers.
And he assured them that if they were united they would win.
And they followed him. And the war began.
They began to fight among the precipices and the cacti.

Lempira's word ran from height to height,
from valley to valley,
                        and from sierra to sierra.
He ascended the highest crag with 30,000 men.
A crag sheer as a lance,
without any path.
                        The Spaniards surrounded him
and the siege lasted 6 months.
Some suggested he make peace
because in the end he was bound to lose,
but he refused the peace offers
and from his crag he defied the Spaniards.

He brought them together in the year *Ix*. And the year *Ix*
was predicted to be of much misery.
A year "of great dearth of water and many suns
which would dry out the cornfields,
and they would have much discord and wars between themselves
AND WITH OTHER PEOPLES
and there would be changes in the world of the Lords
and of the priests,
on account of those wars
AND THOSE WHO WISH TO BE LORDS WILL NOT PREVAIL."
That year *Ix* (1535–36)
the year of many miseries!
was the year of Montejo's arrival in Honduras
and the arrival of Pedro de Alvarado!
        And Lempira rose up in that year *Ix* . . .

And the end of "Katun 13 Ahau" was approaching

y el final de un "BAKTÚN".
Pero los Chilanes habían dicho que no había que temer.
Que habría un nuevo amanecer al morir el "BAKTÚN":
el 5º amanecer. Y decían los Chilanes:
"Ésta es la cara del Katún, del 13 Ahau:
Se quebrará el rostro del sol
Caerá rompiéndose sobre los dioses de ahora."

Y Nahau Pech el Gran Sacerdote había profetizado:
"En el tiempo en que el sol quedará detenido en lo alto
oh Nobles Itzalanos, cuando el regidor sienta piedad,
habrán pasado cuatro katunes
y entonces será conocida verdaderamente la voluntad de Dios.
Vosotros me preguntaréis qué es lo que yo aconsejo,
oh Nobles Itzalanos.
Salid a esperar a vuestro huésped en medio del camino,
oh gente de Itzá!
Son los Padres de la comarca los que llegan.
Por la boca del jefe Pech, el sacerdote, sale esta profecía,
para la época del cuarto katún, justo al fin del katún
oh Nobles Itzalanos."

Eran los días de plantar un nuevo árbol YAXCHE (la Ceiba)
que al final de cada época plantaban en las plazas
para la nueva época, y ya estaban plantando el YAXCHE:
eran las CRUCES que plantaban en las plazas (el YAXCHE
a cuya sombra descansarían los buenos cuando morían:
"debajo de cuyas ramas y sombra
descansarían y se holgarían todos siempre")
Era el final de la 4ª época, y empezaba el 5º baktún.

Pero Lempira no escuchó los anuncios del nuevo baktún.
Lempira defendía un baktún condenado a perecer.
Ni escuchó la profecía de Chilam Balam
el cantor de Cabal-chen (Maní) que decía:
"En el día 13 Ahau
será establecida la nueva edad del tiempo
asignado a Itzá y a los de Mayapán, oh Señores Itzalanos.
Es ella la insignia de Hunab-ku erguida;
el tronco del árbol enhiesto vendrá a anunciar a las gentes
que surge la nueva aurora para el mundo.
Ya se habrá producido largo período de discordia, de anarquía,
cuando vendrá llevado por manos sagradas este signo,
oh Nobles Itzalanos . . .
Se abrirá un amanecer en los cuatro puntos cardinales.
He aquí que llega nuestro Dios oh gente de Itzá,
recibid a nuestro "hermano mayor" oh gente de Tantún.

and the end of a "BAKTUN."
But the Chilams had said there was nothing to fear.
That there would be a new dawn when the "BAKTUN" died,
the 5th dawn. And the Chilams said:
"This is the face of the Katun, of the 13 Ahau:
The face of the sun will break
It will fall smashing itself over the present gods."

And Nahau Pech the High Priest had prophesied:
"In the days when the sun will halt on high
O Noble Itzalans, when the ruler feels compassion,
four katuns will have passed
and then the true will of God will be known.
You will ask me what I advise
O Noble Itzalans.
Go out to await your guest in the middle of the road,
O people of Itzá!
Those who are arriving are the Fathers of the Land.
From the mouth of Chief Pech, the priest, this prophecy comes,
in the time of the fourth katun, right at the end of the katun
O Noble Itzalans."

It was the time for planting a new YAXCHE tree (a ceiba)
which at the end of each epoch they planted in the squares
for the new epoch, and they were already planting the YAXCHE:
these were the CROSSES they planted in the squares (the YAXCHE
in the shade of which the good would rest when they died:
"beneath the branches and shade of which
all would rest and be at leisure forever")
It was the end of the 4th epoch, and the 5th baktun was beginning.

But Lempira did not heed the tidings of the new baktun.
Lempira defended a baktun condemned to die.
Nor did he heed the prophecy of Chilam Balam
the singer of Cabal-chen (Maní) who said:
"On the day 13 Ahau
will be established the new age of time
assigned to Itzá and to those of Mayapán, O Itzalan Lords.
It is the insignia of Hunab-ku raised up;
the upright tree trunk will come and announce to the peoples
that the new dawn is arising for the world.
Already there will have been a long period of discord, of anarchy,
when this sign will come borne by sacred hands,
O Noble Itzalans . . .
A dawn will break in the four cardinal points.
Behold our God is arriving O people of Itzá,
receive our "older brother" O people of Tantún.

Recibid a vuestros huéspedes, los hombres barbados, los del Este,
los portadores del signo divino, oh Nobles de Itzá.
Buena es la palabra de la divinidad que viene hacia vosotros
para que se cumpla la renovación de la vida.
Nada tenéis que temer, oh Nobles, del que está arriba de la tierra;
es el único Dios que os ha creado,
y esto por sí solo os prueba que su Palabra es propicia . . .
Grande es la anarquía que comienza.
Restaurado es el Árbol de la Vida del mundo.
Que se le dé conocimiento a todas las gentes
de la insignia de Hunab-ku erguida.
Adoradla, oh Itzalanos. Debéis adorar esta insignia enhiesta
y creer en la palabra del verdadero Dios
que viene del cielo a hablaros.
Multiplicad vuestra buena voluntad oh Itzalanos,
ahora que está el nuevo amanecer por iluminar el universo
y la vida está por entrar en una Edad nueva.
Tened fe en mi mensaje, yo soy Chilam Balam
y he interpretado la palabra del verdadero Dios."

Alonso de Cáceres le envió una embajada
"que aceptase la paz y obedeciese al Rey de Castilla
y le prometía tratarlo bien." Y mató los mensajeros.
Decía: que no quería conocer otro señor ni saber otra ley
ni tener otras costumbres de las que ya tenía.
Duró el sitio 6 meses. Los últimos 2 meses no dormían,
ni las noches ni los días, tirando flechas día y noche.
Hasta que un día el Cap. Cáceres le envió otra embajada:
un soldado a caballo que se puso a un tiro de arcabuz
diciéndole que *admitiese la paz que se le ofrecía*
mientras otro soldado en las ancas del caballo
le dispararía con el arcabuz. Y salió Lempira
al borde del peñón. Tenía grandes penachos
como el ave *q'uc*, que agitaba el viento de la sierra.
Estaba todo cubierto de una armadura de algodón.
A sus pies se extendían todas las sierras
y se abrían los precipicios erizados de cactus.
Y sus plumas de quetzal se movían en el viento.
Y dijo Lempira desde la alta peña: "La guerra
no habrá de cansar a los soldados ni espantarlos
y aquel que más pueda vencerá . . ." Y las rocas
repitieron el eco, los valles repitieron su voz:
                              ". . . venceráaaaaaa . . ."
El soldado de las ancas le apuntó, y disparó
mientras él hablaba. El tiro le dio en la frente
atravesando el bello morrión empenachado
y Lempira cayó rodando con sus armas sierra abajo

Receive your guests, the bearded men, the men from the East,
the bearers of the divine sign, O Nobles of Itzá.
Good is the word of the divinity which comes toward you
so that the renewal of life may be fulfilled.
You have nothing to fear, O Nobles, from him who is above the earth
he is the only God who created you,
and this alone proves to you that his Word is auspicious . . .
Great is the anarchy that is beginning.
Restored is the world's Tree of Life.
Let knowledge be given to all peoples
of the insignia of Hunab-ku raised up.
Adore it, O Itzalans. You should adore this insignia held on high
and believe in the word of the true God
who comes from the heavens to speak to us.
Multiply your good will O Itzalans,
now that the new Dawn is about to light up the universe
and life is about to enter a new Age.
Have faith in my message, I am Chilam Balam
and I have interpreted the word of the true God."

Alonso de Cáceres sent him an envoy
"that he should accept peace and obey the King of Castille
and he promised to treat him well." And he killed the messengers.
He said that he had no wish to know another master or to know another law
or to have customs other than the ones he already had.
The siege lasted 6 months. The final 2 months they did not sleep,
neither by night nor by day, firing arrows day and night.
Until one day Capt. Cáceres sent him another envoy:
a soldier on horseback who came within crossbow range
telling him *to accept the peace being offered to him*
while another soldier on the horse's haunches
would fire at him with the crossbow. And Lempira came out
to the edge of the crag. He wore huge plumes
like the *q'uc* bird, which the sierra breeze ruffled.
He was entirely covered in cotton armor.
At his feet all the sierras stretched out
and the precipices opened up bristling with cacti.
And his quetzal feathers fluttered in the wind.
And Lempira said from the high crag: "War
does not tire soldiers nor frighten them
and the most able will triumph . . ." And the rocks
repeated the echo, the valleys repeated his voice:
                                        ". . . will triiiiiiiumph . . ."
The soldier on the haunches aimed at him, and fired
as he was speaking. The shot caught him in the forehead
passing through the beautiful plumed helmet
and Lempira fell rolling down the sierra with his weapons

mientras aún seguían hablando los valles.
  Y el día antes Lempira había andado muy triste . . .

Era el año *bisexitl* cuando murió Lempira (1536–37)
Un mal año, de días aciagos. Su letra era *"Cuauc"*
y reinaba en él *"Hozanek"*, el "Bocab" negro del oeste,
el ser subterráneo y malo. Un año pésimo de gran mortandad,
y los muchos soles les habrían de matar los maizales
y las muchas hormigas y pájaros comerse lo que sembrasen.
Este año llevaban al Occidente un tronco de madera negra de *Yaxex*
con la imagen del "Bocab" negro
y con una calavera en él y un hombre muerto,
y encima del árbol ponían al negro zopilote,
llamado "Kub", en señal de mortandad grande,
y encendían un gran fuego por las noches
y caminaban descalzos sobre las brasas calientes
para remediar los malos agüeros de este año . . .

El día antes Lempira había andado muy triste.
  Pero los demás se rindieron alegres
  con caracoles y atambores y atabales.

while the valleys were still speaking.
      And the day before, Lempira had gone around very sad . . .

It was the *bisexitl* year when Lempira died (1536–37).
A bad year, of fateful days. Its letter was *"Cuauc"*
and *"Hozanek"* reigned over it, the black "Bocab" of the West,
the subterranean and evil being. A terrible year of great mortality,
and the many suns were going to kill the cornfields
and the many ants and birds would eat whatever they sowed.
This year they were bringing to the West a trunk of black *Yaxex* wood
with the image of the black "Bocab"
and with a skull on it and a dead man,
and on top of the tree they placed the black buzzard,
called "Kub," as a sign of great mortality,
and they lit a huge fire by night
and walked barefoot over hot embers
in order to remedy the bad auguries of this year . . .

The day before, Lempira had gone around very sad.
      But the rest were happy to surrender
        with cries of delight and drums and timbrels.

Salió el Rey y se sentó en su sillón real,
y se sentaron los flamencos en bancas, más abajo.
Mosiur de Xevres a la derecha del Rey
y el Gran Canciller a la izquierda.
Y junto a mosiur de Xevres el Almirante de las Indias,
y después el obispo del Darién.
Junto al Gran Canciller el obispo de Badajoz;
y Bartolomé de las Casas arrimado a la pared.
Y se levantaron mosiur de Xevres y el Gran Canciller
subieron la grada de la peana lentamente,
se arrodillaron junto al Rey
y hablaron con él unas palabras en voz baja.
Se levantaron, hicieron una reverencia,
y volvieron a sus puestos. Después de un silencio
habló el Gran Canciller: "Reverendo obispo,
su Majestad manda que habléis."
Se levantó el obispo del Darién
y pidió hablar a solas con el Rey y su Consejo.
El Gran Canciller le hizo una seña y se sentó.
Hubo otro silencio.
Se levantaron mosiur de Xevres y el Gran Canciller,
hicieron una reverencia al Rey y se arrodillaron
y hablaron con él unas palabras en voz baja.
Volvieron a sentarse. Después de otro silencio
dijo el Gran Canciller: "Reverendo obispo,
Su Majestad manda que habléis si tenéis que hablar."
Se levantó el obispo del Darién y dijo:
"Muy poderoso Señor:
El Rey Católico vuestro abuelo, que haya santa gloria,
despachó una armada a la tierra firme de las Indias
y fui nombrado obispo de esa primera población
y como fuimos mucha gente y no llevábamos qué comer,
la más de la gente murió de hambre, y los que quedamos,
por no morir como aquéllos, ninguna otra cosa hemos hecho
sino robar y matar y comer. El primer gobernador fue malo
y el segundo muy peor . . . Todo eso es verdad. Pero
en lo que a los indios toca, son siervos *a natura*.
Son los siervos *a natura* de que habla Aristóteles . . ."

Cesó de hablar el obispo y hubo otro silencio.
Se levantaron mosiur de Xevres y el Gran Canciller,
se arrodillaron junto al Rey y hablaron en voz baja,
se volvieron a sus puestos y hubo otro silencio.

XVIII / 110

The King came out and sat on his throne,
and the Flemish sat on benches, lower down.
Monsieur de Xevres on the King's right
and the Grand Chancellor on the left.
And beside Monsieur de Xevres the Admiral of the Indies
and next the bishop of Darién.
Beside the Grand Chancellor the bishop of Badajoz;
and Bartolomé de las Casas against the wall.
And Monsieur de Xevres and the Grand Chancellor rose
and slowly mounted the step of the dais,
they knelt down before the King
and spoke a few words with him in hushed voices.
They rose, bowed,
and returned to their places. After a silence
the Grand Chancellor spoke: "Reverend bishop,
his Majesty commands you to speak."
The bishop of Darién rose
and asked to speak alone with the King and his Council.
The Grand Chancellor signaled to him and he sat down.
There was another silence.
Monsieur de Xevres and the Grand Chancellor rose,
bowed to the King and knelt down
and spoke a few words with him in hushed voices.
They sat down again. After another silence
the Grand Chancellor said: "Reverend bishop,
His Majesty commands you to speak if you have something to say."
The bishop of Darién rose and said:
"Most powerful Lord:
The Catholic King your grandfather, now in God's Glory,
dispatched an armada to Terra firma of the Indies
and I was appointed bishop of that first settlement,
and since we were many and we took nothing to eat,
most of the people died of hunger, and those of us who remained,
so as not to die like them, have done nothing other than
steal and kill and eat. The first Governor was bad
and the second very much worse . . . All that is true. But
as concerns the Indians, they are slaves *a natura*.
They are the slaves *a natura* of whom Aristotle speaks . . ."

The bishop ceased talking and there was another silence.
Monsieur de Xevres and the Grand Chancellor rose,
knelt before the King and spoke in hushed voices,
they returned to their places and there was another silence.

Después dijo el Gran Canciller: "Míser Bartolomé,
Su Majestad manda que habléis."
Se levantó Bartolomé de las Casas, se quitó el bonete,
hizo una reverencia y dijo:
"Muy alto y poderoso señor:
Yo soy de los más antiguos que han pasado a las Indias
y ha muchos años que estoy allá, en los que han visto mis ojos,
no leído en historias que pudieran ser mentirosas, sino
palpado, por así decirlo, con mis manos, tantas crueldades
cometidas en aquellos mansos y pacíficos corderos;
y uno de los que a estas tiranías ayudaron fue mi padre.
No son siervos *a natura*, son libres *a natura*!
Son libres, y tienen sus reyes y señores naturales
y los hallamos pacíficos, con sus repúblicas bien ordenadas,
proporcionados y delicados y de rostros de buen parecer
que pareciera que todos ellos fueran hijos de señores.
Fueron creados simples por Dios, sin maldades ni dobleces
obedientes, humildes, pacientes, pacíficos y quietos.
Así mismo son las gentes más delicadas y flacas
tiernos en complexión y menos hechos al trabajo
y que más fácilmente mueren de cualquier enfermedad
que ni hijos de príncipes son más delicados que ellos
aunque ellos sean hijos de labradores. Son paupérrimos
y no poseen ni quieren poseer bienes temporales
y por eso no tienen soberbias ni ambiciones ni codicias.
Su comida es pobre como la de los Padres del Desierto.
Su vestido, andar desnudos, cubiertas sus vergüenzas
o cuando mucho cubiertos con una manta de algodón.
Sus camas son esteras, o redes que llaman hamacas.
Son limpios y vivos de entendimiento y dóciles.
Y los españoles llegaron como lobos y tigres,
como lobos y tigres donde estas ovejas mansas.
La isla de Cuba quedó yerma, hecha una soledad,
y antes estaba llena de mansísimos corderos.
En la Española no quedan más que doscientas personas.
Las Islas de San Juan y Jamaica están asoladas.
Islas que eran más graciosas y fértiles
que la huerta del Rey en Sevilla
ahora sólo tienen 11 personas que yo vide.
Islas tan felices y ricas! Y sus gentes
tan humildes, tan pacíficas y tan fáciles de sujetar,
no como bestias, pero pluguiera a Dios que como bestias
los hubieran tratado y no como estiércol de las plazas
y aun menos que eso. Quemaban vivos a los señores,
a fuego manso, y yo los vi morir dando alaridos,
dando gritos extraños. Y si huían
a encerrarse en los montes, en las sierras,

Then the Grand Chancellor said: "Míser Bartolomé,
His Majesty commands you to speak."
Bartolomé de las Casas rose, removed his biretta,
bowed, and said:
"Most high and powerful lord:
I am of the oldest who went across to the Indies
and many years have I spent there, during which my eyes have seen,
not read in histories which could be deceitful, but
felt, so to speak, with my hands, so many cruelties
committed upon those meek and peace-loving lambs;
and one of those who abetted these tyrannies was my father.
Slaves they are not, they are free *a natura!*
They are free, and have their natural kings and lords
and we found them very peace-loving, with their republics well-ordered,
well-proportioned and delicate and with comely faces
such it would seem they were all the children of lords.
They were created simple by God, without wickedness or duplicity
obedient, humble, patient, peace-loving and tranquil.
Similarly they are the most delicate and frail people
gentle in complexion and least adapted to work
and who most easily die from whatever illness
that not even the children of princes are more delicate than they
although they are the children of laborers. They are most poor
and possess nothing neither do they wish to possess earthly goods
and neither are they proud, ambitious or covetous.
Their diet is frugal like that of the Desert Fathers.
Their apparel, to go naked, their private parts
at best covered with a cotton apron.
Their beds are straw mats, or nets which they call hammocks.
They are clean and quick to understand and docile.
And the Spanish arrived like wolves and tigers,
like wolves and tigers to the place of these gentle sheep.
The island of Cuba was left barren, turned wilderness,
and before it was full of most gentle lambs.
In Hispaniola no more than two hundred people remain.
The islands of San Juan and Jamaica are laid waste.
Islands which were charming and fruitful
as the King's gardens in Seville
now have only 11 people that I saw.
Such rich and fertile islands! And their people
so humble, so peace-loving and so easy to subject,
not like wild beasts, but would to God that like wild beasts
they had been treated and not like dung on the streets
and even less than that. They burned the lords alive,
on slow fires, and I saw them die screaming,
uttering strange cries. And if they fled
to hide in the hills, in the mountains,

los perseguían con lebreles, perros bravísimos.
Ellos pelean desnudos, sus armas son harto flacas,
y sus guerras como juegos de cañas, y aun de niños.
Enviaron a los hombres a las minas
y a las mujeres a trabajar en las estancias,
y murieron ellos en las minas y ellas en las estancias.
Sus hacendejas quedaban destruidas, llenas de hierba.
Y las criaturas nacidas chiquitas perecían
porque las madres no tenían leche en las tetas,
y se ahorcaban desesperados con los hijos
y las mujeres tomaban hierba para no parir los hijos.
Y robaban las huertas de los indios,
manteniéndose de sus comidas pobres.
Se los llevaban en los navíos a vender.
Llegaban donde estaban trabajando en sus oficios
con sus mujeres y sus hijos, y los hacían pedazos.
Ellos estaban inermes y desnudos
contra gente a caballo y tan armada.
Los herraban en la cara con el hierro del Rey.
Y es para quebrar el corazón del que los haya visto
desnudos y hambrientos cuando los llevan a vender,
o cuando van a llevar la carga de los españoles,
desnudos y temblando, con su redecilla al hombro.
Toman aquellos corderos de sus casas
y les ponen el hierro del Rey.
Todas estas escenas vieron mis ojos y ahora temo decirlas
no creyendo a mis ojos, como si las haya soñado.
Su Majestad: no están hechos al trabajo
porque son de naturaleza delicadísimos.
Y no hay gentes más mansas ni de menos resistencia
ni más hábiles ni aparejados para el yugo de Cristo."
. . . .
Se levantaron mosiur de Xevres y el Gran Canciller.
Se arrodillaron junto al rey y hablaron en voz baja.
Hubo un gran silencio.
Después se levantó el Rey y entró en su cámara.

they pursued them with greyhounds, the fiercest of dogs.
They fought naked, their weapons are most feeble indeed,
and their wars like jousts with canes, and even childlike.
They sent the men to the mines
and the women to work on the farms,
and died they did, men in the mines and women on the farms.
Their plots of land were destroyed, overrun with weeds.
And the babes born tiny perished
because the mothers had no milk in their breasts,
and they hanged themselves along with their children
and the women ate herbs so as not to give birth.
And they stole the Indians' plots,
surviving on their meagre food.
They carried them off to ships to be sold.
They arrived where they were busy at their tasks
with their women and their children, and tore them to pieces.
They were defenseless and naked
against people on horses and so well-armed.
They branded them with the King's iron.
And it is enough to break the heart of anyone seeing them
naked and hungry as they are taken off to be sold,
or when they go to carry the Spaniards' cargo,
naked and trembling, with their small net over their shoulder.
They take those lambs from their houses
and put the King's iron on them.
All these scenes my own eyes saw and now I fear to tell them
scarce believing my eyes, as though I have dreamed them.
Your Majesty: they are not suited to work
because they are most frail by nature.
And there are no people meeker nor less resistant
nor more apt nor inclined to the yoke of Christ."
. . . .
Monsieur de Xevres and the Grand Chancellor rose.
They knelt before the King and spoke in hushed voices.
There was a long silence.
Then the King rose and entered his chamber.

En Santiago de Guatemala y en San Salvador
se reían los conquistadores
        del libro *De unico vocationis modo*
de Fr. Bartolomé de las Casas
y decían que si "con palabras y con persuaciones"
reducía a los indios al gremio de la iglesia
y ponía en práctica lo que escribía en retórica
ellos dejarían las armas . . .
        Se darían por soldados y capitanes injustos.
Y le decían:
Que por qué no iba donde los indios bravos
con sólo "palabras y santas exhortaciones".
No había otra provincia que conquistar
        que la de Tuzulutlán,
llena de ríos, y lagunas, y pantanos
y bosques tristes donde se levantan tantos vapores
        que siempre está lloviendo,
y los indios eran los más feroces y bárbaros
imposibles de domar
y llamaban a esta Provincia Tuzulutlán,
                        "Tierra de Guerra".
A esta Provincia se ofreció ir Fr. Bartolomé de las Casas.
A sujetar los indios sin armas ni soldados
sino solamente con la palabra de Dios.
        . . . Lo que había escrito en "retórica". En literatura.
Y no pidió Fr. Bartolomé de las Casas ningún sueldo,
gastos de viaje, X cantidad de pan,
vino, barriles de conservas, etc., a la semana, o al mes, o al año
ni el Obispado de la tierra.
Única condición:
        Que los indios no se ENCOMENDARÍAN a nadie.
        Que serían vasallos libres de Su Majestad.
Y los frailes hicieron trovas, o versos, en quiché.
Versos con sus consonancias e intercadencias
contando la creación del mundo, la caída del hombre,
el destierro del paraíso, el diluvio, la muerte
del hijo de Dios y su resurrección. Enseñaron los versos
a cuatro indios mercaderes de Guatemala
que iban a comprar y vender al Quiché.
Les pusieron música
al son de los instrumentos de los indios
"acompañándolos con un tono vivo y atiplado
porque los instrumentos de los indios eran bajos y roncos".

In Santiago de Guatemala and in San Salvador
the conquistadors laughed
        at the book *De unico vocationis modo*
by Fr. Bartolomé de las Casas
and said that if "with words and persuasions"
he brought the Indians into the society of the church
and put into practice what he wrote in rhetoric
they would lay down their arms . . .
        They would adjudge themselves unworthy soldiers and captains.
And they asked him:
So why did he not go to the fierce Indians
with merely "words and holy exhortations"?
There was no other province to conquer
        except the province of Tuzulutlán,
full of rivers, and lakes, and swamps
and sad forests where so many vapors rise up
        that it is always raining,
and the Indians were the most ferocious and barbaric
impossible to tame
and they called this Province Tuzulutlán,
                    "Land of War."
Fr. Bartolomé de las Casas offered to go to this Province.
To subjugate the Indians without weapons or soldiers
but simply with the word of God.
        . . . What he had written in "rhetoric." In literature.
And Fr. Bartolomé de las Casas asked for no salary,
traveling expenses, X quantity of bread,
wine, barrels of preserves, etc., per week, or per month, or per year
nor the Bishopric of the land.
Sole condition:
        That the Indians should not be tied to anyone's ENCOMIENDA.
        That they should be free vassals of His Majesty.
And the friars composed couplets, or ballads, in Quiché.
Ballads using their rhymes and intercadences
recounting the creation of the world, the fall of man,
the banishment from paradise, the flood, the death
of the son of God and his resurrection. They showed the verses
to four Indian merchants in Guatemala
who went to buy and sell in the Quiché.
They set them to music
to the sound of the Indians' instruments
"accompanying them with a lively and high-pitched tone
because the instruments of the Indians were low and hoarse."

Y Fr. Bartolomé les dio tijeras, cuchillos, espejuelos
y otras cosas de Castilla.
Llegaron los mercaderes a la casa del Cacique.
Pusieron la tienda, y llegó la gente a ver y comprar
las cosas nuevas. Pidieron un *teplanastle*
y sacaron las sonajas y cascabeles de Guatemala
y al son de los instrumentos comenzaron a cantar los versos.
Y nunca habían oído esos instrumentos juntos.
Y oyeron cantar cosas que nunca habían oído.
El Cacique se quedó callado,
aguardando que otra vez cantasen. Al otro día
volvieron a cantar, y llegó la gente a oir los versos.
Ocho días duraron los cantares.
Y el Cacique los hacía repetir
en público y en secreto.
Y les pidió que le explicaran más lo que cantaban.
Ellos dijeron que no sabían más. Que no era su oficio
Pero que los padres se lo podrían explicar.
Y él preguntó: ¿Que quién eran los padres?
Pues el Cacique nunca había oído hablar de los Padres.
Los Mercaderes se los pintaron vestidos de blanco y negro,
cortados los cabellos en forma de guirnalda
y que no comían carne ni querían oro ni mantas ni plumas
ni cacao.
Que no eran casados
ni tenían pecado porque no trataban con mujeres.
Que cantaban día y noche las alabanzas de Dios.
Tenían muy lindas imágenes y ante ellas se ponían de rodillas.
Y que si los enviase a llamar vendrían de buena gana
a explicarle lo que habían cantado en esas coplas.
Y el Cacique envió a un hermano suyo con los Mercaderes
a Santiago, y le encargó que observara bien a los Padres
en la ciudad de Santiago, y ver si tenían oro.
Recibieron al hermano del Cacique los Padres en Santiago
y él observaba en silencio lo que los padres hacían
(sin que ellos notaran que fueron mirados).
Regresó a su tierra con el Padre que pidieron.
El Cacique le hizo grandes fiestas,
        enramadas, arcos triunfales,
no le miraba a la cara en señal de respeto,
le barrían el suelo porque iba descalzo.
Y el Cacique derribó sus ídolos y los quemó.
Ya no sacrificaban papagayos.
                        Y todas las tardes
cantaban las coplas.
                  Habían cesado las aguas,
Y Fr. Bartolomé de las Casas fue también a Tuzulutlán

And Fr. Bartolomé gave them scissors, knives, lenses
and other things from Castille.
The merchants arrived at the Cacique's house.
They set up their stall, and the people came to see and buy
the new things. They asked for a *teplanastle*
and they brought out the timbrels and small bells of Guatemala
and to the sound of the instruments began to sing the verses.
And they had never heard those instruments together.
And they heard things they had never heard.
The Cacique remained silent,
waiting for them to sing again. The following day
they sang again, and the people came to hear the verses.
Eight days the singing lasted.
And the Cacique made them repeat them
in public and in secret.
And he asked them to explain further what they were singing.
They said that they knew no more. That it wasn't their job.
But that the Fathers could explain it to him.
And he asked: So who are the fathers?
For the Cacique had never heard speak of the Fathers.
The Merchants described them to him as dressed in black and white,
their hair cut in the shape of a garland
and that they ate no meat and wanted neither gold nor cloaks nor feathers
nor cocoa.
That they were not married
nor had any sin because they had no dealings with women.
That day and night they sang the praises of God.
They had very beautiful images and before them they knelt.
And that if he sent for them they would willingly come
to explain to him what they had sung in those stanzas.
And the Cacique sent a brother of his with the Merchants
to Santiago, and charged him to observe the Fathers closely
in the city of Santiago, and to see if they had gold.
The Fathers received the Cacique's brother in Santiago
and he observed in silence what the Fathers did
(without them noticing they were being studied).
He returned to his land with the Father they requested.
The Cacique laid on great festivities for him,
      decorations with branches, triumphal arches,
they didn't look at his face as a sign of respect,
they swept the ground before him because he went barefoot.
And the Cacique overturned his idols and burned them.
They no longer sacrificed parrots.
                       And every evening
they sang the verses.
             The rains had ceased,
and Fr. Bartolomé de las Casas went also to Tuzulutlán

la "Tierra de Guerra".
                     Les predicaban en el campo.
Llamaron a todos a vivir juntos en un pueblo
(porque estaban esparcidos en los montes).
Y Fr. Bartolomé llegó a Santiago de Guatemala
con el Cacique Don Juan.
                  Había llegado el Adelantado
a ver al Cacique Don Juan: se había quitado su sombrero
de tafetán rojo y se lo había puesto al Cacique.
Lo llevaron a ver las calles y las tiendas de Santiago
dando orden a las tiendas que le dieran lo que pidiera
y sacaron todas las mercaderías y las cosas más curiosas
y todo lo miraba con naturalidad, sin ninguna admiración
"como si hubiera nacido en Milán . . ."
     El Adelantado y el Obispo
le habían ofrecido cosas de valor,
       y nada quiso recibir
sino tan sólo una pintura de Nuestra Señora.

Fray Bartolomé llamó a la "Tierra de Guerra" la Vera Paz.

the "Land of War."
                            They preached to them in the countryside.
They called on them all to live together in a town
(because they were scattered in the hills).
And Fr. Bartolomé came to Santiago de Guatemala
with Cacique Don Juan.
                             The Adelantado had arrived
to see Cacique Don Juan: he had removed his hat
of red taffeta and had placed it on the Cacique.
They took him to see the streets and the shops of Santiago
giving orders to the shops to give him whatever he asked for
and they brought out all the merchandise and the most curious things
and he calmly looked at it all, without any amazement
"as if he had been born in Milan . . ."
           The Adelantado and the Bishop
had offered him things of value,
        and he would accept nothing
except a painting of Our Lady.

Fray Bartolomé called the "Land of War" Vera Paz.

Gonzalo Fernández de Oviedo viene a Castilla
y cuenta de los mameyes, que saben a melocotones
y a duraznos, o mejor que duraznos, y huelen muy bien
y son de más suave gusto que el melocotón; del guanábano
que es un árbol muy grande y hermoso
y la fruta es de una pasta como manjar blanco,
espesa y aguanosa y de lindo sabor templado;
y del guayabo, que cuando está en flor huele tan bien
(en especial ciertas flores de guayabo),
huele como el jazmín y el azahar,
y por dentro unas frutas son rosadas y otras blancas
y donde mejor se dan es en Darién
y es muy buena fruta y es mejor que manzanas;
y los aguacates, que llaman perales, pero no son perales
como los de España, sino que hacen ventaja a las peras.
El coco es una fruta como una cabeza de hombre
con una carnosidad blanca como de almendra mondada
y de mejor sabor que las almendras, y de ella hacen leche
mejor que de ganados, y en medio hay una agua clarísima,
la más sustancial, la más excelente, la más preciosa cosa
que se pueda pensar ni beber,
lo mejor que en la tierra
se puede gustar.
Y quitado el manjar hacen vasos de esta fruta.
Y una fruta que llaman piñas, que nace de un cardo,
y es de color de oro, y una de las mejores del mundo,
y de más lindo y suave sabor y vista,
y su olor es a durazno y membrillo
y con una o dos de ellas huele toda la casa
y su sabor es a melocotón y moscatel
y no hay tan linda fruta en la huerta de Fernando I
en Nápoles,
ni en el Parque del Duque de Ferrara en el Po
ni en la huerta portátil de Ludovico Sforza.
Y hay un árbol o planta, monstruo entre los árboles,
que no se puede determinar si es árbol o planta
y ningún otro árbol o planta hay de más salvajez ni tan feo;
y es de tal manera que es difícil describir su forma,
más para verlo pintado por mano del Berruguete,
o de aquel Leonardo de Vinçi, o Andrea Mantegna,
que para darlo a entender con palabras:
sus ramas son pencas espinosas, disformes y feas,
que primero fueron hojas o pencas como las otras,

Gonzalo Fernández de Oviedo returns to Castille
and tells of mameys, which taste of melocoton
and of peach, or tastier than peaches, and smell very nice
and have a subtler flavor than peaches; of the soursop
which is a very large and beautiful tree
and the fruit is pulp-like like white flesh,
firm and juicy and with a lovely strong taste;
and of the guava, which when in flower smells so fine
(certain guava blossoms especially),
smells like the bloom of orange and jasmine,
and some fruits are pink inside and others white
and where it grows best is in Darién
and it is a very good fruit and better than apples;
and the avocados, which they call pears, but they are not pears
like those in Spain, but they are superior to pears.
The coconut is a fruit the size of a man's head
with white flesh like a peeled almond
and better tasting than almonds, and from it they make better
milk than cows' milk, and inside it there is a very clear water,
the most substantial, the most excellent, the most wonderful thing
you could imagine or drink,
the finest thing you can taste
on earth.
And when the meat is removed they make vessels from this fruit.
And a fruit they call pineapple, which grows on a thistle,
and is the color of gold, and one of the best in the world,
and with the most wonderful soft taste and appearance,
and its smell is of peach and quince
and with one or two of them the whole house smells
and it tastes of peach and muscatel
and there is no prettier fruit in the orchard of Fernando I
in Naples,
nor in the Duke of Ferrara's Park in Po,
nor in the portable garden of Ludovico Sforza.
And there is a tree or plant, a monster among trees,
which you cannot tell whether tree or plant
and no other tree or plant exists that is wilder or uglier;
and it is such that it is difficult to describe its shape,
better to see it painted by the hand of Berruguete,
or that Leonardo da Vinci, or Andrea Mantegna,
than to try to explain it with words:
its branches are thorny fleshy stems, misshapen and ugly,
which were first leaves or stems like the others,

y de aquellas hojas o pencas nacieron otras,
y de las otras, otras, y éstas alargándose
procrean otras, y éstas otras, otras,
y así de penca en penca se hace rama.
Y tiene una fruta carmesí, como un muy fino carmesí,
cubierta toda ella de espinas como un vello,
y con ella se pintan los labios las mujeres,
con color carmesí y con color rosado, mejor
que como se pintan las mujeres en Valencia o Italia.
Y un árbol de calabazas que en Nicaragua llaman guacal
de las que hacen vasos para beber, como tazas,
tan gentiles y tan bien labradas y de tan lindo lustre
que puede beber en ellas cualquier príncipe
y les ponen sus asideros de oro, y son muy limpias
y sabe muy bien en ellas el agua.
Hobo es un árbol de una sombra sanísima
y los que andan de camino los buscan para dormir.

Y cuenta del beori:
Estos animales beoris
son del tamaño de una mula mediana,
su pelo es más espeso que el del búfalo y no tiene cuernos,
aunque algunos los llaman vacas. El gato cerval
es como los gatos pequeños y mansos que hay en las casas
pero es más grande que el tigre y más feroz.
Las raposas son negras, más negras que un terciopelo muy negro.
El oso hormiguero es casi a manera de oso en el pelo
y no tiene cola, y el hocico lo tiene muy largo,
y la lengua larguísima, y con ella lame los hormigueros.
Los armadillos son de cuatro pies,
ni más ni menos que un caballo encubertado
con sus costaneras y coplón, como un caballo de armas,
y es del tamaño de un perrillo y no hacen mal y es cobarde.
El perico ligero es el animal más torpe del mundo,
para andar cincuenta pasos necesita un día entero.
Tienen cuatro pies y uñas largas como de ave,
y una cara casi redonda, como de lechuza
y ojos pequeños y redondos y la nariz como de un monico,
la boca chiquita, y mueve la cabeza como atontado;
su voz sólo suena de noche y es un continuado canto,
de rato en rato, cantando seis puntos, como quien canta
la, sol, fa, mi, re, ut.
así este animal dice
ah, ah, ah, ah, ah.
y después que ha cantado
vuelve a cantar lo mismo
ah, ah, ah, ah, ah.

and from those leaves or stems others sprouted
and from the others, others, and as they grow,
they procreate others, and these others, others,
and so from stem to stem a branch is made.
And it has a crimson fruit, like a very fine crimson,
entirely covered in thorns like body hair,
and with it the women paint their lips,
with crimson color and pink color, better
than the women in Valencia or Italy paint themselves.
And a pumpkin tree which in Nicaragua they call *guacal*
from which they make vessels to drink from, like cups,
so light and so well worked and of such a pretty luster
that any prince could drink from them
and they put gold handles on them, and they are very clean
and the water in them tastes very good.
Hobo is a tree which casts a very wholesome shade
and wayfarers look out for it so as to sleep there.

And he tells of the *beori*:
These *beori* animals
are the size of a medium mule,
their hair is thicker than the wild ox's and they have no horns,
although some call them cows. The ocelot
is like the small tame cats that are kept in houses
but it is larger than the tiger and more ferocious.
The foxes are black, blacker than a very black velvet.
The anteater is much like the bear in its hair
and it has no tail, and it has a very long snout,
and an exceedingly long tongue, with which it licks the anthills.
Armadillos have four feet,
caparisoned more or less like a horse
with its ribs and carapace, like a war horse,
and it is the size of a small dog and is harmless and is a coward.
The sloth is the slowest animal in the world,
to walk fifty paces it takes a whole day.
They have four feet and long nails like a bird,
and an almost round face, like an owl,
and small round eyes and a nose like a small monkey,
a tiny mouth, and it moves its head as though dull-witted;
its voice is heard at night and it is a sustained song,
from time to time, singing six tones, as one sings
la, sol, fa, mi, re, ut.
so this animal says
ah, ah, ah, ah.
and after it has sung
it sings the same thing again
ah, ah, ah, ah.

y esto hace de noche y no se oye cantar de día
y es animal nocturno y amigo de las tinieblas.
No muerde ni es ponzoñoso y no hay animal tan feo
ni que parezca más inútil que éste.
Hay zorrillos chiquitos como gozques,
muy burlones y traviesos, casi como monicos.
Hay unos perrillos pequeños, gozques,
que tienen en casa, y son mudos,
porque jamás ladran ni gañen
ni aullan ni gritan ni gimen
aunque los maten a golpes
y si los matan mueren sin quejarse ni gemir.

El pica-flor
tiene el pico largo y delgado como un alfiler
y es pajarito tan chiquito como la cabeza del pulgar.
Se mantiene del rocío y la miel y el licor de las flores,
sin sentarse sobre la rosa;
avecica de tanta velocidad
que al volar no se le ven las alas.
Se duerme o se adormece en octubre
y despierta o revive en abril
cuando hay muchas flores.
Su nido es de flecos de algodón
y en una balanza de pesar oro
pesan dos tomines él y su nido.
Sutil como las avecicas
que en las márgenes de las horas de rezar
ponen los iluminadores.
Es de muy lindos colores su pluma,
dorada y verde y de otros colores y la usan para labrar oro.
Al atardecer salen los cocuyos, como linternas;
sus ojos resplandecen como lumbres,
a su luz hilan y cosen y tejen y bailan los indios
y con uno de ellos se puede leer una carta.
Y hay ciertos leños podridos que están ligerísimos y blancos
y de noche relumbran como brasas.

Hay unos zopilotes, que son unas gallinas negras,
y comen muchas suciedades, indios y animales muertos,
pero huelen como a almizcle
y son muy importunas y amigas de estar en el pueblo
para comerse los muertos.
Los picudos tienen un pico muy grande
y un plumaje muy lindo y de muchos colores
y el pico es tan grande como un jeme o más,
vuelto para abajo, y la lengua es una pluma,

and this it does at night and is never heard to sing by day
and it is a nocturnal animal and fond of the dark.
It does not bite neither is it poisonous and there is no animal as ugly
or that seems more useless than this one.
There are tiny little raccoons like yappers,
very playful and mischievous, almost like young monkeys.
There are some little dogs, yappers,
which they keep in the houses, and they make no sound,
because they never bark or yelp
or howl or cry out or moan
even being beaten to death
and if they kill them they die without complaining or whining.

The humming-bird
has a long thin beak like a needle
and it is a tiny bird the size of the top of a thumb.
It lives off the dew and honey and the nectar of flowers,
without settling on the rose;
it beats its wings so fast
that when it flies you cannot see its wings.
It goes to sleep or dozes in October
and wakes or comes back to life in April,
when there are many flowers.
Its nest is of tufts of cotton
and in a balance for weighing gold
together with its nest it weighs two *tomins*.
Slight as the tiny birds
which the illuminators place
in the margins of books of hours.
Its plumage is of very pretty colors,
golden and green and other colors and they use it to work gold.
At dusk the fire-beetles come out like lanterns;
their eyes shine like fires,
by their light the Indians spin and sew and weave and dance
and with one of them you can read a letter.
And there are certain rotten logs that are very light and white
and at night they shine like red coals.

There are some buzzards, which are black hens,
and they eat many filthy things, dead Indians and animals,
but they smell of musk
and they are very bothersome and fond of being in the town
to eat the dead.
Toucans have a very large beak
and a very beautiful multicolored plumage
and the hooked beak is as long as five or six inches,
or more, and the tongue is a feather,

y da grandes silbos y hace agujeros con el pico.
Y-uana es una manera de sierpe con cuatro pies
muy espantosa de ver y muy buena de comer;
son muy feas y espantables pero no hacen mal
y no está averiguado si son animal o pescado
porque andan en el agua y los árboles y por tierra
y tienen cuatro pies, y son mayores que conejos,
y tienen la cola como lagarto, y la piel toda pintada,
y en el espinazo unas espinas levantadas
y agudos dientes y colmillos, y es callada,
que ni gime ni grita ni suena,
y se está atada dondequiera que la aten
sin hacer mal alguno ni ruido,
diez y quince y veinte días,
sin comer ni beber cosa alguna,
y tiene las manos largas
y uñas largas como de ave
pero flacas y no de presa.

Los petreles son menores que tordos y son muy negros,
son aves muy veloces que vuelan a ras del mar,
subiendo y bajando conforme el subir y el bajar del mar,
y se ven por todo el camino de las Indias en el gran mar Océano.
Las fragatas son aves negras que vuelan muy alto
y las naos las ven veinte y treinta leguas y más, mar adentro,
volando muy alto.
Los pájaros bobos son menores que gaviotas
y cuando ven los navíos se vienen a ellos
y cansados de volar se sientan en las gavias, y son negros.
Los alcatraces pasan siempre volando sobre Panamá,
cuando crece la mar del Sur, cada seis horas,
y vienen en gran multitud volando sobre la marea,
y caen veloces desde lo alto y toman las sardinas
y se vuelven a levantar volando y vuelven a caer
y otra vez a levantarse, sin cesar,
y al bajar el mar se van los alcatraces
continuando su pesca, y detrás van volando las fragatas
quitándoles su presa.
Hay muchos cuervos marinos en la mar del Sur,
en aquella costa de Panamá, y vienen todos juntos
buscando la sardina, y cubren el mar con grandes manchas.
Y el mar parece un terciopelo o paño muy negro
y se van y vienen con la marea como los alcatraces.
Y pasan innumerables aves por Cuba todos los años:
vienen desde la Nueva España y atraviesan Cuba
y van hacia el mar del Sur. Y por el Darién
pasan todos los años viniendo de Cuba

and it gives loud whistles and makes holes with its beak.
I-guana is a kind of serpent with four feet
very frightful to see and very tasty to eat;
they are very ugly and frightening but they do no harm
and it has yet to be determined whether they are animal or fish
because they go in the water and the trees and on the land
and they have four feet, and are bigger than rabbits,
and they have a tail like a lizard, and the skin all painted,
and along the backbone some erect spines
and sharp teeth and fangs, and it is quiet,
not whining or calling out or making a sound
and it remains tied wherever they tie it
without doing any harm or making a noise,
ten and fifteen and twenty days,
without eating or drinking anything,
and it has large hands
and nails like a bird's
but thin and not claw-like.

Petrels are smaller than thrushes and they are very black,
they are very swift birds that fly above the sea surface,
going up and down as the sea rises and falls,
and you see them all the way to the Indies in the great Ocean sea.
Frigates are black birds which fly very high
and ships see them twenty and thirty leagues and more, out to sea,
flying very high.
Boobies are smaller than seagulls
and when they see ships they come to them
and tired of flying they sit on the topsails, and they are black.
Pelicans always pass flying over Panama,
when the South Sea swells, every six hours,
and they come in great multitudes flying above the tide,
and they dive swiftly from on high and take the sardines
and they shoot up flying again and dive again
and again they shoot up, without stopping,
and when the sea goes out the pelicans move off
continuing to fish, and behind them the frigates fly
snatching their catch from them.
There are many cormorants in the South Sea,
on that coast of Panama, and they all come together
looking for sardines, and they cover the sea in huge patches.
And the sea looks like a very dark velvet or cloth
and they come and go with the tide like the pelicans.
And untold birds pass heading for Cuba every year:
they come from New Spain and cross Cuba
and fly toward the South Sea. And by Darién
they pass every year coming from Cuba

y atraviesan la Tierra Firme hacia el polo Austral
y no se les ve volver.
Por quince y veinte días
desde la mañana hasta la noche el cielo se cubre de aves
aves muy altas, tan altas que muchas se pierden de vista,
y otras van muy bajas, con respecto a las más altas,
pero muy altas con respecto a las cumbres,
y cubren todo lo que se ve del cielo a lo largo del viaje,
y a lo ancho gran parte de lo que se ve del cielo
y no se pueden ver sus plumas porque vuelan muy alto,
y no vuelven.
Este paso de las aves es en Santa María la Antigua del Darién,
en Tierra Firme, y pasan en el mes de marzo.

Él tenía una casa en el Darién.
Las casas allá son de cañas atadas con bejucos
y el techo de paja o yerba larga, muy buena y bien puesta,
y cuando llueve, uno no se moja, y es como la teja.
Como cubren las casas en los villajes y aldeas de Flandes
(pero la yerba es mejor que la de Flandes). Y él tenía una casa,
dice, que pudiera aposentar un señor, con muchos aposentos
altos y bajos, y con un huerto de muchos naranjos
dulces y agrios, y cidros y limones, y un hermoso río
lo cruzaba por enmedio. Y el sitio era gracioso y sano
y de lindos aires y bella vista sobre aquella ribera.
Pero ahora el Darién se despobló. Lo despobló Pedrarias
alegando que era malsano (porque lo fundó Balboa su yerno).
Y su casa se está destruyendo, en un pueblo despoblado.
Todos los vecinos se han estado yendo. Ya no queda nadie
en Santa María la Antigua del Darién, donde está su casa.

and they cross Terra firma toward the Austral pole
and you never see them return.
For fifteen or twenty days
from morning to night the sky is covered with birds,
birds very high, so high that many are lost from sight,
and others fly low, in comparison to the higher ones,
but very high in comparison to the mountain tops,
and they cover all there is to see of the sky the length of the journey,
and a large part of what can be seen of the sky breadthwise,
and you cannot see their feathers because they fly very high,
and they never return.
This passage of birds is in Santa María la Antigua in Darién,
in Terra firma, and they pass in the month of March.

He had a house in Darién.
The houses there are made of canes tied with reeds
and the roof of straw or long grass, very good and well arranged,
and when it rains, one does not get wet, and it is like tiles.
Like they cover the houses in the hamlets and villages of Flanders
(but the grass is better than that of Flanders). And he had a house,
he says, fit to accommodate a lord, with many rooms
upstairs and below, and with an orchard with many sweet and bitter
orange trees, and citrons and lemons, and a beautiful river
cut through the middle of it. And the spot was elegant and wholesome
and with fine air and a beautiful view along the banks.
But now Darién has become deserted. Pedrarias drove the people away
alleging that it was unhealthy (because Balboa, his son-in-law, founded it).
And his house is falling into ruin, in a deserted town.
All the neighbors have been leaving. Now no one is left
in Santa María la Antigua del Darién, where he has his house.

En Santiago de los Caballeros de Guatemala
hay un viejo regidor. Un viejo conquistador,
de barba blanca, con una hija por casar,
casi sordo y casi ciego. Apenas oye las campanas
lejanas, como las campanas de Medina del Campo . . .

Recuerda Medina del Campo, donde su padre fue regidor.
El castillo de la Mota, rojo (ladrillos rojos), y alrededor Castilla
y Castilla . . . Oh cómo recuerda. Mientras va envejeciendo
y las cosas se van haciendo más y más lejanas
las recuerda más y más. Recuerda aquella estrella en la frente
del caballo *Motilla* de Gonzalo de Sandoval,
que era un caballo castaño . . . Y él murió en Castilla.
Ceceaba un poco . . . Pedro de Alvarado tenía
treinta y cuatro años, y la cara muy alegre,
y los indios le llamaban Toniatú, "el sol".
Recuerda la yegua alazana de Pedro de Alvarado,
y el caballo castaño zahino de Cortés.
Recuerda todos los nombres de los compañeros muertos.
Y recuerda todas sus muertes. Hernán Cortés
murió en Castilleja de la Cuesta. Alvarado
en Jalisco. Olid, degollado en Honduras.
Juan Velázquez de León en los puentes de Tenochtitlán.
Diego de Ordaz murió en el río Marañón.
Gonzalo de Alvarado en Oaxaca, Juan Alvarado en el mar.
Medina de Ríoseco, "el Galán", murió en los puentes,
Gonzalo Domínguez, muy esforzado y gran jinete,
murió en poder de los indios. Un Morón, de Ginés,
bien esforzado y buen jinete, en poder de los indios.
Aquel Mora, de Ciudad Rodrigo, en Guatemala,
y Francisco Corral, muy valiente, en Veracruz.
Y los Solises: Solís, el anciano, en poder de los indios.
Solís "Casquete" murió de su muerte en Guatemala.
Solís "Tras la puerta" (mirando siempre tras la puerta)
murió de su muerte. Solís "el de la Huerta", de su muerte.
Juan de Limpias Carvajal, que ensordeció en la guerra,
murió de su muerte. Martín López todavía vive en México.
A Martín Vendaval lo llevaron vivo a sacrificar.
Los hermanos Florianes murieron en poder de indios.
Bernaldino de Coria murió de su muerte.
Un Meza, artillero, murió ahogado en un río.
Sindos de Portillo dejó sus indios y sus bienes
y se metió a fraile franciscano. Hizo muchos milagros.

In Santiago de los Caballeros de Guatemala
there is an old alderman. An old conquistador
with a white beard, a daughter still to be married,
almost deaf and almost blind. He can hardly hear the distant
bells, like the bells of Medina del Campo . . .

He remembers Medina del Campo, where his father was alderman.
The red (red-bricked) castle of la Mota, and around Castille
and Castille . . . Oh how he remembers. As he grows older
and events are becoming more and more distant
he remembers them more and more. He remembers that star on the forehead
of Gonzalo de Sandoval's horse *Motilla*,
which was a chestnut horse . . . And he died in Castille.
He lisped slightly . . . Pedro de Alvarado was
thirty-four years old, and his face very happy,
and the Indians called him Toniatú, "the sun."
He remembers Pedro de Alvarado's sorrel mare
and Cortés's frisky chestnut horse.
He remembers all the names of his dead companions.
And he remembers all their deaths. Hernán Cortés
died in Castilleja de la Cuesta. Alvarado
in Jalisco. Olid, beheaded in Honduras.
Juan Velázquez de León on the bridges of Tenochtitlán.
Diego de Ordaz died in the river Marañón.
Gonzalo de Alvarado in Oaxaca, Juan Alvarado at sea.
Medina de Ríoseco, "the Gallant," died on the bridges,
Gonzalo Domínguez, very brave and a great horseman,
died at the hands of the Indians. One Morón, from Ginés,
very brave and a great horseman, in the hands of the Indians.
That Mora, from Ciudad Rodrigo, in Guatemala,
and Francisco Corral, very courageous, in Veracruz.
And the Solíses: Solís, the old man, at the hands of the Indians.
Solís "Helmet" died a natural death in Guatemala.
Solís "Behind the door" (always looking behind the door)
died naturally. Solís "the Garden one," naturally.
Juan de Limpias Carvajal, who went deaf in the war,
died a natural death. Martín López is still alive in Mexico.
Martín Vendaval was taken to be sacrificed alive.
The Florián brothers died at the hands of the Indians.
Bernaldino de Coria died a natural death.
One Meza, a gunner, drowned in a river.
Sindos de Portilla abandoned his Indians and his possessions
and became a Franciscan friar. He performed many miracles.

Francisco de Medina, de Medina del Campo,
también se hizo fraile franciscano. Alonso de Aguilar,
el de la "Venta de Aguilar" entre Veracruz y Puebla,
se metió a fraile dominico y fue muy santo.
Gaspar Díez, otro buen soldado, de Castilla la Vieja,
vivió de ermitaño en los pinares de Guajalcingo.
Un Lerma, se aburrió y se fue con los indios,
y nunca se supo de él. Un Enríquez
se ahogó por el peso y el calor de las armas.
Jerónimo de Aguilar, el intérprete, murió de mal de bubas.
Tarifa "de las Manos Blancas" que sólo hablaba del pasado,
se ahogó con su caballo en el Golfo Dulce
y nunca aparecieron ni él ni su caballo.

De quinientos cincuenta que pasaron con Cortés
no quedan vivos más que cinco en toda la Nueva España.
¿Y sus sepulcros? Son los vientres de los indios
que comieron sus piernas y sus muslos y sus brazos,
y lo demás fue echado a los tigres y a las sierpes
y alcones que tenían enjaulados.
Esos son sus sepulcros y allí están sus blasones.
Sus nombres debían estar escritos en letras de oro.
Ahora sólo cinco están vivos, muy viejos y enfermos,
y lo peor de todo, muy pobres, cargados de hijos,
y con hijas por casar, y nietos, y poca renta,
sin dinero para ir a Castilla a reclamar.
Y ninguno de sus nombres los escribió Gomara,
ni el doctor Illescas, ni los otros cronistas.
Sólo del Marqués Cortés hablan esos libros.
Él fue el único que descubrió y conquistó todo,
y todos los demás capitanes no cuentan para nada.

Por eso comenzó a escribir la "Verdadera Historia".
Las cosas que él vió y oyó, y las batallas
en las que él estuvo peleando. Tal vez se alabe mucho . . .
¿Y por qué no? ¿Lo dirán acaso las nubes
o los pájaros que en aquellos tiempos pasaron por alto,
que cuando peleaban en las batallas pasaron volando?
¿Lo escribieron Gomara, o Illescas en su *Pontifical*
o Cortés, cuando le escribía a Su Majestad?

Pero ha leído lo que escribieron Gomara e Illescas
y Jovio, y ve que escriben con elegancia,
mientras sus palabras son groseras y sin primor.
Manejan la pluma como él manejaba la espada.
Él es sólo un soldado.
                    Y dejó de escribir . . .

Francisco de Medina, from Medina del Campo,
also became a Franciscan friar. Alonso de Aguilar,
who kept the "Aguilar Inn" between Veracruz and Puebla,
became a Dominican friar and was very holy.
Gaspar Díez, another fine soldier, from Castilla la Vieja,
lived as a hermit amid the pine groves of Guajalcingo.
One Lerma, grew bored and went off with the Indians,
and nothing more was heard of him. One Enríquez
drowned from the weight and heat of his weapons.
Jerónimo de Aguilar, the interpreter, died of syphilis.
Tarifa "of the White Hands" who spoke only of the past,
drowned with his horse in the Golfo Dulce
and neither he nor his horse ever surfaced.

Out of five hundred and fifty who crossed over with Cortés
no more than five are left alive in the whole of New Spain.
And their graves? They are the stomachs of the Indians
who ate their legs and their thighs and their arms,
and the rest was thrown to the tigers and serpents
and falcons which they kept in cages.
Those are their graves and there are their escutcheons.
Their names should be written in letters of gold.
Now only five are living, very old and infirm,
and worst of all, very poor, burdened with sons,
and with daughters unmarried, and grandchildren, and little income,
with not enough money to go to Castille to claim their rights.
And Gomara wrote down none of their names,
neither did doctor Illescas, nor the other chroniclers.
Those books speak only of the Marquis Cortés.
He alone discovered and conquered everything,
and all the other captains count for nothing.

That's why he began to write the "True History."
The things he saw and heard, and the battles
in which he himself fought. Perhaps he is prone to brag . . .
And why not? Do you think the clouds will proclaim it
or the birds which at those times flew on high,
which flew overhead as they fought in the battles?
Did Gomara write it, or Illescas in his *Pontifical*
or Cortés, when he wrote to His Majesty?

But he has read what Gomara and Illescas and Jovio
wrote, and he sees that they write with elegance,
while his words are crude and lacking in beauty.
They handle the pen as he handled the sword.
He is just a soldier.
                    And he stopped writing . . .

Pero las cosas no fueron como las cuenta Gomara . . .

Cortés no hundió los barcos secretamente,
como lo dice el Gomara. Todos ellos lo pidieron.
Dijeron que ellos los pagarían si los cobraban.
Y les quitaron las anclas y los cables y las velas.
¿No eran acaso españoles para no ir adelante?

Y después la larga marcha, subiendo,
                              hacia Tenochtitlán.

En Tlascala un viento frío venía de las sierras
y no tenían para abrigarse más que las armas.
Cholula con sus torres blancas parecía Valladolid.
El Popocatepetl echaba fuego y la tierra temblaba.
Y Diego de Ordaz vio Tenochtitlán desde la cumbre,
allá lejos,
             una ciudad sobre el agua,
                              como Venecia.

Los embajadores de Moctezuma llegaron con presentes
a decirles otra vez que no pasaran adelante, que no
llegaran a México. Y cuando se iban acercando a México
iban con miedo.
              ¡La entrada en la gran calzada!
La laguna llena de palacios con terrazas
y las torres y los grandes cúes blancos
reflejados en el agua, las torres de Coyoacán
y las torres de Texcoco y las torres de Tacuba
temblorosas sobre el agua,
                    como cosa de encantamiento,
como las que se cuentan en Amadís de Gaula.
Y creían que soñaban.
                    Puentes de trecho en trecho,
y la calzada derecha a México llena de gente,
unos que entraban y otros que salían de México,
y las torres y las cúes también llenos de gente
y la laguna llena de canoas que iban y venían,
y grandes ciudades en la tierra y en el agua,
y delante la gran ciudad de México.
¡Y ellos no eran más que cuatrocientos!
Ahora todo está en el suelo, todo está perdido.
Ahora no hay ni laguna sino siembras de maizales.
Las calzadas estaban llenas de señores y caciques
con ricas mantas de colores y plumas y libreas:
el señor de Texcoco, y el señor de Ixtapalapa,

But things were not as Gomara tells them . . .

Cortés did not secretly sink the boats,
as Gomara tells. It was at everyone's request.
They said they would all pay if they were charged for them.
And they removed the anchors and the cables and the sails.
Could they be true Spaniards if they wouldn't press on?

And then the long march, climbing,
                              toward Tenochtitlán.

In Tlascala a cold wind blew from the sierras
and they had nothing but their weapons to shelter them.
Cholula with its white towers resembled Valladolid.
Popocatepetl was belching fire and the earth was trembling.
And Diego de Ordaz saw Tenochtitlán from the mountain top,
there in the distance,
                    a city upon water,
                              like Venice.

Moctezuma's envoys arrived with gifts
to tell them again they should not proceed, they should not
go to Mexico. And as they approached Mexico
they were afraid.
                The entry onto the great causeway!
The lake full of palaces with terraces
and the towers and the enormous white temples
reflected in the waters, the towers of Coyoacán
and the towers of Texcoco and the towers of Tacuba
shimmering upon the water,
                              like something enchanted,
like the things told in Amadís de Gaula.
And they thought they were dreaming.
                    Bridges at intervals,
and the right-hand causeway to Mexico full of people,
some entering and others leaving Mexico,
and the towers and the temples also full of people
and the lake full of canoes coming and going,
and mighty cities on land and on water,
and ahead the mighty city of Mexico.
And they were no more than four hundred!
Now it is all in the ground, all is lost.
Now not even the lake is there but fields of maize.
The causeways were full of lords and caciques
wearing lavish colored cloaks with feathers and liveries:
and the lord of Texcoco, and the lord of Ixtapalapa,

el señor de Tacuba y el señor de Coyoacán.
Y Moctezuma en sus andas ya venía cerca,
debajo del palio de plumas verdes y de oro,
vestido de oro, plata, perlas y pedrerías,
y le iban barriendo el suelo donde iba a pasar.
¡Todo se le representa ahora como si lo estuviera viendo!

Y la plaza: los gritos de los vendedores de oro y plata,
piedras preciosas, plumas, mantas, cosas labradas,
esclavos y esclavas, algodón, henequén, cacao,
cueros de tigres y leones y venados, y los vendedores
de chía, frijoles, legumbres, yerbas, gallinas,
gallos, conejos, liebres, venados, perrillos,
las fruteras con sus frutas, las tinajas pintadas,
los cañutos de olores con liquidámbar y tabaco . . .
—Como eran los días de feria en Medina del Campo.
Las acequias con canoas que traían flores y frutas,
y el gran cu en medio de los grandes patios
(más grandes que la plaza de Salamanca)
el gran cu con las gradas llenas de sangre,
y desde el cu se veía toda la ciudad, y las ciudades
blancas, en la laguna y alrededor de ella,
con las tres calzadas que entraban en México
y el acueducto recto y largo de Chapultepec,
y los canales con sus puentes y canoas,
unas que venían y otras que volvían con sus cargas,
y los cúes y los adoratorios y las torres
blancas bajo el sol. Y abajo en la gran plaza
el gentío que compraba y vendía, y subía el rumor
y se oía a una legua de distancia. Y arriba del cu
Huichilobos con los ojos hechos de espejos,
cubierto de pedrerías y oro y aljófar y sangre,
y todo el piso y las paredes bañadas de sangre.
Y más arriba estaba el tambor, el gran tambor
de cueros de sierpes, que cuando sonaba
su sonido era tan triste como si fuera del infierno
y se oía a más de dos leguas de distancia.

Y los españoles oían de noche desde sus lechos
los espantosos silbidos de las serpientes,
los temorosos bramidos de los leones,
los aullidos tristes de los lobos
y los gritos de las onzas y tigres del Emperador Moctezuma
que gritaban cuando tenían hambre
o se acordaban que estaban encerrados.

Y cuando huyeron de Tenochtitlán a medianoche,

the lord of Tacuba and the lord of Coyoacán.
And Moctezuma on his litter was approaching,
beneath the canopy of green and gold feathers,
dressed in gold, silver, pearls, and precious stones,
and they were sweeping the ground where he was to pass.
He pictures it all now as though he were seeing it!

And the square: the cries of the sellers of gold and silver,
precious stones, feathers, cloaks, carved things,
male and female slaves, cotton, henequen, cocoa,
skins of tigers and lions and deer, and the sellers
of chía, beans, vegetables, herbs, hens,
cocks, rabbits, hares, deer, little dogs,
women fruit-sellers with their fruit, the painted jars,
cane vessels of scent with liquidambar and tobacco . . .
—Like market days in Medina del Campo.
The gullies with canoes which brought flowers and fruit,
and the huge temple amid the immense patios
(bigger than the square in Salamanca)
the mighty temple with its steps covered in blood,
and from the temple you could see the whole city, and the white
cities, in the lake and around it,
with three causeways that led into Mexico
and the long straight aqueduct of Chapultepec,
and the canals with their bridges and canoes,
some coming and others returning with their cargo,
and the temples and the shrines and the towers
white beneath the sun. And below in the great square
the crowd buying and selling, and the roar rose up
and could be heard a league away. And on top of the temple
Huichilobos with eyes made of mirrors,
covered in precious stones and gold,
and the whole floor and the walls bathed in blood.
And higher up was the drum, the huge serpent-skin
drum, which when it sounded
had a sound as sad as though it came from hell
and it could be heard for a distance of two leagues.

And from their beds at night the Spaniards heard
the horrendous hiss of the serpents,
the frightful roars of the lions,
the sad howls of the wolves,
and the screeching of Emperor Moctezuma's ounces and tigers,
which screeched when they were hungry
or remembered they were in captivity.

And when they fled from Tenochtitlán in the middle of the night,

en silencio, pasando despacio por los puentes,
bajo la lluvia ¡cómo sonó el tambor aquella noche!
De pronto en el silencio el gran tambor empezó a sonar
y la oscuridad se llenó de gritos y de flechas
y la laguna de canoas. No había luna
y no veían a los que disparaban desde los azoteas
y desde el agua. Llovía, y los caballos resbalaban
y caían en el agua. Habían levantado los puentes,
y cruzaron los canales sobre los caballos muertos,
indios muertos y petacas, y por el peso de oro
los españoles caían al agua, abrazados al oro.
Siguieron por la calzada avanzando entre las lanzas,
dando cuchilladas en la oscuridad sin saber a quién,
y arriba en el gran cu el tambor tocando y tocando.
Cortés lloró cuando vio venir a Pedro de Alvarado,
a pie, con la lanza en la mano, bañado de sangre,
con cuatro soldados, y detrás de él no venían más.

Y lloró en Tacuba bajo el Árbol de la Noche Triste
mirando Tenochtitlán de noche bajo la luna,
con sus torres y sus puentes y el gran cu de Huichilobos.
¡Y qué doloroso el sonar del tambor de Huichilobos
las noches en que llevaban a sacrificar los compañeros
por las gradas del gran cu, y los hacían bailar
delante de Huichilobos, y los ponían sobre piedras
y con cuchillos de pedernal les abrían el pecho
y ofrecían el corazón bullendo a Huichilobos
y los cuerpos iban rodando por las gradas
y los indios abajo se los comían con chilimole,
y las sobras se les daban a los leones y los tigres!
Y en las torres los tambores y atabales tristes
no dejaban de sonar, y el maldito tambor
con el sonido más triste que se podía inventar
se oía desde muy lejos. Él temía la muerte.
Lo habían ya dos veces llevado a sacrificar
y antes de entrar en batalla se le ponía
una como grima y tristeza en el corazón,
y le temblaba el corazón, porque temía la muerte.

El viejo ha vuelto a leer otra vez esas crónicas
y ve que no cuentan nada de lo que pasó en Nueva España.
Están llenas de mentiras. Ensalzan a unos capitanes
y rebajan a otros. Dicen que estuvieron en las conquistas
los que no estuvieron en ellas. Entonces coge la pluma
y empieza otra vez a escribir, sin elegancia,
sin policía, sin razones hermoseadas ni retórica,
según el común hablar de Castilla la Vieja.

in silence, creeping slowly beneath the bridges,
in the rain, how the drum sounded that night!
Suddenly in the silence the great drum began to sound
and the darkness was filled with shouts and with arrows
and the lake with canoes. There was no moon
and they could not see who was firing from the flat roofs
and from the water. It was raining, and the horses lost their footing
and fell into the water. They had raised the bridges,
and they crossed the canals over the dead horses,
dead Indians, and cases, and due to the weight of the gold
the Spaniards fell into the water, embracing the gold.
They went along the causeway, advancing through the spears,
making knife-thrusts in the darkness not knowing at whom,
and high up on the mighty temple the drum beating on and on.
Cortés cried when he saw Pedro de Alvarado approaching,
on foot, with a lance in his hand, covered with blood,
with four soldiers, and behind him no more came.

And he cried in Tacuba under the Tree of the Sad Night
gazing on Tenochtitlán by night under the moon,
with its towers and its bridges and the great temple of Huichilobos.
And how sorrowful the sounding of the drum of Huichilobos
the nights they were taking their companions to be sacrificed
up the steps of the great temple, and they made them dance
in front of Huichilobos, and they laid them out on stones
and with large flint knives they opened their chests
and offered the bubbling hearts to Huichilobos
and the bodies cascaded down the steps
and the Indians below ate them with chilimole,
and the leftovers were given to the lions and the tigers!
And in the towers the drums and the sad timbrels
never ceased to resound, and the accursed drum
with the saddest sound that could be invented
could be heard very far away. He feared death.
Twice they had led him to be sacrificed
and before entering battle disgust
and sadness would grip his heart
and his heart trembled, because he feared death.

The old man has reread those chronicles
and he sees that they tell nothing of what happened in New Spain.
They are full of lies. They exalt some captains
and belittle others. They say some took part in the conquests
who did not take part in them. Then he picks up the pen
and starts writing again, without elegance,
without propriety, without beautified arguments or rhetoric,
according to the common speech of Castilla la Vieja.

Porque el agraciado componer es decir la verdad.
Aunque tal vez no haga sino gastar papel y tinta . . .
Porque él nunca había escrito. Él es sólo un soldado.
Pero escribe también para sus hijos y sus nietos,
para que sepan que él vino a conquistar estas tierras.
Su historia si se imprime verán que es verdadera.
¡Y ahora que lo escribe se le representa todo
delante de los ojos como si fuera ayer que pasó!
Irá escribiendo con su pluma, despacio, despacio,
corrigiendo los errores con cuidado, como el piloto
que va descubriendo las costas, echando la sonda . . .

Ya es tarde. El cuarto se está oscureciendo.
Las campanas de Santiago de los Caballeros de Guatemala
suenan lejanas, lejanas, como las campanas
                                   de Medina del Campo.

Because graceful composition is the telling of the truth.
Though he may be doing nothing more than wasting paper and ink . . .
For he had never written. He is only a soldier.
But he writes also for his children and his grandchildren,
so they might know that he came to conquer these lands.
His history if it is printed they will see is truthful.
And now as he writes it he pictures it all
before his eyes as though it happened yesterday!
He will go on writing, slowly, slowly,
correcting his errors with care, like the pilot
who proceeds mapping the coasts, casting his line . . .

It is late now. The room is growing dark.
The bells of Santiago de los Caballeros de Guatemala
ring distantly, distantly, like the bells
of Medina del Campo.

La última tarde del año fue triste y nublada
y en derredor de la nao saltaban peces grandes
como caballos, dando grandes bufidos.
Los bufones: presagiadores de tempestad.

Pero el primer día del año 1545
amaneció con el cielo sereno y el mar azul
y el viento próspero. Manadas de toninas
rodeaban la nao. En el camarón de proa
los frailes llevaban un altar con un Nacimiento
y el Niño Dios envuelto en heno. Y después de la misa
Fray Bartolomé dijo el sermón.
A lo lejos se veían tierras azules.
PADRES Y HERMANOS MÍOS: Miramos ya
las cumbres de los montes
de la tierra que vamos a pisar.
                              Es Yucatán.
Tenía infinitas gentes, porque es tierra abundante,
llena de frutas. La tierra no tiene oro
pero tiene miel y cera más que ninguna otra de las Indias.
Tiene trescientas leguas en torno. Se gobernaba
con el mejor sistema político de las Indias
y no tenía vicios ni pecados
y se pudieran hacer grandes ciudades de españoles
y vivir allí como en un paraíso terrenal.
Pero llegó un Gobernador a este Reino
y mató a los que estaban en sus casas sin ofender a nadie.
Y como no tenían oro, sacó el oro de sus cuerpos.
Y regresaban cargados de gente vendida,
comprada con vino y aceite y vinagre,
cambiados por tocinos, cambiados por caballos.
La doncella más bella, una arroba de vino.
Un tocino. El hijo de un príncipe
(o que parecía un hijo de un príncipe)
comprado por un queso. Cien personas por un caballo.

Mientras hablaba estaba la nao en calma
y el viento no movía ni una ola ni una vela.
Después que cantaron vísperas y completas
comenzó a soplar un aire muy manso
y la nao poco a poco fue acercándose a tierra.
Iban con la sonda en la mano sondeando el puerto
y al oscurecer encendieron fuego en la gavia

The last afternoon of the year was sad and cloudy
and around the ship large fish frolicked
like horses, snorting loudly.
The clowns: harbingers of storm.

But the first day of the year 1545
day broke to a serene sky and blue sea
and the wind flourishing. Herds of dolphin
encircled the ship. In the bow cabin
the friars had an altar with a Manger
and Baby Jesus swaddled in hay. And after mass
Fray Bartolomé gave the sermon.
In the distance you could see the blue lands.
MY FATHERS AND BROTHERS: We've seen
the tops of the mountains
of the land we are about to walk.
                              It's the Yucatán.
It had an infinity of people, because the land is abundant,
full of fruit. The land has no gold
but it has more honey and wax than any other of the Indies.
It measures three-hundred leagues around. It was governed
with the best political system of the Indies
and had no vices or sins
and it was possible to make large cities of Spaniards
and to live there as in an earthly paradise.
But the Governor arrived in this Kingdom
and he killed those who were in their homes giving offense to no one.
And since they had no gold, he extracted gold from their bodies.
And they returned loaded with sold people,
bought with wine and oil and vinegar,
exchanged for salt pork, exchanged for horses.
The most beautiful maiden, an arroba of wine.
A salted hog. The son of a prince
(or what seemed to be a prince's son)
bought for a cheese. One hundred people for a horse.

While he spoke the ship was in calm
and the wind moved not a wave nor a sail.
After they sang vespers and compline
a very gentle breeze began to blow
and the ship gradually drew toward the land.
They proceeded with the sounding line in hand sounding the port
and when it grew dark they lit a fire in the crow's nest

y les respondieron de tierra. Avanzaron
hasta tres brazas de fondo, y echaron el ancla
y esperaron a que amaneciera.

and from the land they answered them. They advanced
to a depth of three fathoms, and dropped anchor
and waited for day to break.

Justicia e regimiento de la çibdad de granada
de la provincia de nicaragua
humillmente besamos los reales pies y manos
no se a fecho relaçion a vuestra magestad
por cabsa de tener los gouernadores desta prouinçia
absoluto ymperio
porque pedrarias davila
despues que degollo al capitan francisco hernandez
procuro por todas las vias anichilar esta provincia
e lo peor de todo vuestra magestad
es que pedrarias davila
e el licenciado francisco de castañeda
alcalde mayor e contador e juan tellez
que tuvo a cargo la tesoreria
cada vno dellos tenian en la mar del sur vn navio
e contrataban con ellos en la çibdad de panama
e porque en aquel tiempo no avia contrataçion
ni tenian de que aprovecharse en los fletes
tomaron por espirente para su ganançia
la destruyçion e desolaçion desta tierra
e llevaban los escuadrones de yndios e yndias
a enbarcar en sus navios
E despues que pedrarias dauila fallesçio
el licenciado castañeda se opuso a la governaçion
hechando en cadenas e otras prisiones
yndios e yndias naturales desta tierra
teniendo respeto solo a su ynterese particular
tuvo presos en la çibdad de leon publicamente
a vn alcalde e a vn regidor desta çibdad
e a otras muchas personas hizo muy grandes agravios
e como tovimos nuevas çiertas que rodrigo de contreras
yerno de pedrarias davila
venia de governador a esta tierra tovimos por çierto
procuraria con todas la fuerças de conplir
lo que por vuestra magestad le fuese mandado
mas como los pecados de los que aca bibimos son tan grandes
no an dado lugar a que oviese efecto la real voluntad
por manera que esta tierra a syempre esperimentado
yugos tan pesados
que si se detoviera algun tiempo el remedio
ovieramos de salir huyendo della
porque si a vuestra magestad hubiesemos de haser relaçion
de todo lo que en esta tierra a subcedido

XXIII / 148

Justice and council of the citie of Granada
in the provynce of Nicaragua
        we humbly kiss the royal hands and feet
no accompt has bene sent your majestie
due to the governours of this provynce injoyinge
        absolut dominion
            because Pedrarias Davila
after he beheaded captain Francisco Hernandez
sought by everie means to annihilate this provynce
and worst of all your majestie
        is that Pedrarias Davila
and the licentiate Francisco Castañeda
magistrate and comptroller and Juan Tellez
who had charge of the treasury
each one of them had a shippe in the South Sea
and they did commerce with them in the cittie of Panama
and because at that tyme there was no trade
nor had they anythynge to take advantage of in cargoes
they looked for theyr profitt in
the destruction and desolation of this land
and brought squadrons of indiens male and female
        to embarke upon theyr shyppes
And after Pedrarias Davila died
the licentiate Castañeda opposed the gouvernement
castyng into chaines and other prisons
male and female indiens native to these parts
havyng respecte onelie to his own interest
publickly in the citie of Leon he held prisoner
a mayor and an alderman of this citie
and to many other people he did great affront
and sith we had certeyne news that Rodrigo de Contreras
        sonne in lawe of Pedrarias
was bound for this land as gouvernor we felt certeyne
he wolde seeke with all his powers to cary out
whatever your majestie had ordered him
yet since the sinnes of us who dwell here are so great
they have not allowed the royal wille to have effect
in the maner that this lande has always suffered
        such heavy yokes
that were the remedie to be delayed sum tyme
        we wolde have quickly to fly from here
because were wee to send accompt to your majestie
of all that hath passed in this land

          de nueve años a esta parte
que ha que rodrigo de contreras a governado
seria haser vn proceso muy grande e de cosas
que vuestra magestad dudamos pudiese creer
          su magestad
                    de las cuatro partes de los repartimientos
de toda esta provinçia las tres e lo mejor de toda la tierra
tiene puestos en su muger e fijos
                    e criados e criadas e parientes
          e paniaguados
estando toda la tierra agraviada de rodrigo de contreras
e de sus tenientes e de su yerno pedro de los rios
se pusieron ynfinitas demandas e querellas criminales
contra el dicho rodrigo de contreras
e sus tenientes
e pedro de los rios
e aviendo visto por muchos e diversos capitulos
los grandes daños e delitos quel dicho rodrigo de contreras
avia cometido e perpetrado en esta tierra
el juez de recidencia se fue desta provinçia
dexando todos los pleytos a cabsas yndeterminadas
syn aver en esta tierra fecho justicia ninguna
e para que esta tierra quede en paz e quietud asimismo suplicamos
a vuestra magestad nos haga merçed de mandar no se provea
de alcalde mayor para esta çibdad de granada
syno fuere a pedimento desta çibdad
e la persona queste cabildo señalare
porque asy conviene al seruiçio de vuestra magestad
e bien desta tierra
                         porque mandando vuestra magestad
que rodrigo de contreras e su yerno pedro de los rios
con sus hijos e mugeres salgan desta provinçia
no queda en ella persona que desasosiegue ni de penas ni
molestias a persona ninguna de los que en ella biven
               desta çibdad de granada de la provincia de nicaragua
               a diez e seys dias de henero de 1545 años.

          S.C.C.R. Magestad
bartolome tello vecino e regidor e procurador
desta çiudad de granada
beso los reales pies i manos de vuestra magestad
i digo que a nueve años por mandado de vuestra magestad
a governado rrodrigo de contreras en esta provincia
del cual emos sido tratados no como uasallos de vuestra magestad
sino como propiamente sus esclauos
hasta agora nos a faltado libertad para dar a vuestra magestad
auiso y verdadera relaçion de las tiranias o prisiones

over the nine yeres
Rodrigo de Contreras has gouverned these parts
it wolde be a verye lengthy process and of thyngs
whych your majestie we dout you could believe
      your majestie
            of the four encomiendas
of all this province three and the best of all the lande
he has under the control of his wife and sonnes
            and servaunts and mayds and relatives
      and protégés
beeyng the hole land affronted by Rodrigo de Contreras
and by his lieutenants and by his son in lawe Pedro de los Rios
endlesse suits and criminel accusations were levelled
ageynest the sayed Rodrigo de Contreras
and his lieutenants
and Pedro de los Rios
and havynge seen through many and diverse chapters
the great harme and crimes whych sayd Rodrigo de Contreras
had committed and perpetrated in this land
the judg of residence departed from this provynce
leavynge all complaynts in undetermined causes
without in this lande any justice havynge bene done
and that this land remayne in peace and tranquillitie thus we begg
your majestie to do us the favour of not providynge
a magistrate for this cittie of Granada
other then it be at the beheste of this citie
and the personne this council shall indicate
because this is what suits best the service of your majestie
and the well beynge of this lande
            because your majestie orderynge
that Rodrigo de Contreras and his son in law Pedro de los Rios
with his sonnes and wyves leave this provynce
no person remaineth here who might disturbe neither with payn nor
trouble any personne of those that live here
      from this cittie of Granada in the provynce of Nicaraqua
      on the sixteenth day of Ianuarie in 1545.

      Sacred Catholyke Emperiell Royal Majestie
Bartolomé Tello resident and alderman and prosecutor
of this citie of Granada
I kisse the royal hands and feete of your majestie
and I say that for nine yeres by order of your majestie
Rodrigo de Contreras has gouverned in this provynce
by whome we have bene treated not as vassalls of your majestie
but more in realitie as his slaves
until nowe we have lacked the freedom to give to your majestie
notice and trewe accompt of the tyrannies or prisons

e malos tratamientos que a husado i del emos rrecebido
procurandonos toda miseria i pobreza para mexor nos sugetar
                estamos espantados
y no podemos saber de donde nos a venido tan gran daño
de quedar vuestros uasallos como quedamos mas agraviados
y enemistados por no hechar de esta tierra
los que an sido y seran causa de muchas disinciones y alborotos
e no se remediar como conviene dexado en esta provincia
a rrodrigo de contreras y a pedro de los rrios su yerno
quedando afrentados por aver pedido contra ellos justicia
siendo como son poderosos tematicos i vengativos
e no eran parte los vezinos para hazer saver
a vuestra sacra magestad lo que pasava en esta tierra
porque el que governava tenia debaxo de su mano y de su llave
el cavildo de la çibdad y los puertos de mar
y caminos de la tierra
de manera que si no fuese lo que el enviava a españa
otra cosa no avia de salir de la tierra
porque ellos no vienen a estas partes sino por su puro ynterese
porque a estas partes vienen a pagar lo que en españa deven
vienen a hazer rricos sus parientes vienen a casar sus hijas
y todo con los indios de vuestra magestad y con el sudor
de los que an conquistado la tierra y derramado su sangre

/al dorso:/ Nicaragua   a su magestad   1545
vna de las cosas mas deseadas que los subditos
y vasallos de vuestra magestad en estas partes deseamos
es la rretitud de la justicia y por esta descendio Dios al mundo
para pagar con su preciosa sangre la libertad
que ya teniamos perdida y pues la amo Dios es justo
la deseemos nosotros porque por donde no ay justicia
no ay vien no ay quietud no ay seguridad no ay rrepublica
porque donde carecen de todo esto se puede llamar
y con rrazon rreyno diuiso
que por tal emos tenido esta miseria tierra
despues de que por nuestros pecados fue Dios servido
que nos cupiese en suerte rrodrigo de contreras . . .

yten no obedece las proviciones de Su Magestad
        dice que se venden a cuarto en Panamá
        aprovecha la hacienda de Su Majestad y las rentas reales
        y las penas de los condenados que se aplican al fisco
        y se paga con ello su salario
yten manda prender al que no hace su voluntad
        y le levanta proceso, deja el proceso pendiente
        va un allegado suyo a decirle que lo van a matar

and bad treatments whych he has employed and from him we have received
givynge to us everie misery and poverty to better subject us
        we live in fear
and cannot tell from where such harme has come to us
as to remayn your vassalls as we remayne more aggrieved
and antagonized for not throwynge out of this lande
those who have bin and wil be the cause of many dissensions and dysturbances
and if not remedied as is fittynge leavynge in this province
Rodrigo de Contreras and Pedro de los Rios his sonne in lawe
continuynge to be afronted for havynge sought justice ageynst them
beeyng as they are persistent and vengefull powerfull men
and the residents were not party to informynge
your sacred majestie of what was goynge on in this lande
because he who gouverned had under his hand and key
the council of the citie and the sea ports
and the land roads
so that unlesse it were sumthyng he was sendyng to Spain
no other thing were to leave the lande
because they only come to these parts out of pure interest
because to these parts they come to pay what in Spain they owe
they come to make theyr relatives ryche they come to marrie theyr daughters
and all with your majestie's indiens and with the sweat
of those who have conquered the land and spilt theyr bloud

/on the back:/ Nicaragua   to his majestie   1545
one of the thyngs most desired that the subjects
and vassals of your majestie in these parts desire
is the rectitude of justice and for this God came into the worlde
to pay with his precious bloode for the libertie
we have presently lost and since God loved it 'tis just
we desire it our selves because where there is no justice
there is no good there is no tranquillitie there is no securitie there is no
                                                Republick
because where they lack all this it can be cauled
and with raison a divided kingdome
whych is how we have had this miserable land
since for our sinnes it pleased God
we should suffer the misfortune of Rodrigo de Contreras . . .

item he does not obey the provysions of Your Majesty
        he says they are two a penny in Panama
        he helps himself to the wealth of Your Majesty & the royal income
        & the penalties of the condemned which correspond to the exchequer
        and pays his own salary from it
item he orders whosoever opposes his will to be arrested
        and brings charges against him, he leaves the case pending
        one of his followers goes to tell him they are going to kill him

si no hace aquello que el gobernador ruega
yten ha cometido robos
    no permite que salgan a pedir justicia fuera de Nicaragua
    los que lo hacen tienen que salir a escondidas y huyendo
yten tiene más de la tercera parte de la provincia
    (él y su mujer y sus hijos)
    ha puesto sus propios escribanos públicos
    para que le revelen las escrituras que se otorgan
    (si son contra él) y el secreto de los cabildos
yten vende los indios libres al Perú
yten ha roto y encubierto procesos
    hace que los testigos declaren contra la verdad
    o que los escribanos asienten lo que no han dicho los testigos
    los cabildos se celebran en su propia casa
    las apelaciones contra él son denegadas
    no son castigados los delitos de sus criados
yten su mujer manda a los alcaldes
yten quita las haciendas particulares de sus dueños
    a unos ha echado en prisiones, a otros a desterrado
    y han muerto en las prisiones y destierros
    el cabildo no hace más que firmar lo que él les da
    no hay registro de las cédulas de encomienda
    falsifica los títulos de encomiendas
    los indios son traspasados de mano en mano con cédulas falsas
    los alcaldes y regidores son puestos por él
    las querellas contra él están metidas en una caja
    y los vecinos se han refugiado en las iglesias o los montes

LOS PUEBLOS QUE POSEEN RODRIGO DE CONTRERAS E SU
                MUGER E HIJOS SON:
    El pueblo de mistega————
    el pueblo de teçuatega————
    otro pueblo abangasca————
    otro pueblo queçaloaque————
    otros dos pueblos que se llaman utega y uteguilla————
    otro pueblo totoa————
    otro pueblo junto a esta ciudad de pescadores————
    otro pueblo junto esta ciudad se dice çebaco————
    la provincia de chira————
    la provincia de nicoya————
    el pueblo de bombacho————
    el pueblo de monimbo————
        etc.
            etc.
                etc.
    (Véase COLECCIÓN SOMOZA)

if he does not do as the governor demands
item he has committed robberies
    he does not permit them to leave Nicaragua to seek justice
    those who do so must leave in secret and taking flight
item he holds more than the third part of the province
    (he & his wife & his sons)
    he has appointed his own public notaries
    so they can reveal to him the deeds which are granted
    if they be against him) and the secrets of the councils
item he sells free Indians to Peru
item he has broken & corrupted court cases
    he makes witnesses testify against the truth
    or gets notaries to put down what the witnesses have not said
    councils meet in his own house
    appeals against him are denied
    the crimes of his servants go unpunished
item his wife controls the mayors
item he takes private estates from their owners
    some he has thrown into prison, others into exile
    and they have died in prison & exile
    the council does nothing more than sign what he gives them
    there is no register of the seals of encomienda
    he falsifies the titles of encomiendas
    Indians are passed from hand to hand using false seals
    mayors & aldermen are appointed by him
    complaints against him are placed in a box
    and the residents have taken refuge in churches or in the hills

THE TOWNS WHICH ARE OWNED BY RODRIGO DE CONTRERAS AND HIS
WIFE AND SONS ARE:
    The town of mistega————
    the town of teçuatega————
    another town abangasca————
    another town queçaloaque————
    two other towns called utega & uteguilla————
    another town totoa————
    another town close to this city of fisherman————
    another town which is called çebaco————
    the province of chira————
    the province of nicoya————
    the town of bombacho————
    the town of monimbo————
        etc.
            etc.
                etc.
(Cf. SOMOZA COLLECTION)

AL MUY ALTO Y MUY PODEROSO SEÑOR EL PRÍNCIPE NUESTRO
SEÑOR
En lo que a los yndios toca
ningund remedio ni alivio an dado
Justiçia ninguna vemos en esta Audiençia
Todos estan acobardados para pedir justiçia

> (Fray Bartolomé de las Casas
> y Fray Antonio de Valdivieso
> al Príncipe Don Felipe)

Su Alteza podía ver qué vida llevaban ellos
(el obispo de Chiapas y el de Nicaragua)
reprendiendo a los que tienen todo el poder
como reyes
          y son verdaderamente aca reyes

Han pensado dejar sus obispados para ir a pedir Justiçia
y no regresar
            hasta que se desarraygue la tyrania
Los remedios que esperan de Su Magestad y Su Alteza:
que les liberten sus ovejas
      los yndios naturales destas Yndias
que se las liberten
              y pongan en toda libertad
   Que la protección dellos se encomiende a los prelados,
no a todos, a los que den muestras de no querer ser ricos
El único remedio:
          quitar los yndios a todos
y desde luego quitarselos a estos tyranos
que quieren hacer mayorazgos
con la sangre de los vasallos del Rey
Porque temen como a la misma muerte estos tyranos
que se ponga un yndio bajo la protección de la Corona Real
              Firman: Fray Bartolomé de las Casas
                      y Fray Antonio de Valdivieso

los obispos de guatimala y chiapa y nicaragua dezimos . . .
(Y dicen al Consejo de Indias los 3 obispos
que ellos pueden hacer justicia en las causas de las personas
miserables y sobre todo cuando son opresas y agraviadas
porque a estas tiene la iglesia bajo su protección y amparo
según el capítulo super quibus damde berborum significationem
y de la distinçion 84 ci y 2° y en la distinçion 8. 7. C 1° y 2°
y de la distinçion 8.8 C 1° etc. etc. etc.)
. . . y como todos los yndios naturales de todas estas yndias
sean las mas myserables y mas opresas y agraviadas afligidas
y desamparadas personas que mas ynjustiçias padezcan y mas carezcan

TO THE MOST HIGH AND VERYE POWERFULL LORD PRINCE OUR
LORD
Concerning the Indiens
no remedie or relief have they given
no Justice doo we see in this Royal Tribunall
All are intimidated from seekyng justice
(Fray Bartolomé de las Casas
and Fray Antonio de Valdivieso
to Prince Don Felipe)

Your Highness could see the life they led
(the bishops of Chiapas and Nicaragua)
reproving those who have all the power
like kings
and truly they are kings here

They have considered leaving their bishoprics to go to seek Justice
and not to return
until the tyrannie is rooted out
The remedies they hope for from Your Majestie & Your Highness:
that theyr sheep be set free
the native Indiens of these Indes
that they be set free
and to them all freedom be graunted
That theyr protection be entrusted to the prelates,
not to everyone, to those who give signs of not desiryng to be ryche
The sole remedie:
to take the Indiens away from everyone
and of course take them away from these tyrants
who wish to create primogenitures
with the bloode of the King's vassalls
Because those tyrants dread like death it self
the Indiens beeyng placed under the protection of the Royal Crown.
Signed: Fray Bartolomé de las Casas
& Fray Antonio Valdivieso

we bishops of Guatimala & Chiapa & Nicaraqua say . . .
(And the 3 bishops tell the Council of the Indies
that they can bring justice in the cause of miserable
persons and above all when they are oppressed and injured
because the church has these people under its protection and refuge
in accordance with the chapter super quibus damde berborum significationem
and of the distinction 84 ci and 2nd and in the distinction 8. 7. C 1st and 2nd
and of the distinction 8.8 C 1st etc. etc. etc.)
. . . and since all the native Indiens of all these Indes
are the most miserable & most opressed & injured & afflicted
& helplesse people who most injustices suffer and lack most

y mayor neçesidad tengan de amparo defension y protecion
de todas las que oy ay en el mundo . . .
. . . porque otras no pueden ser mas pusilanymes
y mas encoxidas que carescan de çiençia y espiriençia
ningunas otras ay tan sinples ni que menos sepan de pleytos
ni juyzios demandas ni respuestas sentençias ni apelaçiones
ni de las maldades calunias cabilaçiones yndustrias dellas
y cautelas de los españoles de quien cada día se an de defender
ningunas otras naçiones jamas se vieron que tan entronado
y arraygado y casi ya natural tengan el miedo
por las nunca otras tales vistas ni oidas ni pensadas
violençias fuerças opresiones tiranyas
robos crueldades ynjustos captiverios guerras iniquas
estragos matanças despoblaçiones de dos mil leguas de tierra
. . . de lo cual se sigue manifiestamente ser estas myseras naçiones
las mas myserables y mas abatidas y peor agraviadas y mas ympotentes
y desamparadas y neçesitadas que ay en el universo orbe . . .
. . . y al juycio eclesiastico pertenece inmediatamente conoçer
y determinar sus causas y hazerles todo cumplimiento de justicia
defender sus vidas y libertad de todas y cualquier personas
deshazer sus agravios quitales sus opresiones liballos
de las violencias y tiranias que cada dia padeçen
y del furor y ceguedad de los que los afligen oprimen e destruyen
y de su ynfernal condiçion y anbiçion como a miserrimas pauperrimas
ynpotentisimas para se defender y de todo consuelo auxilio y favor
y socorro de solatisimas y sin comparacion desamparadas
y destituidas personas . . .
                    (Respondieron los señores presidente
                    y oidor de la dicha real audiencia:
                                        que no ha lugar)

and have greatest neede of refuge defense & protection
of any that exist in the Worlde today . . .
. . . because others may not be more pusillanimous
& more timid that lack knowledg & experience
none others are there as simple nor who know less of lawsuits
nor courts writs nor replies sentences nor appeals
nor of the iniquities calumnies caviling devices of them
and guile of the Spaniardes from whom everie day they must defend
themselves
no other nations ever saw in them selves so enthroned
and rooted and almost naturally the fear
of heretofore never seen & heared & thought
tyrannous violences forces oppressions
thefts cruelties unjust imprisonments iniquitous wars
devastation killyngs depopulations of two thousand leagues of lande
. . . of whych they continue manifestly to be these wretched nations
the most miserable & most downtrodden & worst injured & most impotent
& helplesse & needie that there existes in the universe Orb . . .
. . . and to ecclesiastical justice it behoves immediately to acquaintt with
and to determine theyr causes and bring them the full execution of justice
to defend theyr lives & libertie from all and any persons
undo theyr grievances remove theyr oppressions and free them
from the violences & tyrannies whych each day they suffer
and from the rage & blindness of those who afflictt oppress & destroye them
and from theyr hellish condition & ambition as the most miserable most poor
most impotent to defend them selves and from all consolation aide & favour
and help most desolate and without equall helplesse
& destitut people . . .

> (Lords president and examiner of the
> Royal Tribunal responded:
> the petition is denied)

"... puñaladas ..."
                    (escribe el Obispo Valdivieso en Marzo del 45
cinco años antes que se las dieran)
"y hubo gente armada para venirmelas a dar"

Y como se han cometido otros delitos sin que se haga nada —dice—
"tampoco se hará aunque maten al obispo"

"La audiencia holgare que me maten ..."
dice en la misma carta al rey.
... oprimidos ...
Los indios cada día son más oprimidos
Y el obispo no es sólo para tener mitra y renta
(dice él). También para remediar las opresiones
Y suplica la autoridad para defenderlos. Si no
que el rey no haga cuenta que les ha dado obispo.
Si no, suplica licencia para renunciar al obispado.
"Mire vuestra alteza que ya no falta en las indias
sino hacer otro rey ..."
                    fray antonio episcopus de nicaragua

"Los agravios de los indios son cotidianos"
                    (en Julio de 45)
Escribe en duplicado, en la misma nao,
por la censura ... Porque hay censura en Nicaragua.
Interceptan las cartas ... Espionaje, etc.
La provincia es pobre, no por falta de riquezas
(dice) sino de buen gobierno.
Por los que han gobernado desasosegando la tierra
(pobladores i conquistadores por igual)
                    Tiene (rrodrigo de contreras)
la tercera parte de los pueblos
   "... señores de esta tierra
como si de sus padres la heredaran ..."
La diferencia de estos con los del Perú:
que estos no necesitan alzarse
porque aquí los que están alzados
son la autoridad ...
"Y tenga vuestra alteza entendido
que si publicamente NOS MATASEN ...."(a él y las Casas)
                    (Sept. del 45)

"... el que aca viniere por prelado

"... a knifing ..."
                    (writes Bishop Valdivieso in March of 45
five years before they attacked him)
"and there were armed people prepared to stab me"

And as other crimes have been committed without anything being done
"nothing will be done either even if they kill the bishop"

"The royal audience might be pleased they should kill me ..."
he says in the same letter to the king.
... oppressed ...
The Indians are every day more oppressed
And the bishop is not merely to have a miter and a living
(he says). Also to put right oppressions
And he begs the authorities to defend them. If not
the king should consider it of no account he has given them a bishop.
If not, he begs license to resign the bishopric.
"Notice your highness that there is nothing left to the Indies
other than to make a new king ..."
                    fray antonio episcopus de nicaragua

"Affronts to the Indians occur daily"
                    (in July of 45)
He writes in duplicate, aboard the ship itself,
because of censorship... Because there is censorship in Nicaragua.
They intercept the letters... Spying, etc.
The province is poor, not for want of riches
(he says) but of good government.
Because of those who have governed creating unrest in the land
(settlers and conquistadors alike)
                    He (rodrigo de contreras) owns
a third of the towns
   "... lords of this land
as though from their fathers they'd inherited it ..."
The difference between these and those in Peru:
that these do not need to rebel
because those who are in rebellion
are the authorities ...
"And understande your majestie
that if they publickly KILL US ...." (he and las Casas)
                    (Sept. of 45)

"... whoever comes here as prelate

o se a de ir al infierno o tornarse a españa . . ."

A tal punto habían llegado las cosas en Nicaragua
que no había más camino para un obispo
    que el infierno o España

Pero la Audiencia de los Confines de Guatemala
le quitó al fin a Rodrigo de Contreras ¡al fin!
la Gobernación y los indios.
Fue a España a gestionar —mover influencias.
Mientras quedaban en Nicaragua los dos hijos.
Hernando Contreras y Pedro Contreras.
Los dos hermanos Contreras.
                           Los dos hermanos tiranos.
Y supo Hernando Contreras que el Real Consejo de Indias
había confirmado lo de la Audiencia de los Confines.
Por las cartas del obispo Valdivieso
habían perdido la Gobernación y los indios.
Él tenía la culpa, el obispo. Por él les habían quitado
la gobernación y los indios.
Se juntó con una banda de exilados del Perú:
Juan Bermejo, partidario de Gonzalo Pizarro,
expulsado por un motín en el Cuzco. Un Castañeda
ex-fraile, ex-lego franciscano, que andaba sin hábito,
y otros. Desterrados del Perú y de Panamá.
Y en un 26 de febrero
reunió Hernando Contreras la gente en su casa
para oir un cantor.
"Con estas armas tenemos" les dijo.
"Para hacer lo que vamos a hacer con estas tenemos."
Se fue con todo el grupo donde el obispo
(que estaba platicando con un fraile).
Hernando Contreras le enterró la daga.
El obispo cayó junto a una tinaja. Le decía
"Acaba ya carnicero"
mientras él le seguía dando puñaladas.
Y gritaba la Catalina Álvarez, la madre.
Después abrieron dos cofres:
uno de oro y plata, el otro de escrituras.
El obispo en su charco de sangre besaba un crucifijo.
Su mano ensangrentada quedó pintada en la pared.
Siempre quedó la sangre viva y roja, dicen,
como si acabara de salir de sus venas.
Juan Bermejo se puso al cuello la cruz pontifical.
Robaron el oro y la plata. Y un guacal de oro del obispo.
Después se juntaron todos en la plaza de León.
Saquearon la caja real con el Tesoro de Su Majestad,

either must go to hell or return to spain . . ."

Things had reached such a state in Nicaragua
that a bishop had no option other
            than to go to hell or to Spain

But the Audience of the Territories of Guatemala
finally removed from Rodrigo de Contreras—finally!—
the Governorship and the Indians.
He went to Spain to negotiate—to lobby.
While his two sons stayed behind in Nicaragua.
Hernando Contreras and Pedro Contreras.
The two Contreras brothers.
                    The two tyrant brothers.
And Hernando Contreras learned that the Royal Council of the Indies
had confirmed the decision of the Audience of the Territories.
Because of bishop Valdivieso's letters
they'd lost the Governorship and the Indians.
He was to blame, the bishop. Because of him they'd taken away
the Governorship and the Indians.
He fell in with a group of exiles from Peru:
Juan Bermejo, a supporter of Gonzalo Pizarro,
expelled because of a mutiny in Cuzco. One Castañeda
ex-friar, ex-Franciscan lay brother, who went around without a habit,
and others. Thrown out of Peru and Panama.
And on a 26 February
Hernando Contreras brought the people together in his house
to listen to a tenor.
"These weapons will do" he told them.
"To do what we are going to do, these will do."
He went with the whole group to see the bishop
(who was talking to a friar).
Hernando Contreras plunged his dagger into him.
The bishop collapsed beside a jug. He said to him
"Finish it off, butcher"
while he continued to stab him.
And Catalina Álvarez, his mother, was screaming.
Then they opened two coffers:
one of gold and silver, the other deeds.
The bishop in his pool of blood was kissing the crucifix.
His bloodied handprint was left on the wall.
The blood stayed bright and red, they say,
as though it had just left his veins.
Juan Bermejo put the pontifical cross around his neck.
They stole the gold and silver. And a gold vessel of the bishop's.
Then they met in the square in León.
They ransacked the royal safe with the Treasure of His Majesty,

la Caja de las 3 llaves (con $15.000) y las marcas reales.
Llamaban a Hernando "General" y
"General del Campo de la Verdad"
y "Capitán General de la Libertad".
Y le envió a su hermano Pedro a Granada
que estaba en Granada en casa de su madre
la daga sin punta con que mató el obispo
(se le quebró la punta cuando lo estaba matando).
El se fue al puerto del Realejo a tomar los barcos
y Bermejo, "Maestre de Campo", a Granada,
a tomar Granada. En el camino del Realejo
ya no lo llamaban "General" sino "Príncipe"
y decían que después sería Rey. Y decía H.C.
que Su Majestad le había quitado la Tierra Firme
y a Nicaragua, que su abuelo Pedrarias había ganado
y al Perú, que se había descubierto por su abuelo,
y no contento con eso había quitado ahora a sus padres
sus indios de Nicaragua. Y él "daría a entender al Rey
que de otra manera se había de tratar los caballeros"
(el plan era quemar los navíos en la costa de Nicaragua,
Guatemala y la Nueva España y Panamá, asaltar Panamá,
ir al Perú, apoderarse del Perú, y declararse REY:
Rey de toda América iba a ser Hernando Contreras).
En el camino ya lo llamaban "Príncipe de Cuzco".

Era en Cuaresma, y en Granada Doña María de Peñalosa
estaba rezando el vía-crucis en San Francisco
cuando llegaron a decirle que su hijo Hernando en León
HABÍA MATADO AL OBISPO Y SE HABÍA ALZADO CONTRA EL REY
Y Doña María no se inmutó. ("Ninguna alteración ni mudanza")
Siguió rezando las estaciones. ¿Heroica serenidad
o ella estaba en el plan? Y en esa Semana Santa
Doña María de Peñalosa dijo también en la iglesia
(rezando tal vez otro vía-crucis) al aya de los Contreras:
"Ya estará Hernando Contreras en Panamá . . ."
Porque el aya había dicho:
                    "¿Dónde estará el Príncipe esta noche?"

Doña María de Peñalosa —la viuda de Balboa.
Hernando Contreras tenía 24 ó 25 años,
y Pedro Contreras tenía 18 ó 19 años
y estaba en Granada en casa de Doña María.
40 días antes en Mombacho (pueblo de los Contreras)
se hacían alpargatas y se hilaba algodón para mechas de arcabuces
y en la costa del lago los indios de los Contreras lavaban con jabón
las cotas de malla.

the Safe with three keys (with ₿15,000) and the royal stamps.
They called Hernando "General" and
"General of the Camp of Truth"
and "Captain General of Freedom."
And he sent to his brother Pedro in Granada
who was in Granada in his mother's house
the dagger without a point with which he murdered the bishop
(the point broke off when he was killing him).
He went to the port of El Realejo to seize the ships
and Bermejo, "Field Master," to Granada,
to take Granada. On the way to El Realejo
they no longer called him "General" but "Prince"
and they said that later he'd be King. And H.C. said
that His Majesty had taken Terra firma and Nicaragua
from him, which his grandfather Pedrarias had won
and Peru, which had been discovered by his grandfather,
and not content with this had now taken from his parents
their Nicaraguan Indians. And he "would teach the King
that knights should be treated differently"
(the plan was to burn the ships on the coast of Nicaragua,
Guatemala, and New Spain and Panama, to attack Panama,
to go to Peru, seize control of Peru, and declare himself KING:
King of all America Hernando Contreras was going to be).
On the way they were already calling him "Prince of Cuzco."

It was Lent, and in Granada Doña María de Peñalosa
was following the Way of the Cross in San Francisco
when they arrived to tell her that her son Hernando in León
HAD KILLED THE BISHOP AND REBELLED AGAINST THE KING
And Doña María did not react. ("No alteration or change")
She continued to pray the stations. Heroic serenity
or was she in on the plan? And in that Holy Week
Doña María de Peñalosa also said in the church
(perhaps following the Way of the Cross again) to the Contreras's governess:
"Hernando Contreras should be in Panama by now . . ."
Because the governess had said:
                              "Where will the Prince be tonight?"

Doña María de Peñalosa—Balboa's widow.
Hernando Contreras was 24 or 25 years old,
and Pedro Contreras 18 or 19
and he was in Granada in Doña María's house.
40 days before in Mombacho (the Contreras's estate)
they were making rope sandals and spinning cotton for the wicks of
                                                            harquebuses
and on the shore of the lake the Contreras's Indians were washing the suits of
chain mail with soap.

Y en casa de Doña María los hermanos chiquitos gritaban
(dice el proceso): "Biba Hernando Contreras".
Y decían: "Agora iremos al Perú".
Bermejo tomó Granada, quemó las fragatas del lago
para que no fueran a dar aviso a Panamá,
y fue con Pedro Contreras a Realejo.
Tomaron el "Galeón de Chile", saquearon sus mercancías
(enviaron a Doña María indios cargados de conservas)
hicieron al "Galeón de Chile" capitana de la armada, tomaron
otro navío y una fragata; los demás navíos los quemaron.
Y partieron para Panamá, para tomarla, y
tomar todos los navíos que hubiera en Panamá
y pasar al Perú y capturar todas las galeras
del mar del sur, y adueñarse de toda la costa
del mar del sur, desde Chile hasta la Nueva España.
Iban quemando todos los barcos que encontraban en el mar.
A una legua de Panamá saltaron a tierra.
Fueron caminando de dos en dos a medianoche
hasta un tiro de ballesta de Panamá,
y después se formaron en escuadrón.
Bermejo dijo un discurso sobre la libertad:
que luchaban por la libertad de todos,
pues hasta entonces habían estado en cautiverio.
Y fueron por el camino de la playa
hasta la casa del Gobernador, con muchas mechas encendidas
gritando ¡VIVA HERNANDO CONTRERAS!
                    ¡LIBERTAD! ¡LIBERTAD!
¡MUERA EL TRAIDOR GOBERNADOR! (que no estaba)
y robaron su casa, rompieron las puertas, las arcas,
y Bermejo daba gritos abajo en la puerta
gritando a Hernando Contreras que le echase la cabeza
del traidor gobernador.
Y fueron a la plaza a reunir gente
y otros recorrían las calles gritando LIBERTAD
        VIVA EL PRÍNCIPE CONTRERAS
            ¡A LA MIERDA EL REY!
y tomaban las armas y los caballos que hallaban
y los llevaban a la plaza. Llevaron al obispo,
Bermejo lo sentó en la picota, y lo iba a matar.
Saquearon las tiendas. Abrieron la cárcel real
y sacaron a los presos. Cogieron la plata del Rey.
Repartían las barras de plata a todo mundo.
A los que salían a las ventanas o encontraban en la calle
les ponían el arcabuz al pecho preguntando quién vivía.
"Vivan quien vuestras mercedes mandaren" respondían.
Pregonaron que todos se juntaran bajo la bandera de Contreras
so pena de muerte. Y decían

And in Doña María's house the little brothers were shouting
(according to the trial): "Long live Hernando Contreras."
And they were saying: "Now we'll go to Peru."
Bermejo took Granada, he burned the frigates in the lake
so they wouldn't go to warn Panama,
and he went with Pedro Contreras to El Realejo.
They seized the "Chilean Galleon," they looted its merchandise
(to Doña María they sent Indians laden with preserves)
they made the "Chilean Galleon" the flagship of the armada, they seized
another ship and a frigate; the remaining boats they burned.
They set sail for Panama, to take it, and
to take all the ships there were in Panama
and proceed on to Peru and capture all the galleys
of the South Sea, and take possession of the entire coast
of the South Sea, from Chile to New Spain.
En route they burned every ship they found in the sea.
One league away from Panama they leapt ashore.
They traveled on in pairs in the middle of the night
to within a crossbow-shot of Panama,
and then they formed into a squadron.
Bermejo made a speech about freedom:
that they were fighting for the freedom of all,
since until then they had all been in captivity.
And they took the path along the beach
as far as the Governor's house, with many torches lit
shouting LONG LIVE HERNANDO CONTRERAS!
                                    FREEDOM! FREEDOM!
DEATH TO THE TREACHEROUS GOVERNOR! (he was away)
and they looted his house, broke the doors, the treasury boxes
and Bermejo shouting down below at the door
shouting to Hernando Contreras to throw him down the head
of the treacherous governor.
And they went to the square to gather the people together
and others ran through the streets shouting FREEDOM!
        LONG LIVE PRINCE CONTRERAS!
            TO HELL WITH THE KING!
and they seized what weapons and horses they found
and brought them into the square. They brought the bishop along,
Bermejo sat him in the pillory, and was going to kill him.
They ransacked the shops. They opened the royal jail
and released the prisoners. They stole the King's silver.
They handed out bars of silver to everyone.
Those who leaned out of windows or they found on the streets
they placed a harquebus against their chest asking who they were for.
"Long live whoever your excellencies ordain" they replied.
They proclaimed that all were to join together under the Contreras flag
under pain of death. And they said

"No venimos a tomar la hacienda de los particulares
sino tan sólo queremos tomar la hacienda del Rey
y poner a todos en Libertad
        Y QUE CADA UNO VIVA COMO QUISIERE"
Y fueron a tomar Nombre de Dios
Bermejo y el "General y Príncipe" Contreras
(Pedro se quedó con los barcos en el mar:
en un barco de Doña María que también capturaron,
de la Línea de Doña María, que estaba en Panamá).
En el camino iban quemando ventas y ahorcando gente
y hasta a un perro que les ladró también lo ahorcaron
y tomaron las partidas de plata de Su Majestad,
saquearon la Aduana, se repartieron las sedas, vinos
y conservas. Ya había llegado aviso a Nombre de Dios.
Vieron que no podían tomarlo. Volvieron a Panamá
y Panamá ya estaba alzada por el Rey. Se retiraron
a una finca enfrente de Panamá. Iban a quemarla.
Pero salieron los de la ciudad con las banderas del Rey.
Pelearon en un cerro. Mataron 80 de los rebeldes
y a otros los prendieron. Otros huyeron a los montes.
En la falda del cerro murió Bermejo de un arcabuzazo.
Su cuerpo fue hecho cuartos y puesto en los caminos.
Pedro se perdió en los manglares y no se supo de él.
Hernando huyó en una canoa por la selva.
Hallaron un hombre en un pantano
que parecía Hernando Contreras.
Lo conocieron dijeron por el sombrero
y por un Agnus Dei de oro que traía al cuello.
Lo hicieron cuartos,
le cortaron la cabeza
y la pusieron en una picota
en una jaula de hierro, en la plaza de Panamá
con el letrero: HERNANDO CONTRERAS

Mientras el aya preguntaba en Granada a Doña María de Peñalosa
    ¿Dónde estará el Príncipe esta noche?

"We are not here to seize the property of individuals
but merely to seize the property of the King
and to set everyone free
          AND FOR EVERYONE TO LIVE AS HE PLEASES"
And Bermejo and the "General and Prince" Contreras
went to take Nombre de Dios
(Pedro stayed behind with the ships in the sea:
on a ship of Doña María's which they also captured,
of the Doña María Line, and which had been in Panama).
En route they burned stores and hanged people
and they even hanged a dog that barked at them
and they took shipments of His Majesty's silver,
they looted the Customs, they handed out silks, wines
and preserves. By now warnings had reached Nombre de Dios.
They saw that they couldn't take it. They returned to Panama
and Panama had now rebelled in support of the King. They withdrew
to a farm close to Panama. They were going to burn it.
But the city's inhabitants came out bearing the King's flags.
They fought on a hill. They killed 80 of the rebels
and captured others. Others fled into the mountains.
On the flanks of the hill Bermejo died from an harquebus shot.
His body was quartered and dumped on the roadside.
Pedro got lost in the mangroves and was never heard of again.
Hernando fled in a canoe through the forest.
They found a man drowned in a swamp
who resembled Hernando Contreras.
They recognized him they said by his hat
and by a gold Agnus Dei he wore around his neck.
They quartered him,
they cut off his head
and they placed it in a pillory
in an iron cage, in the square in Panama
with the sign: HERNANDO CONTRERAS

While the governess in Granada asked Doña María de Peñalosa
Where will the Prince be tonight?

Comenzó a retumbar el Momotombo.
Desde lejos se oían los rugidos
como truenos dentro de la tierra.
Como un tambor de guerra. Todas las noches
la tierra tenía temblores. Un río de fuego
bajaba del volcán, y el lago iba subiendo.
El agua del lago tenía un sabor a azufre.
Las mujeres no parían, y si parían
se morían las criaturas. Llegó la plaga.
      El Momotombo
seguía bramando. El lago seguía subiendo.
Después de otro terremoto hubo Cabildo Abierto
y acordaron abandonar la ciudad DESCOMULGADA
(por el asesinato del obispo).
      Salieron con el Santísimo Sacramento,
el Alférez Mayor adelante, con la cruz y la insignia,
y llegaron a un llano verde, junto a Sutiaba.
El Alférez Mayor puso el estandarte real en un guásimo.
Pusieron la cruz donde iba a estar la Catedral
y el Alcalde con el cordel y el cuadrante trazó la plaza,
y le puso horca y cuchillo en nombre del Rey
y trazó las calles rectas en el campo,
el lugar de Nuestra Señora de la Merced
San Francisco
      La Yglesia de San Sebastián.

Allá lejos junto al lago el Momotombo
de cuando en cuando seguía bramando.
El agua seguía subiendo
         y la ciudad *maldita*
con la mano de sangre en el muro todavía pintada
se iba hundiendo
      y hundiendo
          en el agua.

Momotombo began to rumble.
The roars could be heard from afar
like peals of thunder within the earth.
Like a war drum. Every night
the earth trembled. A river of fire
was descending from the volcano, and the lake was rising.
The lake water tasted of sulphur.
Women did not give birth, and if they gave birth
the babes died. The plague had arrived.
         Momotombo
continued to roar. The lake continued to rise.
After a further earthquake an Open Council was held
and they agreed to abandon the EXCOMMUNICATED city
(because of the bishop's murder).
         They came out with the Blessed Sacrament,
the Lieutenant Major in front, with the cross and the insignia,
and they reached a green plain, close to Sutiaba.
The Lieutenant Major placed the royal standard in a large tree.
They planted the cross where the Cathedral was going to be
and the Mayor with measuring line and quadrant traced out the square,
and designated the site of execution in the King's name
and traced out the straight streets in the field,
the place of Our Lady of Mercy
San Francisco.
         The Church of Saint Sebastian.

There in the distance by the lake, Momotombo
from time to time continued to roar.
The water continued to rise
                    and the *accursed* city
with the bloodied hand still painted on the wall
was sinking slowly
                    down down
                         into the water.

Glossary

Abangasca. An Indian town at the time of the Conquest. The site is now in the city of Granada, Nicaragua.

Acajutla. Coastal town in present southwestern El Salvador and site of a battle between Pedro de Alvarado and the Pipils in 1524.

Acalán (also *Acalá*). Region of the Putún Maya on the Candelaria River, Campeche. An important commercial center, it served as a major interior crossroads between the Gulf of Mexico and the Gulf of Honduras.

Acla. Once an important city in the Bay of Caledonia, northwest of the Isthmus of Panama. Site of Balboa's execution, ordered by Pedrarias Dávila in 1519.

adelantado. Provincial governor; a crown appointment of considerable power and prestige.

Agua, Volcán de. One of the largest of several geologically young, active volcanoes on the south side of Lake Atitlán in Guatemala. It erupted in 1541, destroying the old capital of Guatemala (now called Ciudad Vieja).

Aguilar, Jerónimo de. Conquistador shipwrecked during a voyage from Darién to Santo Domingo off the coast of Catoche in Yucatan, Mexico. He was rescued and held captive by the inhabitants of the area for eight years, during which time he learned Maya; found later by Cortés, Aguilar became an interpreter. He is believed to have died in 1526 or 1527.

Ahau. Last and most important day of the twentieth Maya month, which corresponds to the Aztec day Xóchitl. Also refers to a king or emperor, monarch, prince, or great noble.

ahau-ahpop ("lord of the mat"). Quiché chronicles used this term to refer to rulers. Their assistants, destined to succeed them, were referred to as *ahpop-camhá*.

ahpop-camhá. Assistants and succesors to the *ahau-ahpop* or Quiché rulers.

Almagro, Diego de. (1475–1538) Conquistador who with Francisco de Pizarro took part in the first (1524) and second (1526–1528) expeditions to Peru, and in the bloody subjugations of the Incas after 1532. He lost out in the division of spoils from the Conquest, but Charles I of Spain granted him the title of Governor of the Territories South of Cuzco. Believing Cuzco was within his jurisdiction, in 1537 he seized the city from Hernando Pizarro, whom he set free. Civil war followed, and Almagro was defeated. He begged for his life and was promised it, but Pizarro had him garroted.

Alvarado, Pedro de. (1486–1541) Notoriously cruel conqueror of Guatemala. Began as chief lieutenant of Cortés in the Conquest of Mexico, but Cortés later sent him out to conquer Guatemala and El Salvador. Alvarado defeated the Quichés under Oxi-Quieh in the battle of Xelajú on February 20, 1524. He went on to subdue the entire area as far south as Cuzcatlán, capital of the Cuzcatec Indians (near present-day San Salvador) by July 1524, and in the same year founded the city of Santiago de los Caballeros (near present-day Tecpan). He spent some time in Cortés's jail, accused of financial irregularities. In 1527 Charles V made him Governor and Captain General of Guatemala, granting him the the rank of *adelantado*. He died on July 4, 1541, in a battle against the Mixtón-area Indians in Nochistlán, Jalisco, Mexico. The prolonged battle was made more difficult by the terrain. Alvarado gave his horse to a wounded soldier and fought on foot. When his scribe spurred his horse, causing it to rear, it stumbled and fell on Alvarado, crushing him to death.

Amadís de Gaula. Perhaps Spain's most celebrated novel of chivalry, attributed to Garcí Ordoñez or Rodríguez de Montalvo. Cervantes praised the novel and its protagonist, Amadís—the perfect gentleman, loyal vassal, and ideal lover—who became a model for Don Quixote.

arroba. Twenty-five pounds.

Atenguillo. Village in Jalisco, Mexico.

Atitlán. Village in Guatemala and site of battle between Pedro de Alvarado and the Zutuhils, under Tepepul, in 1524. Also a lake of the Guatemalan highlands, edged by volcanoes, in the Department of Solalá.

atole. Drink prepared with cornmeal gruel.

Audience of the Territories. A colonial court with special jurisdiction over civil cases and appeal cases within specific geographical regions or provinces.

Audiencia. Technically, a Spanish colonial court but also assigned wide administrative powers and therefore by extension, territorial division in the colonial system.

axóyatl. Within its present context, the term appears to be a variation of the Nahuatl term "xochiyaoyotl." Broadly speaking, the term refers to festivities. Narrowly defined, it refers to a war of flowers, a mutually agreed upon war, or a tournament exercising warriors and providing captives for sacrifice.

Azcapotzalco. Capital of the Tepanec state (1250–1428) until it was conquered by the alliance of Tenochtitlán and Texcoco. At one time located on the edge of Lake Texcoco and founded by Otomí and Teotihuacán groups. It is now part of present Mexico City.

baktun. Maya unit of time equal to 20 *katuns*, 400 *tuns*, or 144,000 days.

Balboa. See *Núnez de Balboa, Vasco.*

Belehé-Qat. Cakchiquel leader who together with Cahi-Imox orchestrated a major uprising against Alvarado in the early stages of the Maya conquest. Later, Belehé-Qat allied with other communities and attempted another rebellion against Alvarado in 1526 at Iximché, where he was defeated. He died in Solalá in 1532.

Beleheb-Tzy. Quiché leader who was captured and killed along with Oxib-Queh (the *ahpop camhá* of the Quiché) by Alvarado in Utatlán during his conquest of the Southern Maya in 1524.

beori. American tapir.

Bermejo, Juan. Spanish adventurer and friend to Hernando Contreras. Encouraged Contreras to murder the bishop of Nicaragua, Antonio de Valdivieso, in 1549, and to pursue his quest to become absolute ruler of America. Joined the Contreras brothers (Hernando and Pedro) in the occupation first of Granada, Nicaragua, and then of Panama in 1549. Panamanians loyal to the crown responded with a fierce rebellion that left all three men dead.

bisexitl. Leap year.

Bocab (also *Bacab*). Maya deities, sons of Itzámná, who supported the sky at four corners of the earth. The Chilam Balam of Chumayel tells of the creation when the 13 lords of the heavens were overcome by the 9 lords of the underworld and the 4 Bacabs were set in place. Each had his own world direction, color, Year Bearer, and name. East: color red, Kan years, called Hobnil; North: color white, Muluc years, called Can; West: color black, Ix years, called Zac Cimi; South: color yellow, Cauac years, called Hozanek.

Boto. Name of a Nicaraguan cacique.

Brusselles. Settlement founded in 1524 by Francisco Hernández de Córdoba on the Nicoya Gulf and present site of the town of Puntarenas. When Hernández de Córdoba's authority was challenged by Pedrarias, he rebelled and moved with his men and supplies to Nicaragua, leaving not a trace of Costa Rica's first Spanish settlement.

Cabal-chen. Refers to Maní, post-classic capital of the Xiu family in Central Yucatan, where one of the 18 extant books of the Book of the Prophet Chilam Balam was written.

Cáceres, Alonso de. Sixteenth-century Spanish explorer and conqueror of Honduras responsible for the murder of the Honduran cacique, Lempira, in 1538.

Cacique. Arawak tribal chief. Subsequently used by Spaniards to refer to all Indian leaders.

Cahi-Imox. Cakchiquel ruler who submitted to Alvarado at Yximché in 1526.

Cakchiquel. Maya tribe of the Guatemalan highlands that shared Toltec ancestry with the Quiché Maya. The Cakchiquel entered Guatemala around 1100 from Tabasco through Chiapas, eventually establishing their capital at Iximché.

Calero, Alonso. Spanish explorer who left with Diego Machuca from Granada, Nicaragua, on April 7, 1539, and discovered the Desaguadero—or Río San Juan outlet—on May 1 of the same year, tracing it to the sea by June 8. After many hardships, he made his way to the port of Nombre de Dios to present himself to an associate justice of the Audiencia, Doctor Robles, and give an account of his discoveries. Robles, who had a rival interest in the area explored, took him prisoner, but Contreras, Governor of Nicaragua, granted him permission to continue his pursuits.

Canek. Cacique of Itzalán, Mexico, in 1532. The capital city of his kingdom was on an island in Lake Itzá where Cortés arrived with his men on route to Honduras.

Carambaru. Small settlement on the Mosquito Coast found by Columbus on his fourth voyage.

Cariay. According to Las Casas, this name refers to a settlement found by Columbus on what is now the Mosquito Coast in eastern Nicaragua. He later called it Huerta ("orchard") because of its fertility.

Cartas de relación. Letters from Hernán Cortés to King Charles I of Spain, which gave a full account of the Spanish conquest.

Casas, Bartolomé de las. (1474–1566) Spanish missionary of the Dominican order and historian, called "the apostle of the Indies." He went to Hispaniola with his father in 1502. Eight years later he was ordained. In 1514, he began working for the abolition of Indian slavery and the forced labor of the *encomienda*. He devoted the rest of his life to that cause, going to Spain to urge the government to action, converting tribes to Christianity, and striving to break the power of Spanish landholders over Indian laborers. For a brief time (1544–1547) he was bishop of Chiapas. Author of *Historia de las Indias, De unico vocationis modo,* and *Brevísima historia de la destrucción de las indias.*

Casas, Francisco de las. Member of the Spanish military who accompanied Cortés during the Conquest of Mexico earning the latter's trust and respect. When Cristobal de Olid rebelled against Cortés in Honduras in 1524, Cortés dispatched Las Casas to restore his authority. Ultimately, however, Cortés doubted the authority of all of his subordinates and set out to Honduras himself.

Castilleja de la Cuesta. Village near Seville, Spain, where Hernán Cortés died in exile in 1547.

Cathay. Old name for Northern China introduced by Marco Polo and used especially during the Middle Ages. Part of the Empire of the Great Kubilai Khan.

Cawek. One of the four original patrilineal descent groups of the Quiché of Utatlán along with the Nihaib, Ahau Quiche, and Sakic.

Ceiba. Small island in Lake Nicaragua.

ceiba (see also *yaxché*). Large tree native to Latin America that measures an average of 30 meters in height and has a large trunk. A sacred tree for the Maya, it is the national tree of Guatemala.

Chapultepec. "Grasshopper hill" in Nahuatl, the Mexica reached it in their migration to the Valley of Mexico. They were driven out, forced to settle on an island in Lake Texcoco. It later became a recreational area for Aztec rulers. Today it is a public park in Mexico City.

Charles V. (1500–1558) Holy Roman Emperor (1519–1556) and Charles I of Spain (1516–1556), son of Joanna the Mad and Philip I (the Handsome), and grandson of Ferdinand of Aragón and Isabella of Castille. He inherited a vast empire and was initially unpopular amongst his Spanish subjects because he increased taxation to finance his imperial ambitions, chose Flemish favorites for high-level crown appointments, and spoke little Spanish. His reign faced the Protestant Reformation in Germany, the dynastic conflict with King Francis I of France, particularly over power in Italy, and the advance of the Ottoman Turks. Withdrew from the throne and later abdicated (1556) retiring to the monastery of Yuste, where he continued an active interest in politics until death.

Chiapas. Most southern Mexican state, it borders Guatemala.

Chichimeca. General term for the people from the Valley of Mexico. Before the 11th century, the Chichimec were nomads on the valley's northern fringes. Although Aztec tradition has it that they were part of the Chichimec, the Aztecs were actually farmers and military aids to the Toltecs. The Chichimec period (950–1300) was one of inter-tribal warfare and political confusion, but it prepared the way for the tributary empire of the Aztec.

chilam (also *chilam* and *chilamboob*). Teachers and prophets and members of the upper echelon of the Yucatec Maya priestly hierarchy. They read sacred scriptures and studied astronomy.

Chilam Balam. Sacred books of the Maya of Yucatan, named after their last and greatest prophet, *Chilam* or *chilan* (interpreter of the gods). The title of the work can be translated as the *Book of the Prophet Chilam*. The prophet Balam lived during the last decades of the fifteenth and the first decade of the sixteenth centuries and he foretold of strangers from the east who would establish a new religion. The fulfillment of his prediction earned him the reputation of a seer, and for years to come he was an authority for other prophecies uttered before his time. The books of Chilam Balam were written in the Maya language but in European script. Each book contains a great variety of material on the history, cultural practices, and the belief-system of the Maya.

Çibola. A vague historical region in present northern New Mexico believed (by the earliest Spanish explorers) to include seven pueblos ("Seven Cities of Cíbola") and to contain vast treasures.

Ciguare. Province north of northeastern India that Marco Polo had described and which Columbus thought he had found when he arrived on the Mosquito Coast of Nicaragua on his fourth voyage.

Cipanga. In medieval legend an island, or islands, east of Asia described by Marco Polo by the name Zipangu. Sought by Columbus, it is generally identified with present-day Japan.

Coanaco. See *Coanococh.*

Coanococh. Second son of Nezahualpilli (son of Netzahualcóyotl) who claimed the crown of Texcoco and was sanctioned by Cuitlahuac of Tenochtitlán. He fled when Cortés entered Texcoco in December 1520.

Cohuanacohtzin. See *Coanococh.*

Colección Somoza. A multi-volume compilation of archival documents on the history of Nicaragua from the arrival of the Spaniards to this continent, it was edited by Andrés Vega-Bolaños in the 1950s.

Comagre (also *Comogre*). Name of an important cacique who was known to have the respect of Indians from all the South of the Isthmus of Darién during the Conquest.

Contreras, Hernando. (1520?–1549) Son of Rodrigo de Contreras and grandson of Pedrarias Dávila. After Rodrigo de Contreras was stripped of his titles and possessions, Hernando decided to take revenge on the person he perceived as being responsible for the dispossession: the bishop of Nicaragua, Antonio de Valdivieso. He murdered Valdivieso (1549) and then proceeded in a quest to make himself absolute ruler of the region from Nicaragua to Peru. Together with his brother, Pedro de Contreras, and his friend, Juan Bermejo, he occupied Granada. They then moved south to Panama and occupied the capital while the governor of the region, Pedro de la Gasca, was out of town. Panamanians loyal to the Crown put up a fierce resistance. Hernando was drowned while fleeing his enemies. His body was beheaded and his head exposed in a cage in the central plaza in Panama.

Contreras, Pedro de. Supported his brother, Hernando de Contreras, in his quest to become absolute ruler of America. During the occupation of Panama, Pedro was left guarding boats in the harbor. He was repeatedly attacked by angry Panamanian loyalists and at first successfully defended himself. He abandoned port pursued by four ships, disembarked at the first opportunity, and headed inland where he disappeared. It is believed that he was killed by area Indians.

Contreras, Rodrigo de. (1502–1558) Appointed Governor of Nicaragua by Charles I in 1534, at Granada. His cruelty prompted the bishop of Nicaragua, Antonio de Valdivieso, and citizens of Granada to petition the king for his removal in 1544. He was stripped of his title and possessions and relieved of his duties in 1548.

Cortés, Hernán. (1485–1547) Spanish conqueror of Mexico (1521). After arriving in Veracruz with 508 soldiers and 100 sailors, he marched inland and, with the help of the Totonacas and the Tlaxcaltecas, defeated Moctezuma and Cuauhtémoc in Tenochtitlan. After destroying and rebuilding the city, Cortés ruled as governor there until 1524 when he left for southern Mexico and Baja California. Numerous accusations and challenges were brought against his governorship and authority. These left him disenchanted and drove him into exile in Castilleja de la Cuesta, Spain, where he died in 1547.

Cosa, Juan de la. Cartographer who sailed as pilot with Christopher Columbus and later made three expeditions to the north coast of South America with Alonso de Ojeda and Americo Vespucci. He died in a skirmish with Indians in 1509 during a mainland expedition.

Coyoacán. City and municipality in Mexico City. Also site of Cuauhtemoc's execution and home to Cortés after the conquest of the city and during the rebuilding of the capital.

cu. Name given by colonial historians to the temples of Indians in the Mexican region. Also a name given by Huasteca Indians to artificial mounds upon which dwellings were built.

Cuauc (also *Cauac*). In the meshing of the Aztec and Maya 365-day calendars with the 260 days of their ritual calendars, the same four days would repeatedly arise to mark the start of a new year. These days were called Year Bearers, determining the luck of the years as well as giving their names to designate them. Aztec Year Bearers were the days Acatl, Calli, Técpatl, and Tochtli; at the time of the Conquest, Maya Year Bearers were Muluc, Ik, Cauac, and Kan. *Cauac* was the nineteenth of the 20 Maya day signs, corresponding to the Aztec Quiáhuitl. Associated with the number 3; its augury was unfavorable.

Cuauhtémoc ("descending eagle," meaning sunset). (1495?–1524) Last of the Aztec rulers, he reigned between 1520 and 1524. Nephew of Moctezuma II and Cuitláhuac. Hanged by order of Cortés in 1524 for planning an alleged rebellion, in Mexico he is venerated today as a national hero.

Cueva, Beatriz de la. Wife of Pedro de Alvarado. After his death in 1541, she was so grief-stricken that she painted the interior of her house black and ordered the entire town of Santiago de los Caballeros to mourn the *adelantado*'s death. Named governor, she appointed her brother, Francisco de la Cueva, lieutenant governor. She died that same year, a victim of the eruption of the Agua Volcano that destroyed the capital of Guatemala.

Cuzcatlán. Capital of the Cuzcatec Indians near present San Salvador, conquered by Alvarado in 1524.

Darién. During the sixteenth century the term referred to the region from today's Canal Zone to Colombia (now the eastern province of Panama separated from the Caribbean by the province of San Blas).

De unico vocationis modo. A treatise by the Dominican priest, Bartolomé de Las Casas, in which he attacked the *encomienda* system and the enslavement of Indians. He advocated full human and legal rights for Indians, and against the cruelty of the conquistadors. He also argued for peaceful means to convert the indigenous populations to Catholicism.

Decades of the History of the Indies. History of the colonial period written by the Italian historian, Pedro Mártir de Anghiera (1457–1526).

Desaguadero. Name given by early explorers and conquistadors to the outlet of the Río San Juan in Nicaragua.

Díaz del Castillo, Bernal. (1492–1581) Conquistador and chronicler. He had served in the New World under various commanders—Pedro Arias de Avila, Diego de Velázquez, Francisco Fernández de Córdoba, and Grijalva— before serving Hernán Cortés (1519) in the conquest of Mexico. His work, *Verdadera historia de los sucesos de la conquista de la Nueva España*, written in his old age in Guatemala, is a fresh, unstudied account of events, scenes, and men he himself had known, with an accent on everyday concerns, the common soldier, and the correction of errors made in previous histories (mainly Francisco López de Gomara's).

Doña Marina. See *Malinche.*

encomienda (from Spanish *encomendar,* meaning "to trust"). A system of tributory labor established in Spanish America that gave the conquistador control over the Indians by requiring them to pay tribute from their lands, which were "granted" to deserving subjects of the Spanish crown. The Indians often rendered personal services as well. In return the grantee was theoretically obligated to protect his wards, to instruct them in the Christian faith, and to defend their right to use the land for their own subsistence. When first applied in the West Indies, the system wrought such hardship that the Indian population was soon decimated. This resulted in efforts by the Spanish king and the Dominican order to suppress encomiendas, but the need of the conquerors to reward their supporters led to de facto recognition of the practice. The crown prevented the encomienda from becoming hereditary, and with the New Laws (1542) promulgated by Las Casas the system gradually died out, to be replaced by the *repartimiento* and finally by debt peonage.

fanega. Dry measure of a hundredweight, about 1.6 bushels.

Fernández de Oviedo, Gonzalo. (1478–1557) A Spanish historian and author of the multi-volume *Historia General y Natural de las Indias,* a comprehensive general and natural history of the Americas beginning with the arrival of Columbus.

Fuego, Volcán de. One of several volcanoes on the south side of Lake Atitlán in Guatemala.

González de Avila, Gil (also Gil González Dávila). (1480?–1526?) Conquistador who from Panama explored the Pacific Coast from Golfo Dulce to Lake Nicaragua between January 21, 1522 and June 25, 1523.

Gracias a Dios. Named by Columbus in 1502, cape in the northeast extremity of Nicaragua that extends into the Caribbean Sea near the border with Honduras. Also a town in Honduras founded by Gonzalo de Alvarado by order of Pedro de Alvarado in 1536.

Granada. City in Western Nicaragua on Lake Nicaragua and known as a stronghold of Nicaragua's landed aristocracy. Founded in 1524 by Francisco Hernández de Córdoba, it was the object of repeated raids by French and English pirates. After independence from Spain in 1821, it became the conservative center, engaging in bloody rivalry with the liberal city of León. The rivalry lead to the founding of Managua in 1885. Granada was captured by the filibuster, William Walker, in 1885.

Great Khan. The Emperor of China, Kubilai Khan (1260–1294), of whom Marco Polo left a portrait, and whose empire Columbus thought he might visit on his voyage to the Indies.

guacal. Bowl-shaped gourd.

Guadalajara. Capital of the southwestern state of Jalisco, Mexico. Site of the death of Alvarado, it was founded by Cristobal de Oñate in 1530 and moved twice because of Indian raids. Finally permanently established in 1542, it became the seat of the audiencia de Nueva Galicia.

Hernández de Córdoba, Francisco (also Fernández de Córdoba). (1475?–1526?) An agent of Pedrarias Dávila, Governor and Captain General of Castilla del Oro. He founded a settlement, Brusselles, on the Gulf of Nicoya, in 1524. The settlement was abandoned in 1527 by order of Diego López de Salcedo, Governor of Honduras.

Herrera y Tordesillas, Antonio de. (1559?–1625) A Spanish historian who was appointed official historiographer of Castille and the Indies under Philip II. Author of *Historia general del mundo en tiempo del rey don Felipe II* and of *Historia general de los hechos de los castellanos en las islas y Tierra Firme del mar Océano* (1601).

Hibueras. Name with which the Spaniards designated the province of Honduras in approximately 1534. At the time, the region was subdivided into two districts, Hibueras encompassed the western part while the rest remained known as Honduras.

Higüeras. See *Hibueras*.

Hispaniola. Island in the central West Indies east of Cuba and West of Puerto Rico now divided between Haiti on the west and the Dominican Republic on the east. First visited by Columbus in 1492 and settled in 1493 becoming the center of Spanish rule in the West Indies.

Hojeda, Alonso de (also *Ojeda*). (1466?–1515?) Sixteenth century explorer and conquistador who accompanied Columbus on his second voyage in 1493. With Juan de la Cosa and Vespucci, he explored the coast of Venezuela and discovered the Island of Curazao in 1499. He was granted one half of the territory known as Tierra firme, which included land between Cape Vela and the Gulf of Urabá.

Hozanek. See *Bocab*.

Huichilobos. Name given by the Spaniards to the Aztec god of war and of the sun, Huitzilopochtli. Originally a tribal god of the Mexica, he became the patron deity of Tenochtitlán. He symbolized the struggle of the Mexicas, "people of the sun," chosen to be warriors. As the god of war he was nurtured by human sacrifice.

Hunab-ku. Supreme, invisible, single creator god of the Yucatec Maya. Possibly an Early Post-classic abstraction of priests; not generally venerated, he was thought of as the father of Itzámná, the most important deity of the Maya pantheon.

Hunaphú (also *Hunhpú*). Twentieth day of the 20-day month of the Quiché Maya of Guatemala. Corresponds to Ahau of the lowland Maya of Yucatán. In the Popol Vuh, the sacred book of the Quiché Maya, Hun Hunaphú and Vucub Hunaphú were sons of the Maya mother-goddess Xmucané. Also an ancient name of a volcano in the Guatemalan Highlands which was renamed Volcán de Agua by the Spanish after an eruption-generated flood destroyed their first capital (today called Ciudad Vieja) in 1541.

Illescas, Gonzalo de. (d. 1633) Spanish priest and author of *Historia pontifical y católica* (1606) and *Jornada de Carlos V a Tunes.*

Itzá. Maya Indians of Yucatan, Mexico and Petén, Guatemala, and probable founders of Chichen Itzá, which they occupied at various times from 514 to 1194. They moved (1450?) south from Campeche to Lake Petén. In spite of sporadic attempts by the Spanish to convert or subdue them after the visit of Cortés in 1525, the Itzá, a strong, independent Maya tribe, remained here until driven from their capital, Tayasal, in 1697.

Itzalan. A person from Itzá.

Itzcoatl ("obsidian snake"). Uncle of Moctezuma I and the Fourth Chief Speaker of the Aztecs who ruled during 1427–1440. His leadership secured independence and alliances for the Aztecs that laid the foundation for their empire. He negotiated the Triple Alliance with Texcoco and Tlacopan, which eventually resulted in the defeat of Atzcapotzalco.

Itzcohuatzin. See *Itzcoatl.*

Itzcuintlán (also *Escuintla*). The modern capital and department of the Pacific coast of Guatemala. Between the fifth and seventh centuries, it was the area of the Tiquisate culture and of the Cotzumalhuapa culture in the Late Classic period.

Ix. Fourteenth day of the twenty-day Maya month, corresponding to the Aztec day Océlotl. The day is related to the Jaguar god.

Iximché (also *Tecpan-Quauhtemalan*). Fortress capital of the Cakchiquel Maya of the Guatemalan highlands which fell to the Spanish, under Alvarado, in 1524. On its ruins Alvarado founded Santiago de los Caballeros de Quauhtemalan. It is also a native word for the breadnut tree (*Brosimum utile*), *ramón* in Spanish.

Iztlán. Valley in the state of Jalisco.

Jalisco. A state in west central Mexico.

Joanna the Mad. (1479–1555) Spanish queen of Castille and León (1504–1555) and daughter of Ferdinand II and Isabella I. She acceded to Castille and León at the death of her mother. Ferdinand II briefly assumed the regency until he was replaced by Joanna's ambitious husband, Philip I. After Philip's death in 1506, Ferdinand again assumed power, for Joanna had become insane. At Ferdinand's death in 1516, Joanna's elder son, Charles (later Holy Roman Emperor Charles V), was proclaimed joint ruler of Castille with his mother. Joanna spent the rest of her life in the castle of Tordesillas.

katún. Contraction of *kal* ("twenty") and *tun*, a period of twenty years in the Maya calendar, or 7,200 days. Ends of katuns were of supreme importance to the lowland Classic Maya, who erected stelae to mark their completion.

La Mota. Castle in Medina del Campo, Spain, where Isabel la Católica died in 1504.

Lempa. Principal river in El Salvador.

Lempira. (1497–1538) Young Honduran Indian leader who led a major rebellion in 1537 against the Spanish. He established his base on a fortified hill known as the Peñol de Cerquín and until 1538 successfully defeated all efforts to subdue him. Inspired by his example, other Indians began revolting, and the entire district of Higueras seemed imperiled. By order of Alonso de Cáceres, Lempira was murdered while negotiating with the Spaniards.

León. Second largest city in Nicaragua, about fifty miles northwest of Managua, near the Pacific Coast. Rebuilt on its present site in 1610 after León Viejo was destroyed by the eruption of Momotombo in 1609.

León Viejo. City in Nicaragua founded by Francisco Hernández de Córdoba in 1524 on the shore of Lake Managua and destroyed in 1609 by the violent eruption of Momotombo and a concurrent earthquake. The city was rebuilt on its present site in 1610. See also *León.*

López de Gomara, Francisco de. (1511?–1566?) Spanish chronicler and secretary to Hernán Cortés. Author of the *Historia de las Indias y conquista de México* and of the *Crónica de la Nueva España* (1553).

Luque, Hernando. Spaniard who collaborated with Almagro and Pizarro in the conquest of Peru and who became Peru's first priest.

Machuca de Suazo, Diego. With Alonso Calero discovered the Desaguadero—or Río San Juan outlet—on April 7, 1539, and traced it to the sea by June 8, 1539.

Malinche (also *Malintzin* and *Doña Marina*). Native American woman from Tabasco, Mexico, who acted as an interpreter for Hernán Cortés during the Conquest. It is also believed she was a mistress to Cortés, although she was married to another Spanish explorer. Originally named Malinatzin, she was baptized Marina by the Spanish.

Malintzin. See *Malinche.*

mamey. The fruit of a tropical American tree (*Mammea americana*), it has a thick, leathery, russet or reddish rind and juicy, yellow or reddish flesh.

Mango (also *Mangi*). Province in southeast China described by Marco Polo. Columbus always referred to Cuba with this name, convinced that Cuba was this region in Asia.

Marañón. A river approximately 1,000 miles long that rises in the Andes in west central Peru and flows northwest toward northern Peru, bends east, and joins the Ucayali to form the Amazon.

Masaya. Town and department of southwestern Nicaragua. A rich agricultural region that now produces cigars, soap, leather goods, footwear, and hats.

Mayali. Group of islands in Lake Nicaragua.

Mayapán. Maya state and seat of the Cocom family of Itzá lineage, who joined the Triple Alliance with Chichen Itzá, the leading city, and Izamal from the tenth to the thirteenth century. After 1200, led by Hunac Ceel, Mayapán subjugated Chichen Itzá and remained dominant until 1450, when a revolt of the Maya nobles, abetted by the rival Xiu family, brought about its fall.

Medina del Campo. Historic city in the province of Valladolid in northwest central Spain.

Moctezuma (Moctezuma II). Moctezuma Xocoyotzin ("angry lord," "youngest lord") was the ninth Aztec ruler (1502–1520). He was the son of Axayácatl, the sixth Aztec king, and the grandson of Moctezuma I. He died while a prisoner of Cortés.

Mombacho. A volcano which rises on the shores of Lake Nicaragua.

Momotombo. A volcano (4,126 feet) in western Nicaragua, northwest of Lake Nicaragua. Its violent eruption in 1609 destroyed the city of León Viejo.

Montejo, Francisco. Governor of Yucatán and of Honduras (1536–1539) who ordered the death of Lempira in 1538.

Montoya, Baltazar. A scribe whose horse stumbled and fell, crushing Pedro de Alvarado to death after a battle in Nochistlán, Jalisco, in 1541.

Naco. Commercial center for the Ulúa valley at the time of the Conquest, situated on an affluent of the Chamelecón river in present-day Honduras.

Nahua Pech. Maya high priest and prophet who, according to the book of the prophet Chilam Balam, lived in the time of Katun 4 Ahau, which ended either in 1487 or 1500. He was probably a member of the Pech family, which governed the province of Ceh Pech at the time of the Conquest.

Netzahualcóyotl ("fasting coyote"). (1402–1472) King of Texcoco and son of Ixtlilxóchitl I, who was slain by Tezozómoc, the Tepanec king of Atzcapotzalco. He later aided the Aztecs in destroying Atzcapotzalco. Netzahualcóyotl, an inspired poet, codified the ancient laws of Texcoco and founded what was probably the first library in the Americas. As an engineer, he helped plan the city of Tenochtitlán, its aqueduct, and the great dike separating the brackish waters of Lake Texcoco from the sweet waters and the fertile chinampas (islands) of Lake Chalco. His concept of the Tloque Nahuaque (an abstract, invisible god) was the closest conceptualization of monotheism in Mesoamerica. He was a contemporary of and counselor to both Itzcóatl and Moctezuma I of Tenochtitlán.

Netzahualcoyotzin. See *Netzahualcóyotl.*

Nicaragua. Name of a powerful cacique from Nicaragua.

Nicoya. Peninsula on the Pacific coast of Costa Rica. It was originally populated by peoples of southern origin who were forced out by Mexican invaders— the northern Chorotega and the Nahuat-speaking Nicarao.

Nicuesa, Diego de. (d. 1511) Governor of Veragua for four years. Present-day Costa Rica and Nicaragua (also called Castilla del Oro) formed part of his grant, which extended from the center of the Gulf of Urabá to the Cape of Gracias a Dios. It was subject to the governor of Hispaniola.

Nito. Important trading center at the Caribbean mouth of the Río Dulce, Guatemala.

Nochistlán. A village in Jalisco, Mexico, on a high rocky eminence, where 10,000 Indian warriors from the Mixtón region staged a revolt. It was also the site of Alvarado's death.

Nombre de Dios. A Spanish port and early settlement on the north coast of Panama, just northeast of Portobelo. Founded in 1510 by Diego de Nicuesa, it included the Veragua region. It was abandoned in 1597 because it was thought to be unhealthful. Until 1584, it was a port for cargo fleets from Spain.

Núñez de Balboa, Vasco. (1475–1519) Conquistador and "discoverer" of the Pacific Ocean. After sailing with Bastidas in 1501, Balboa probably went to Hispaniola. In 1510, fleeing from creditors, he hid on a vessel that took Martín Fernández de Enciso to Panama. After reaching Darién, he took command of the vessel, deposed the incompetent Enciso, and sent him to Spain as a prisoner. Rarely guilty of the cruelty characteristic of other conquistadors, Balboa won the friendship of the Indians, who accompanied him on his epic march across the Isthmus. Toward the end of September 1513, he reached the Pacific and claimed it and all shores washed by it for the Spanish crown. His discovery came too late to offset Enciso's complaints at the court of Spain, which led to Balboa's replacement by Pedrarias Dávila. Pedrarias married Balboa to his daughter (in her absence) and thus obtained rights to Balboa's grants and titles. In 1519, while Balboa was preparing for an expedition to Peru, he was arrested, accused of treason, and beheaded in Acla, by order of Pedrarias.

Olid, Cristobal de. (1488–1524) Spanish conquistador who first served Diego Velázquez, governor of Cuba, and later Cortés in the conquest of Mexico. Was sent by Velázquez to the coast of Yucatán on an abortive expedition to find out the whereabouts of Juan de Grijalba.

Oñate, Cristobal de. (1504?–1567) Spanish conquistador and founder of Guadalajara, Mexico (1530), he was Governor and captain general of Nueva Galicia three times.

Ophaz. Unspecified area of Asia which Columbus thought he had found.

Ophir. Ancient country rich in gold and of unknown location, perhaps in the Arabian peninsula.

Oquici. Ruler of Atzcapotzalco during the Conquest who was hanged in 1524, along with Cuauhtémoc, for allegedly inciting a rebellion against the Spaniards.

Otomí. Language group principally settled in the region north and west of the Valley of Mexico. It is referred to in one legend as the Otontlaca or Chichimec origin. It moved into the Valley of Mexico after the Chichimec invasion of Xólotl. Their leader married a daughter of Xólotl and established the Kingdom of Xoltocan, subsequently incorporated into the Tepanec empire under Tezozómoc. Conquered by the Aztecs and later by the Spaniards, the remnants of the Otomí peoples remain in the mountains north of the Valley of Mexico.

Oxib-Queh (also *Oxib-Quieh*). Leader of the Quichés who was defeated by Alvarado in the decisive battle at Xelajú on February 20, 1524.

Panquiaco. An Indian leader of Panamá and son of the cacique Comogre. He is said to have given Vasco Núñez de Balboa 4,000 ounces of gold and sixty slaves (prisoners of war). He also told Balboa of the existence and location of the Pacific Ocean.

Pedrarias Dávila (also *Pedro Arias de Avila*). (1440?–1531) Made Governor and Captain General of Nicaragua by royal decree in March of 1527, he died in office in 1531. He was known for his greed, ambition, and cruelty (particularly toward Indians).

Peñalosa, María de. The oldest daughter of Pedrarias Dávila and of Isabel of Bobadilla who married Vasco Núñez de Balboa. After Balboa's execution in 1519, she married Rodrigo de Contreras and with him had two sons, Hernando and Pedro de Contreras.

Philip II. (1527–1598) King of Spain (1556–1598) who ascended to the throne following the abdication of his father, Holy Roman Emperor Charles V (Charles I of Spain). Known as an energetic and effective ruler, Philip often used religion to advance his political aims, which resulted in cruel persecution. Like his father, he relied heavily on taxation to counter the effects of depopulation and colonial overexpansion, breeding resistance among his subjects both at home and in the colonies. Philip lived and died at the Palace of Escorial and was succeeded by his son Philip III; married to Anne of Austria.

pinole. Aromatic powder formerly used for flavoring chocolate. In Mexico and Central America, a flour made from any of various cereals. In Central America, a refreshing drink made with ground toasted corn, honey, and water.

Pipil. Conquest-period term loosely applied to the speech and culture of various Nahuat-speaking groups whose influence penetrated southern Mesoamerica and Central America from the Mexican highlands.

Pizarro, Francisco. (1476–1541) Conqueror of Peru who accompanied Hojeda to Colombia in 1510 and was with Balboa when he reached the Pacific. Hearing of the wealth of the Incas, in 1524, he formed a partnership with Diego de Almagro and Fernando de Luque (a priest who secured funds). His first expedition to Peru reached the San Juan River, part of the present boundary between Ecuador and Colombia. On the second expedition, Pizarro explored the swampy coast of southern Peru before returning to Panama. After a trip to Spain to secure funds, he sailed south, landing at Tumbes (1532), and ascended the Andes to Cajamarca. There he enticed the Inca, Atahualpa, into the power of the Spanish, took him captive, secured a substantial ransom, then had him executed. The conquest of Peru was completed with the capture of Cuzco, which was later defended against Inca forces led by Manco Capac. Pizarro consolidated his conquest by founding Lima and allotting land and Indians in *encomienda* to his followers. He alienated Almagro, which ultimately was his downfall. Some of Almagro's supporters surprised Pizarro one night at dinner; he was overpowered and slain.

pochote. Large spiny tree.

Pocosol. Nicaraguan cacique.

Puñonrostro, Francisco Arias Dávila de (Count of). Grandson of Pedrarias Dávila who unsuccessfully sued the Spanish chronicler Antonio Herrera y Tordesillas for defaming his grandfather in his multi-volume history, *Historia general de los hechos de los castellanos en las islas y Tierra Firme del mar Océano* (1601).

quetzal. Large Central American bird with a compressed crest and brilliant plumage (the upper parts and throat are iridescent green and the underparts crimson). In the male, the upper tail coverts often exceed two feet in length. The national bird of present-day Guatemala, it has also given its name to the nation's basic monetary unit.

Quetzalcoatl ("feathered serpent"). Ancient deity and legendary ruler of Mexico. The name is also that of a Toltec ruler, who is credited with the discovery of maize, science, the arts, and the calendar. It is unclear whether the ruler took his name from the god or, as a great ruler, was honored in life and was later deified. Quetzalcoatl, the god of civilization, was identified with the planet Venus and with the wind; he represented the forces of good and light pitted against those of evil and darkness, which were championed by Tezcatlipoca. According to one epic legend, Quetzalcoatl, deceived by Tezcatlipoca, was driven from Tula, the Toltec capital, and wandered for many years until he reached his homeland—the east coast of Mexico—where he was consumed by divine fire, his ashes turning into birds and his heart becoming the morning star.

Quetzaltenango. Center of the ancient Quiché kingdom of Xelajú. Currently a metropolis in the western highlands and the second-largest city in Guatemala.

Quiché. Most important group of ancient southern Maya, from the western highland of Guatemala.

Quisay. Name given by Marco Polo to Hang-chow or Hang-chou, a city of the Chekiang province of Eastern China, where the Fu-ch'un river empties into Hangchow Bay.

Robles, Doctor. An associate justice (*oidor*) of the Audiencia.

Royal Audience of the Indies. A court based in Spain, made up of royal appointees from both church and state, and overseeing legal issues pertaining to the Indies.

San Lúcar (San Lúcar de Barrameda). A seaport in the province of Cádiz in southwestern Spain at the mouth of the Guadalquivir river.

San Salvador. Second largest city in Central America. Founded in 1525, after some difficulties, it was officially recognized in its current location. In the colonial Kingdom of Guatemala, the city served as the capital of the province of El Salvador and, after 1786, of the Intendancy of San Salvador. After independence, it served as the capital of the state of El Salvador until 1835, as capital of the Federation of Central America to 1839, and thereafter as capital of the Republic of El Salvador.

Santa María la Antigua. Present-day Antigua, Guatemala. The third capital of Guatemala, it was destroyed by an earthquake in 1773.

Santa María la Antigua del Darién. Town founded by Vasco Núñez de Balboa in the region of Darién. This territory was controlled by the governor of Nicaragua, Diego de Nicuesa. Together with Martín Fernández de Enciso, Balboa resisted Nicuesa's governorship, resulting in the latter's death in 1511.

Santiago de los Caballeros Guatemala. First capital of the colony of Guatemala, founded in 1524 by Alvarado in the former fortress capital of the Cakchiquel Maya, Iximché. The city was later moved (in 1527) to the Valley of Bulbuxyá (from a word meaning "spring" or "gushing water") at the foot of the Volcán de Agua. An eruption of this volcano in 1541 destroyed the city on September 10. A new capital, *Santa María la Antigua*, was begun in the Valley of Ponchoy soon afterward.

Soconusco. Important area of trade and geographic region formed by the narrow Pacific coastal plain of southern Mexico, backed by a hilly piedmont area, extending eastward along the Isthmus of Tehuantepec and southward into Guatemala.

Solentiname. Archipelago in the southern part of Lake Nicaragua. Here, on Mancarrón island, Cardenal established a contemplative community (Our Lady of Solentiname) on February 13, 1966, which became a haven for writers, artists, and young FSLN activists. Because of the community's association with Sandinista militants, it was bombed by Somoza's National Guard in 1977.

Sweet Water Sea. Translation of Mar Dulce, which refers to Lake Nicaragua.

Tacuba. Principal center of the Tepanecs in the Valley of Mexico. Tacuba became one of the largest cities (apart from Tenochtitlán) during the fifteenth and sixteenth centuries. The site is now occupied by Tlacopan and part of present Mexico City.

Tantún. Associated with the Island of Cozumel, it was a place of holy pilgrimage.

tapextle. Stretcher made of cane or light wooden slabs and used to carry the sick and the dead.

Tayasal. Island in Lake Petén-Itzá, Guatemala; the last stronghold of the Itzá-Maya, conquered by the Spanish in 1697.

Tecún-Umán. Quiché leader killed by Alvarado in the battle of Xelajú in 1524. Now considered a national hero of Guatemala.

Tegusgalpa (also *Tegucigalpa*). The capital of Honduras.

Temilotzin. Warrior of high ranking who fought with Cuauhtemoc.

tenate. Leather bag or sack used by Indian miners to carry extracted metals and stones or other goods. Also a unit of volume.

Tenochtitlán. Capital of the Mexica Aztecs, founded on a mud flat in Lake Texcoco in 1396 and future location of Mexico City. There was an adjoining island called Tlatilulco. Both islands were inhabited by Mexica people, but in 1473 the inhabitants of Tlatilulco were defeated by Tenochtitlán. The city was divided into four large quarters, with the temples of Huitzilopochtli and Tlaloc in the center and a total population that probably reached 150,000. Each quarter was further divided into calpulli (smaller social units). Access to the mainland was over causeways that also carried aqueducts. The city was besieged and destroyed by Hernán Cortés in 1521 and was reconstructed soon thereafter as a Spanish colonial city.

Tepanecas. Traditionally one of the seven Aztec tribal groups believed to have left the legendary Chicomoztoc ("seven caves") in 1168, starting the migration to the Valley of Mexico. Meaning "those on the rocks" in Nahuatl, their name may relate to their first settlement in the Pedregal, an area of volcanic outcroppings at present-day San Angel in Mexico City. Under

Tezozómoc they founded the Tepanec empire, ruling the Valley of Mexico from their capital, Atzcapotzalco, until subdued by the Mexica under Itzcoátl in 1428.

Tepec. Valley in the Mexican state of Jalisco.

teplanastle. See *teponaxtle.*

teponaxtle. Nahuatl name for a Mesoamerican musical instrument consisting of a horizontal wooden cylinder (a hollowed-out log). The upper surface had two carved tongues that were struck with rubber-tipped mallets (*olmaitl*) to produce two pitches. Called *tunkul* by the Maya, *cuiringa* by the Tarascans, *nicache* by the Zapotecs, *nobiuy* by the Otomí. The drum often represented a crouching man or an animal.

Tetlepanquetzal. Ruler of Tacuba at the time of the Conquest. Cortés accused him of inciting a rebellion in 1524 and sentenced him to hang along with Cuauhtémoc in Coyoacán.

Tetlepanquetzatzin. See *Tetlepanquetzal.*

Texcoco. City-state across the lake from Tenochtitlán and originally settled by the Otomí, who called it Katenikko. The capital of the Acolhuacán state and a member of the Triple Alliance with Tenochtitlán, Texcoco grew with the accession of Netzahualcóyotl in 1430. He and his son Netzahualpilli made it the intellectual center of the Valley of Mexico. Cortés built ships there for his attack on Tenochtitlán.

Tierra firme. Name given by Spanish explorers to the mainland of what would become Central and South America.

tlacatl. A Nahuatl word for "man" also used to refer to helpers or servants.

Tlacopan. The smallest member of the Triple Alliance with Tenochtitlán and Texcoco in the fifteenth century and now part of Tacuba in Mexico City.

Tlascaltecas. Traditionally one of the seven tribes believed to have emigrated from legendary Chicomoztoc ("seven caves") in 1168, eventually reaching the Valley of Mexico. Also known as Teochichimec, they settled in southern Acolhuacán before being ousted by the Tepanec, Colhua, and Mexica. Some then migrated to Chalco, others to the area of present Tlaxcala.

Tlaxcala. The smallest Mexican state, with a capital of the same name, bounded by the states of Mexico, Hidalgo, and Puebla. Also the city-state reputedly founded in 1328 whose symbol was a white heron and which became an ally of Cortés in 1519 against Tenochtitlán.

Toluca. A subdivision of the plateau of Anahuac in central Mexico. Also a city in the state of Mexico about 35 miles southwest of present-day Mexico City.

tomin. A silver coin used in some parts of Spanish-speaking America at the time of the Conquest, when it was valued at thirty centimes of a peseta.

Toniatuh (also Tonatiú). Mexican sun god associated with the young war deity Huitzilopochtli, who was the sun itself. Also the name given by the Indians to Pedro de Alvarado.

Tori. A Nicaraguan cacique.

Toscanelli, Paolo. (1397–1482) Florentine physician and cosmographer with whom Columbus is said to have corresponded prior to his voyages and whose maps Columbus used to chart his westward voyage. Toscanelli's belief that the Far East could be reached more directly by sailing west than by rounding the Cape of Good Hope and crossing the Indian Ocean strongly influenced Columbus's venture.

Tumanamá. Panamanian chief.

Tuzulutlán. Area in present-day Chiapas, Mexico, inhabited by the Rabinal, an Indian people who defeated successive Spanish attempts at conquest. Renamed Verapaz ("true peace") after the Dominicans—under the aegis of Bartolomé de Las Casas—had brought them peacefully under Spanish authority.

Tzutuhil. Maya linguistic group, related to the Quiché and Cakchiquel, who settled on the shores of Lake Atitlán, Guatemala. The ruins of their capital, Tziquinaha, stand in a place now called Chuitinamit. After conquering the Tzutuhil in 1524, the Spaniards moved them across a bay of Lake Atitlán to the site of present-day Santiago Atitlán.

Urabá. A bay in the northwest coast of Colombia, at the inner end of the Gulf of Darién. Also refers to a region of Colombia east of Pacific Darién Province that was the hub of a trading network linking the Isthmus with the Caribbean and the Cordilleran regions of Colombia.

Utatlán. The Nahuatl name (*Tecpan Utatlán*) for Gumarcaah, the last capital of the Quiché Maya, conquered by Alvarado in 1524. It was later renamed Santa Cruz del Quiché.

Valdivieso, Antonio de. Dominican priest from Burgos, Spain, appointed bishop of Nicaragua in 1544 by Charles I of Spain. Like Bartolomé de Las Casas, whom he befriended, he protected the indigenous peoples and denounced Spanish cruelty and atrocities. His denunciations succeeded in having the governor of Nicaragua, Rodrigo de Contreras, stripped of his titles and possessions. Rodrigo de Contreras's son Hernando took revenge on Valdivieso by stabbing him to death in 1549.

Vela. Cape on the Pacific coast of Costa Rica.

Veragua. Name given by Columbus to the Panamanian coast between the Valiente peninsula and Point Toro. Also a river in Panamá that flows into the Caribbean.

Xicalanco. An important commercial center situated on the Laguna de Términos by the Gulf coast of Campeche, Mexico.

Xuchipila. A valley in Jalisco.

Yari. A river in Nicaragua.

yaxché. (see also *ceiba*). Tree considered sacred by the Maya.

Yucatán. 55,400 square-mile peninsula dividing the Gulf of Mexico from the Caribbean Sea. Located on it are the Mexican states of Yucatan, Quintana Roo, and Campeche, as well as Belize and parts of northern Guatemala. During the pre-Hispanic era, the peninsula was the center of Maya civilization. The Maya ruins here include Chichen Itzá, Uxmal, and Tulum.

Zaiton. A town in southeastern China described by Marco Polo as one of the great ports of the East in the time of Kubilai Khan (1260–1294). Present day Ch'üan-chou (Chuan-chow) or formerly Tsin-kiang in Fukien province.

Zapotitlán. Town and municipality in Jalisco, Mexico.

ERNESTO CARDENAL is a poet, priest, and revolutionary. His opposition to the Nicaraguan dictator Somoza nearly cost him his life. He was later Minister of Culture in the Sandinista government. Cardenal's works include *Cosmic Canticle, Zero Hour and Other Documentary Poems, In Cuba,* and *Golden UFOs.*

JOHN LYONS, translator of Cardenal's *Cosmic Canticle,* is the author of a study of Cardenal.

TAMARA WILLIAMS is Associate Professor of Spanish at Hamilton College.